European Monetary Integration & Domestic Politics

European Monetary Integration & Domestic Politics

Britain, France, and Italy

James I. Walsh

LYNNE RIENNER PUBLISHERS
BOULDER
LONDON

Published in the United States of America in 2000 by
Lynne Rienner Publishers, Inc.
1800 30th Street, Boulder, Colorado 80301
www.rienner.com

and in the United Kingdom by
Lynne Rienner Publishers, Inc.
3 Henrietta Street, Covent Garden, London WC2E 8LU

Library of Congress Cataloging-in-Publication Data
Walsh, James I.
European monetary integration and domestic politics : Britain, France, and Italy / James I. Walsh.
p. cm.
Includes bibliographical references and index.
ISBN 1-55587-823-7 (hard : alk. paper)
1. Foreign exchange rates—Government policy—Great Britain. 2. Foreign exchange rates—Government policy—France. 3. Foreign exchange rates—Government policy—Italy. 4. Monetary policy—European Economic Community countries. 5. European Monetary Union. I. Title.
HG3943.W34 2000
332.4'5—dc21 99-055594

British Cataloguing in Publication Data
A Cataloguing in Publication record for this book
is available from the British Library.

Printed and bound in the United States of America

∞ The paper used in this publication meets the requirements of the American National Standard for Permanence of Paper for Printed Library Materials Z39.48-1984.

5 4 3 2 1

Contents

Tables and Figures

Tables

Figures

Acknowledgments

Much of this book is about debt, so it is only right that I begin by expressing some of mine. My biggest debts are to Stephen J. Silvia and C. Randall Henning. Steve Silvia taught me what it means to be a scholar and a teacher from the day I entered graduate school and gave me enthusiastic help with this project. Readers will recognize the intellectual debt I owe to Randy Henning's work; he also provided continuous encouragement, criticism, and advice.

Maria Green Cowles, Louis W. Goodman, and Peter Lewis offered comments and suggestions from the beginning. Giulano Amato, Fabrizio Saccomani, and James Lee read and commented on earlier versions of the entire manuscript. Bruce Western and John McCormick convinced me to turn my work into this book, and Bridget Julian and an anonymous reviewer provided useful advice about how I might restructure the project.

For comments and conversations that helped me sharpen my arguments and analysis, I am grateful to David Andrews, Michelle Egan, Jonathon Golub, Dorothee Heisenberg, Erik Jones, Lori Lindberg, John McCormick, Andrew Moravcsik, Thomas Oatley, Peter Lewis, Martin Rhodes, Daniel Verdier, and Bruce Western. I also thank the following individuals who commented on earlier versions of parts of the manuscript: Karen Alter, Mark Aspinwall, Thomas Banchoff, William Bernhard, David Cameron, James Caporaso, William C. Cromwell, Harvey Feigenbaum, Robert Isaak, Thomas Johnson, Mattias Kaelberer, Karl Kaltenthaler, Kathleen McNamara, George Ross, Anthony Zito, and participants in workshops at Duke University, the Center for European Studies at Harvard University, the Jean Monnet Fellows Colloquium at the European University Institute, and the Center for German and European Studies at Georgetown University.

For funding, I thank American University for a fellowship that financed field research in London, Brussels, and Paris in 1995 and the European Community Studies Association for the Jacques Delors Fellowship at the European University Institute during the 1995–1996 academic year. Daniel Gros and Erik Jones were kind enough to allow me to set up shop at the Centre for European Policy Studies and helped me to navigate my way around the European Commission, and Bill Burros at the European Community Studies Association kindly advised me about getting settled in Florence.

Finally, I thank my parents, James and Elizabeth, for their support and encouragement, and Michelle Benes for the chance to talk about the really important topics.

—James I. Walsh

1

Politics and Exchange Rates

In one sense this is a book about the esoteric subjects of international finance: exchange rates, capital flows, foreign exchange market intervention, and so on. But in a more important sense, it is about politics. International financial developments produce winners and losers, and in this book I explain how these winners and losers mobilize political resources to influence public policy.

More specifically, the book explains why countries responded to similar economic challenges since the 1970s in quite different ways. Consider briefly the experiences of Britain, France, and Italy. Each saw high inflation, currency depreciation, and speculative attacks against exchange rates in the mid-1970s. Governments responded with monetary policies in ways that influenced the level and stability of their currencies in different ways. French authorities devalued the franc's exchange rate in the early 1980s in order to maintain the international competitiveness of manufacturing firms. They stabilized the currency in the European Monetary System (EMS), then the European Union's institution for monetary policy cooperation, only when it was at a competitive level. Italian governments pursued exchange-rate policies somewhat similar to those of the French by participating in the EMS but devaluing the lira in the early 1980s and mid-1990s to keep industry competitive. In contrast, British decisionmakers generally treated the exchange rate as a residual of domestic monetary conditions and in the early 1980s and again in the 1990s favored currency appreciation that reduced domestic inflation but undermined the competitiveness of British industry.

Governments in Britain, France, and Italy also had different preferences regarding the rules of European monetary institutions intended to promote the coordination of national monetary policies. The French and Italians supported strengthening such institutions by pooling sovereignty over monetary and exchange-rate policy. Officials in both countries worked closely with their German counterparts to create the EMS in 1978 and the 1991 Maastricht Treaty's plan for economic and monetary union, and in 1999 they replaced their national currencies with the single European currency. With one exception, British authorities refused to participate in European monetary institutions.

The central goal of this book is to explain these differences in exchange-rate policies and institutional preferences. In doing so, I do not seek to develop new theories of the politics of economic policy or of international institutions. Instead, the principal contribution of this book is empirical; I test the explanatory power of existing theories with evidence drawn from the British, French, and Italian experiences. Understanding the origins of exchange-rate policies and preferences regarding the rules of international institutions is important for both practical and analytical reasons. In analytical terms, I take as a starting point the verdict of much of the academic literature that domestic politics has a strong influence on economic policies.[1] But what exactly is it about domestic politics that matters? I tackle this question by comparing the ability of two general understandings of domestic groups' exchange-rate preferences and national policies to explain the pattern of political conflict and policy choices in Britain, France, and Italy from the mid-1970s through 1998.[2] The first uses an open-economy model with rational-choice assumptions about preferences and lobbying to explain exchange-rate policy as the outcome of a political struggle between groups insulated from and exposed to the international economy. The second is consistent with rational-choice assumptions but considers how groups' preferences and political influence are defined by the institutions of the domestic political economy. I find that this second, institutional explanation does a better job than the sparse open-economy approach in accounting for cross-national differences in preferences and policies.

Understanding exchange-rate preferences and policies is a precondition for analyzing the issues that governments raise during negotiations over the rules of international monetary institutions. I use evidence from the British, French, and Italian experiences to evaluate two explanations for such rules. The first focuses on bargaining among states with different preferences and holds that those with a preponderance of power have the greatest influence over the rules of international institutions. The second posits that decision-makers in different countries learn through structured interaction to come to agreement on institutional rules. In particular, authorities in countries that experienced economic policy failure in the 1970s, such as France and Italy, learned about and adopted some of the institutional preferences of more successful countries such as Germany. In contrast to much recent literature, I conclude that learning and communication had only a modest influence on officials' preferences during international negotiations.

At a more practical level, currency volatility increased sharply throughout the world after the breakdown of the Bretton Woods monetary institutions in the early 1970s and is alleged to have had many negative consequences. It may distort international trade and investment flows, undermine the effectiveness of domestic monetary policy in controlling inflation, and reduce public confidence in a government's ability to manage the economy. It can also make life unpredictable for employers and workers in the manufacturing sector by leading to unforeseen changes in the prices of exports and imports and by making planning, production, and marketing decisions more difficult for this important source of innovation, productivity increases, and economic growth. Exchange-rate policy may not be the sole, but is certainly an important, cause of currency volatility.

It is important to understand why governments sometimes are willing to coordinate their economic policies in order to prevent currency volatility. This is particularly interesting in western Europe, where the member states of the European Union have long discussed the possibility of replacing national currencies and potentially conflicting economic policies with a single currency managed by a supranational central bank. The successful conclusion of this project in 1999 is a spectacular example of international cooperation and an important step in European integration.

Furthermore, exchange-rate policy has become an increasingly important—and contentious—aspect of economic management because of the integration of national financial markets. The reasons have to do with the relationships among national monetary policy autonomy (the ability to hold domestic interest rates at levels different from those of other countries), stable exchange rates, and international capital mobility. Each of these may be a desirable goal in itself, but all three are incompatible with each other. Governments must choose among

- monetary policy autonomy and fixed exchange rates with low international capital mobility,
- monetary policy autonomy and international capital mobility with varying interest rates and volatile exchange rates, or
- fixed exchange rates and international capital mobility with low monetary policy autonomy.[3]

Increases in international capital mobility have made the first option—policy autonomy and stable exchange rates—increasingly problematic. Given the depth and size of contemporary international financial markets, restricting international investment to retain policy autonomy can impose large costs on the domestic economy.[4] Governments increasingly chose between retaining policy autonomy with a potentially volatile currency or giving up policy autonomy to maintain a stable exchange rate.[5]

Policy choices are limited by the increase in international capital mobility that has occurred since the 1970s. When capital mobility was low, governments were free to adopt different monetary policies and maintain stable exchange rates. This freedom disappears when capital moves across international borders because asset holders will invest in the country whose monetary policy produces the highest expected returns, thus forcing a convergence of returns on short-term financial assets and of interest-rate policies.[6] For example, real short-term interest rates—that is, nominal interest rates deflated by the inflation rate—in Britain, France, and Italy went from being negative and divergent in the 1970s to being positive and convergent beginning in the early 1980s.[7] Although capital mobility makes it difficult to implement an autonomous monetary policy, it is still possible to influence the exchange rate. For example, if the central bank pushes interest rates below rates prevailing overseas, investors sell the currency and purchase foreign currency assets. This reduces demand for the domestic currency relative to foreign currencies, resulting in the depreciation of the exchange rate.

The effects of exchange-rate changes on economic activity are straightforward. When a currency depreciates (or, in the context of an international monetary institution, is devalued), the prices of goods denominated in the currency decline relative to goods denominated in foreign currency. Imports denominated in foreign currency become more expensive, whereas exports denominated in the domestic currency become less expensive. Demand for the cheaper domestically produced goods increases at the expense of demand for foreign currency goods. Conversely, currency appreciation (or revaluation) switches demand from domestic goods to foreign goods.

In the remainder of this chapter I explore these issues in more detail. The next section defines exchange-rate policy, lays out the openness and institutional explanations for cross-national variations in policy, and describes the research design used to evaluate these explanations in subsequent chapters. The following section elaborates on the definitions of, explanations for, and methods of evaluation of the rules of international institutions. The chapter concludes with an overview of the structure of the remainder of the book.

Explaining Exchange-Rate Policy

Defining Exchange-Rate Policy

The exchange rate is the market price of one currency in terms of another. In this book I investigate policies that influence the stability and level of exchange rates. An exchange rate is stable when its value does not change much over time. The exchange rate may be at a competitive level so that the prices of domestic goods are equal to or less than prices for goods produced overseas using similar inputs, or it may appreciate above this level. The level of the exchange rate can be measured in nominal or real terms. The nominal exchange rate is just that—the price of one currency in terms of another. The real exchange rate takes account of changes in prices in different countries to measure the competitiveness of their products. It is calculated as $r = P/P_f$, where r is the real exchange rate, P is the domestic inflation rate, and P_f is the inflation rate in the foreign country. If domestic inflation increases, the real exchange rate (r) appreciates and raises the prices of domestic goods compared to foreign goods, even if the nominal exchange rate remains unchanged. This distinction between real and nominal exchange rates is important because on many occasions the pound, franc, and lira depreciated in nominal terms but appreciated in real terms since domestic inflation was high.

The first dependent variable in this book is not the stability or level of the exchange rate but exchange-rate *policy*, defined as the authorities' attempts to influence the market exchange rate. Policy is only one of many factors that determine actual exchange rates.[8] There are a number of instruments the authorities use in different combinations to influence the exchange rate, including

- public declarations in favor of or against a particular exchange rate;
- intervention on the foreign exchange market by purchasing or selling the domestic currency;
- imposition of capital controls that limit investors' ability to buy and sell currency;
- participation in an international monetary institution to secure assistance from other countries; and
- changes in domestic monetary and fiscal policies, such as changes in interest rates.

I do not attempt to explain exactly which of these instruments governments use, but rather the general pattern of policy activity and the importance attached to the exchange rate when compared to other goals.[9]

The Openness Explanation

The openness explanation holds that groups' exchange-rate policy preferences are a function of their dependence on international trade and investment.[10] Exchange-rate changes alter the returns to, and lead to conflicting policy preferences on the part of, two broad groups.[11] The first group is producers of tradable goods, whose products can be exported and are priced on world markets (although subsidies, tariffs, and transport costs drive a wedge between domestic and world prices). The principal producers of tradable goods in advanced capitalist democracies are manufacturing industries. The second group is producers of nontradable goods, whose products are sold only in the domestic market and whose prices are determined by domestic supply and demand. Examples include most services (including many financial services) and products protected from foreign competition by high trade barriers, such as many agricultural and military goods.

The tradable and nontradable goods sectors have different preferences regarding changes in the level of the currency. Depreciation decreases the price of tradable goods produced domestically compared to tradable goods produced overseas. It allows domestic producers of tradable goods to cut their prices compared to their foreign competition with little effect on profitability or to leave prices unchanged and to reap higher profits. Depreciation also reduces the relative prices of nontradable inputs such as land and labor. Depreciation hurts producers of nontradable goods by raising domestic currency prices of domestic and imported tradable goods that they consume. Thus, tradable goods producers prefer policies that stabilize the currency at a competitive level, whereas producers of nontradable goods prefer policies that appreciate the currency in real terms.

These groups also have different preferences regarding the stability of the currency. As discussed earlier, there are two broad policy options when capital is internationally mobile. The first is to allow the currency to float (or fluctuate) against other currencies and to give the authorities the autonomy to pursue a monetary policy different from that of other countries. The second option is to fix the exchange rate to another currency, perhaps by participating in an international monetary institution, and to match that country's monetary policy. Nontradable goods producers, whose demand is concentrated in the domestic market, prefer a floating exchange rate. This allows the authorities to respond to changes in the domestic economy by raising or lowering interest rates. Any resulting changes in the exchange rate do not greatly affect nontradable goods producers since they do not face foreign competition. But such currency changes do affect producers of tradable goods. International investors, traders, and manufacturing industry value the predictability of returns from domestic and international sales and investments that is produced by currency stability. It is true that they can reduce uncertainty about exchange-rate changes with various forms of inexpensive insurance available in well-developed financial markets, including currency futures, options, swaps, and other derivative contracts. However, such insurance is not widely available for more than one year, making it difficult to hedge against the longer-term risks of exchange-rate fluctuations that influence planning, production, marketing, and investment decisions.[12]

The openness explanation forecasts the following pattern of preferences and policy choices. First, producers of tradable and nontradable goods should have different preferences regarding the degree to which exchange-rate policy tries to stabilize the currency at a competitive level. Tradable goods producers favor such policies; producers of nontradable goods oppose them. Individuals and firms within these groups lobby the government to implement the policies that they prefer. Second, the openness approach concludes that the influence of these groups is a function of their relative size. When more of a national economy is open to international trade and investment, governments try to secure the political support of tradable goods producers by pursuing policies that keep the currency stable and at a competitive level.[13]

The Institutional Explanation

The openness explanation is a parsimonious model of the cleavages surrounding exchange-rate policy and the political influence of different groups. An alternative adds more structure to the explanation of preferences and policies by focusing on institutional arrangements. Many studies emphasize the important role that institutions such as executive-legislative relations, the legal system, or legislative procedures play in influencing groups' political *strategies* for achieving a given policy preference.[14] In this section, I focus on how institutions also shape groups' preferences, organizational capacity, and power.[15]

A key difference between the openness and institutional explanations concerns their conceptions of the intensity with which groups hold their preferences. Both agree that industry has a strong preference for keeping the currency at a competitive level. Industry also prefers a stable currency to ease predicting future demand patterns and investment requirements. But producers of nontradable goods may not hold strong exchange-rate policy preferences. C. Randall Henning argues that banks are crucial in this regard. Banks have an overriding preference for low inflation since unexpected increases in inflation can reduce the spread between the prices of banks' liabilities (such as borrowed funds and deposits) and returns on their assets (such as loans). But this does not tell us much about banks' exchange-rate policy preferences, which requires knowledge of the institutional environment in which they operate.[16]

Where banks and other financial firms do not have strong, institutionalized ties to manufacturing industry, as in Britain, industry meets more of its external financing needs through savings and sales of equity and bonds to investors. Banks and other financial intermediaries may manage the sale of these liabilities and provide short-term loans to industrial firms to cover operating expenses. But only rarely do banks invest directly in or lend to industrial firms on a long-term basis, and any such investments can be sold on well-developed financial markets. Banks, therefore, are insulated from many of the effects of exchange-rate changes on the competitiveness of industry. There are only two situations in which banks express preferences regarding the exchange rate. First, banks favor steps that could reduce exchange-rate volatility, such as participation in an international monetary institution, when this seems likely to address their overriding preference for low inflation. Second, banks with substantial international activities favor a modest appreciation of the currency to attract banking clients and investment from overseas.[17]

Where banks and industry have strong, institutionalized ties, as they do in France and Italy, industrial firms are more dependent on bank loans because secondary markets for bonds and equity are small and illiquid. This produces a situation of mutual dependence between banks and industry. Industry relies heavily on banks for external funds, and banks have a direct interest in industrial firms' profitability and ability to repay their debts. Banks also have detailed information about the profitability, competitiveness, and expansion strategies of their industrial clients. This leads banks to adopt their industrial clients' preferences for stabilizing the exchange rate at a competitive level. A relatively small number of banks can aggregate and organize the preferences of many industrial firms, and efficiently channel these preferences to decisionmakers. The close professional links between bankers and industrialists make this political coalition relatively easy to organize and sustain over time, according to Henning: "Consensus building . . . is greatly facilitated by existing channels of routinized communication that derive from the long-standing institutional connections between banks and firms." Bankers' strong ties with finance ministers and central bank officials make it easier for the preferences of industrial firms to get a hearing from important decisionmakers.[18]

Hypotheses

In this section, I use data regarding international trade and finance and the structure of bank-industry ties in Britain, France, and Italy to develop hypotheses about exchange-rate policy that are based on the openness and institutionalist explanations of exchange-rate politics. Quantitative data highlight four important characteristics regarding the openness of the British, French, and Italian economies. First, their tradable goods sectors (defined as manufacturing industry) were of roughly equal size. The value added by manufacturing industry as a percentage of gross domestic product (GDP) averaged 20.6 percent in Britain, 21.4 percent in France, and 22.4 percent in Italy for the period 1983–1993.[19] Second, from the 1970s to the 1990s, Britain was more open to trade with the rest of the world than were France and Italy. Third, from the 1970s to the 1990s, trade with the European Union as a percentage of gross domestic product was roughly equal in the three countries (see Table 1.1). Fourth, Britain was much more open to international capital movements than France and Italy. Foreign assets as a percentage of the money supply is a rough measure of the integration of domestic and international finance. The mean of foreign assets as a percentage of the money supply in Britain outstripped the figures for France and Italy by factors of six and sixteen, respectively, from the 1970s to the 1990s.[20] The British pound sterling was more widely traded on foreign exchange markets and used to denominate more external bank loans and bond issues than the French franc and the Italian lira.[21] British securities markets were much more integrated with overseas markets.[22] London is one of the world's three major financial centers, serving as the headquarters for some of the most internationally oriented banks and financial firms.

Table 1.1 Trade Patterns

		1971–1980	1981–1990	1991–1999
Trade with the EU as a percentage of GDP	Britain	18.9	22.9	21.7
	France	18.6	21.9	22.1
	Italy	18.5	19.5	20.2
Trade with the rest of the world as a percentage of GDP	Britain	23.4	19.4	17.7
	France	13.5	15.0	13.5
	Italy	16.5	16.3	14.0

Source: Calculated from *European Economy* 66 (1998): 138–141, 146–149.

British banks long have had weaker ties to industry than do their continental counterparts. Weak bank-industry ties in Britain date to the nineteenth century, when commercial banks and equity markets formed to finance the development of small industrial firms.[23] In contrast, French and Italian governments restructured their national financial institutions after World War II to channel capital to industry through the banking sector.[24] Quantitative evidence demonstrates that the structure of British industrial firms' liabilities still differ from those of French and Italian firms. Funds borrowed from banks comprised a larger proportion of industry's total liabilities in France and Italy than in Britain (see Table 1.2, line 1). Between 1981 and 1992, borrowed funds as a percentage of industrial firms' liabilities were, on average, about 10 percent higher in France than in Britain and about 20 percent higher in Italy than in Britain. As a consequence, British

Table 1.2 Indicators of Bank-Industry Ties (means of annual data)

	Indicator	Britain	France	Italy
1.	Industrial firms' borrowed funds as a percentage of liabilities, 1981–1992[a]	13.4[b]	23.8	32.9
2.	Industrial firms' equity as a percentage of liabilities, 1981–1992[c]	47.2[b]	31.9	23.9
3.	Debt-equity ratios of nonfinancial enterprises, 1980, 1984–1990[d]	1.07	1.94	3.06[e]
4.	Stock market capitalization as a percentage of GDP, 1982–1990[f]	74.9	19.7	12.9
5.	Gross bond issues: ratio of financial to nonfinancial enterprises, 1979–1992[g]	0.42	3.68[h]	4.12

Notes:

a. Data exclude trade credit, accounts payable, and long-term bonds. Data for French firms include short-term loans from banks and long-term borrowed funds. Data for British firms include short-term loans from banks and long-term borrowed funds from banks. Data for Italian firms include short-term and long-term funds borrowed from banks and affiliates. *Source:* Calculated from Organization for Economic Cooperation and Development, *OECD Financial Statistics Part 3: Non-Financial Enterprises Financial Statements 1993* (Paris: OECD, 1993), pp. 52–53, 60–61, 89.

b. Data are for 1983–1990.

c. *Source:* Calculated from OECD, *OECD Financial Statistics Part 3,* pp. 52–53, 60–61, 89.

d. Organization for Economic Cooperation and Development, *Financial Market Trends* 53 (October 1992): 20.

e. Data are for 1984–1990.

f. *Source:* Marcello de Cecco and Giovanni Ferri, "Origini e natura speciale dell'attivitá di banca d'affari in Italia," Banca d'Italia Temi de Discussione No. 242 (Rome: Banca d'Italia, December 1994), p. 33.

g. Nonfinancial institutions include public and private enterprises. Data for France after 1983 include industrial development (CODEVI) funds. *Source:* Calculated from Organization for Economic Cooperation and Development, *OECD Financial Statistics Monthly: Domestic Markets,* various issues and pages.

h. Data are for 1979–1990.

firms relied more heavily on equity finance—the sale of shares to individual and institutional investors. On average, 47.2 percent of British industrial firms' liabilities took the form of equity, whereas the corresponding figures for French and Italian firms were only 31.9 percent and 23.9 percent (Table 1.2, line 2). The result was much higher debt-equity ratios for nonfinancial firms in France and Italy than for those in Britain (Table 1.2, line 3). British firms also financed a greater proportion of their investment through retained earnings and relied on bank loans primarily for short-term working capital, rather than long-term investment capital.[25] It is not surprising that the stock exchange was much larger and more liquid in Britain than in France and Italy. Table 1.2, line 4 presents data on the capitalization of the French, Italian, and British stock markets for most of the 1980s. On average over this period, the British stock market was almost four times as large as the French market and six times as large as the Italian market. Total capitalization increased in all three countries in the 1980s, growing by a factor of 2.3 in Britain, 5.4 in France, and 3.0 in Italy. Despite this growth, the British market remained qualitatively larger than the other two. Another source of strong bank-industry ties in France and Italy was the fact that the vast majority of issuers of new corporate bonds were financial corporations (Table 1.2, line 5). Banks loaned much of the money they raised in the bond market to nonfinancial firms; in other words, corporate bonds served as another form of bank intermediation. British financial firms issued relatively small quantities of bonds, instead relying on money markets to raise funds.

These average figures obscure some changes in the financing of French, and to a lesser extent Italian, industry. During the 1980s and early 1990s, French firms' borrowed funds as a percentage of liabilities declined by just under 50 percent, and equity as a percentage of liabilities rose by over 10 percent. As a consequence, French firms' debt-equity ratios fell by about 30 percent while the ratio for Italian firms fell by 10 percent. Despite these changes, French and Italian firms' reliance on bank lending for funds remained much higher than that of British firms.[26] Chapter 5 explores the relationship between these changes in bank-industry ties and exchange-rate politics in detail.

The structure of industrial firms' ownership and management differed in important ways as well. In Britain, institutional investors such as pension funds were the largest category of equity owners.[27] Investors tended to hold equity in individual firms for short periods, selling particular stocks (or equities in general) when poor results were reported. Pension funds in particular focused on maximizing short-term returns and on spreading their funds over a wide variety of investments to reduce risk. These strategies limited investors' willingness and ability to hold a particular firm's debt or equity during periods of low profitability or to try to influence management decisions. French and Italian patterns of equity holdings were quite different. Nonfinancial firms, banks, and the state owned more shares, quite often in the form of long-term interlocking shareholdings. Beginning in the mid-1980s, the Italian and especially French states began privatizing their equity stakes; to facilitate these sales the authorities took steps to improve the liquidity and openness of domestic securities markets and to enhance the attractiveness of equities for small investors. Nonetheless, the state retained a good deal of influence by selling sizable stakes in privatized banks and firms to "hard cores" of long-term investors.[28]

With these data in hand, we can compare the preferences and policies forecast by the openness and institutionalist explanations. Both predict that industry in all three countries would favor exchange-rate policies aimed at stabilizing the currency at a competitive level. The openness explanation forecasts that the international orientation of British finance would lead it to lobby more strongly for currency stability than its counterparts in France and Italy. The institutionalist approach expects the opposite pattern of preferences. British finance should have had a strong preference for low inflation and supported exchange-rate stabilization only when it produced that outcome; because of their close links to industry, French and Italian banks should have given higher priority to exchange-rate stability. Turning to policy choices, the openness explanation predicts that the overseas exposure of British finance and the trade dependence of industry on the European market should lead British authorities over time to attach greater importance to stabilizing sterling at a competitive level against other European currencies. In contrast, the institutionalist explanation foresees that weak bank-industry ties would lead British authorities to focus on domestic economic policy, whereas French and Italian governments, facing a unified coalition of banks and industry, would give priority to stabilizing the exchange rate at a competitive level.

International Institutions

Defining International Institutions

Oran Young's useful and widely accepted definition holds that international institutions (or regimes) are "practices consisting of recognized roles linked together by clusters of rules or conventions governing relations among the occupants of these roles."[29] The rules of international institutions can help states to engage in mutually advantageous cooperation in three ways. First, they facilitate the exchange of information among states about their goals, behavior, and expectations, making it easier to detect and punish defection from a commitment to cooperate. Second, established rules can change the costs and benefits of cooperation. For example, the adoption of a single currency makes it impossible for a member state to defect from monetary union without going through the costly and risky process of reintroducing a national currency. Third, institutions lengthen governments' time horizons and trust in each other, making them more willing to engage in cooperation that imposes short-term costs but provides long-term gains.[30] But why do states come to accept some institutionalized rules but not others? Two research programs in international politics—distributional bargaining and learning—explain what drives agreement on specific rules.

The Distributional Bargaining Explanation

This explanation holds that rules of international institutions distribute any burdens arising from cooperation in different ways. States bargain to create rules that distribute these costs away from themselves, and the institutions that emerge from their bargaining reflect the preferences of the most powerful states.[31] The principal source of power is a credible threat not to participate in any new institution, that is, to continue with the status quo or another nonnegotiated outcome. In other words, the state with the least to gain from creating new rules has the most power to set the institution's rules.[32]

Studies in this tradition conclude that Germany has had the most influence over the rules of European monetary institutions. Three factors made it possible for Germany to credibly threaten not to agree to new rules that did not closely match its preferences. First, Germany was in a position to resist demands that it adjust policy to eliminate balance-of-payments disequilibria and unwanted changes in market exchange rates. Adjustment takes the form of changing the exchange rate, altering fiscal and monetary policies, or imposing controls on the movement of capital overseas.[33] A country with an appreciating currency, as was typically the case with the German mark after 1973 because of Germany's low inflation, could respond effectively to market pressures to revalue by purchasing government securities in the secondary market with the currency it issued.[34] In contrast, countries with depreciating currencies—such as France and Italy—could not offset currency outflows indefinitely by selling their holdings of foreign currency reserves. They eventually ran out of reserves and had to raise interest rates or impose capital controls if they wished to keep the currency stable.[35] Germany preferred to maintain this asymmetrical distribution of the burdens of adjustment, whereas France and Italy preferred changing the rules so that Germany had to adjust policy to keep exchange rates stable.[36]

A second reason for Germany's credible threat to veto changes was that it benefited disproportionately from the rules of the status quo institution, the EMS. The EMS stabilized the mark and dampened its appreciation against other participating currencies, which benefited German firms exporting to Europe.[37] A final reason was that Germany's central bank, the Bundesbank, as well as important interest groups, opposed any European rules that could subordinate monetary policy autonomy or the goal of internal price stability to exchange-rate stabilization. The Bundesbank's independence and political standing in German politics made governments wary about agreeing to international rules that did not accord with the central bank's preferences.[38]

The Learning Explanation

The learning explanation has much in common with the constructivist understanding of international politics. Constructivists stress that preferences and bargaining strategies are not innate but are informed by a state's environment. Sustained communication—often facilitated by an international institution—can lead governments to exchange ideas about how the social world operates.[39] Such communication may induce them to learn and adopt similar ideas about the goals and tools of economic policy cooperation.[40] These commonly accepted ideas can serve as "focal points" that suggest specific rules for international institutions.[41] Some explanations of European integration that draw on the neofunctionalist theoretical tradition also emphasize how supranational institutions can facilitate such communication and learning.[42]

A good example is Kathleen McNamara's book *Currency of Ideas,* in which she argues that governments learned the advantages of a specific set of rules for monetary policy cooperation in three steps.[43] First, during the 1970s and early 1980s, the authorities in many countries—but not in Germany—experimented with loose monetary policies, floating exchange rates, and fiscal expansion. These policies produced inflation and currency depreciation but had little positive effect on growth and employment. An important reason for this policy failure was a rapid increase in international capital mobility that allowed investors to withdraw funds from states pursuing inflationary policies. The second step involved a process of "complex learning" that changed political leaders' ideas not only about the most effective policy tools but also about the overall goals of policy.[44] During the 1980s, governments adopted neoliberal ideas that held that loose monetary policies and depreciation increase inflation but do not promote growth and employment. But many specific varieties of neoliberalism existed, including targeting the money supply or exchange rate or increasing the political independence of central banks, and it was not clear how to choose among them. The third step started with the observation that the German version of neoliberalism produced superior economic outcomes in the turbulent 1970s and 1980s. German authorities employed a model of neoliberalism that emphasized low inflation and small budget deficits, exchange-rate stability, and central bank independence. Governments in other member states learned about and began to emulate this model; many stabilized their exchange rates in the EMS, adopted versions of monetary targeting, and raised interest rates to reduce inflation. The success of the German model also convinced these governments to change their preferences regarding the rules of European monetary institutions. During the 1970s, most favored rules that would lead to the rapid integration of decisionmaking power and subordinate central banks to political authorities. But by the late 1980s, they were convinced by German arguments in favor of gradual integration and central bank independence. In the 1990s, they agreed to and implemented the Maastricht Treaty plan for a monetary union managed by an independent European Central Bank and limited to member states with low inflation, stable exchange rates, and sustainable fiscal positions.

Germany was more than a passive model that some other countries chose to emulate. Sustained interaction in the EMS provided German authorities with a forum in which to communicate ideas to their European counterparts.[45] The existence of an international institution such as the EMS facilitated learning by providing a forum in which authorities developed commonly understood ideas about appropriate monetary policy goals and instruments, which reduced the importance of bargaining power in reaching agreements.

The work of McNamara and others represents an important advance in at least two respects. First, it moves beyond a tendency to equate rising international capital mobility with pressures for monetary integration.[46] Integration in the form of the EMS and then the Maastricht Treaty were only two of many possible responses to capital mobility and economic stagnation. Second, the focus on failure as promoting learning and a redefinition of interests is a useful advance over much of the recent constructivist work in international politics, which does not adequately explain the mechanisms that lead officials to adopt some ideas and institutions but not others.[47]

Evaluating the Explanations

It is not possible to compare directly the distributional bargaining and learning explanations for the rules of European monetary institutions, since both conclude that such rules would accord closely with German preferences. However, they do have different expectations about the *processes* by which states create such rules, and these differences make it possible to estimate the importance of distributional bargaining and learning. In particular, these explanations have quite different expectations about the bargaining positions and strategies of states other than Germany. The distributional bargaining approach holds that bargaining positions are a reflection of the preferences of powerful domestic groups, whereas the learning explanation holds that policy failure and interstate communication play an important role in shaping preferences. If the distributional bargaining approach more accurately reflects the process of rule creation, we should see little change in states' bargaining positions unless a shift occurred in the underlying preferences and power of domestic groups. But if learning is more important, states' bargaining positions should converge toward the German position during the 1980s and 1990s, after they experienced policy failure and learned the advantages of the German model of economic policy.

Plan of the Book

The following chapters use evidence from Britain, France, and Italy from 1973 to 1998 to evaluate explanations of exchange-rate policy and the rules of international institutions. Chapters 3 and 5 analyze groups' preferences and national policies regarding exchange-rate instability, depreciation, and appreciation. Chapters 2 and 4 investigate how states agreed on rules for international institutions by analyzing the negotiations of the EMS in 1978, the failure to reform the system's rules in the 1980s, and the negotiation of the Treaty of European Union's sections on economic and monetary union in 1988–1991. The final chapter discusses more recent institutional developments.

I use congruence and process-tracing procedures to evaluate the causal relationships discussed in the previous two sections.[48] The congruence procedure simply compares the predicted and actual relationships between underlying structural conditions and outcomes that are relatively easy to observe. For exchange-rate politics, this includes the co-variation between the independent variables of bank-industry ties and openness with the dependent variable of exchange-rate policies; for international negotiations, it includes the relationship between the independent variables of bargaining power and policy failure and the dependent variable of the rules of European monetary institutions. The advantage of the congruence procedure is that most of the information regarding the independent and dependent variables identified by each theory is easy to observe. But it does not directly measure the key intervening variables—groups' preferences and national bargaining positions. Process tracing, in contrast, allows me to directly examine "the decision process by which various initial conditions are translated into outcomes."[49] In particular, I look for evidence in the available historical record regarding the preferences and lobbying activities of banks and industry in the three countries to see if the openness or institutionalist accounts of exchange-rate politics have greater support. I also investigate national bargaining positions to see if these converged on the German model, as posited by the learning approach, or remained quite different, as the distributional bargaining approach expects.

The information in these chapters is drawn from a number of published sources, including official documents and reports, treaties, newspapers and trade journals, memoirs, and secondary literature. To complement the published record, I conducted interviews with current and former officials from central banks, foreign affairs and finance ministries, international organizations, and European, national and sectoral interest groups, as well as current and former politicians, bankers, businesspeople, and academics.

The last chapter begins by summarizing the two major empirical findings. First, the institutions linking banks and industry play a more important role than openness in explaining domestic groups' preferences as well as governments' policy choices. Particularly important are the differences between exchange-rate politics in Britain and those in France and Italy. British finance and industry consistently held divergent exchange-rate policy preferences, despite the fact that the economy was quite open to trade and investment with continental Europe. Faced with a divided private sector, British governments' policy choices privileged domestic economic considerations and the preferences of finance over those of industry by allowing sterling to float and appreciate. Banks and manufacturing firms in France and Italy tended to hold similar exchange-rate policy preferences, and governments in these countries generally tried to stabilize their exchange rates at a competitive level. The second finding is that the distributional bargaining approach does a better job than the learning approach in explaining the dynamics of bargaining over the rules of European monetary institutions. Governments' institutional preferences were stable from the 1970s to the 1990s, despite policy failure and continued interaction with Germany in the EMS. I also show that more recent institutional developments, such as the negotiation in the mid-1990s of the Stability and Growth Pact limiting governments' fiscal policies and the introduction of a single European currency in 1999, are consistent with the distributional bargaining explanation. The chapter concludes with discussions of the findings' implications for the analysis of foreign economic policy and international institutions as well as the politics of Europe's single currency.

Notes

1. There is a large and diverse literature here; important statements include Thomas Ferguson, "From Normalcy to New Deal: Industrial Structure, Party Competition, and American Public Policy in the Great Depression," *International Organization* 38, no. 1 (1984): 41–94; Peter Gourevitch, *Politics in Hard Times: Comparative Responses to International Economic Crises* (Ithaca, NY: Cornell University Press, 1986); Peter J. Katzenstein, ed., *Between Power and Plenty* (Madison: University of Wisconsin Press, 1978); Helen Milner, *Resisting Protectionism* (Princeton: Princeton University Press, 1988); D. Michael Schafer, *Winners and Losers: How Sectors Shape the Developmental Prospects of States* (Ithaca, NY: Cornell University Press, 1994); and Ronald Rogowski, *Commerce and Coalitions* (Princeton: Princeton University Press, 1989).

2. A third explanation looks at how governments try to establish a credible

reputation for low inflation by committing to a policy rule such as a fixed exchange rate or independence for the central bank. This theory does not explain why decisionmakers adopt different rules. An interpretation consistent with a focus on domestic politics is that the definition and implementation of monetary policy rules depends on the preferences of domestic groups. See Francesco Giavazzi and Marco Pagano, "The Advantages of Tying One's Hands: EMS Discipline and Central Bank Credibility," *European Economic Review* 32 (1988): 1055–1082; and John T. Woolley, "Policy Credibility and European Monetary Institutions," in *Euro-politics: Institutions and Policymaking in the New European Community*, ed. Alberta Sbragia (Washington, DC: Brookings Institution, 1992).

3. Marcus Fleming, "Domestic Financial Policies Under Fixed and Floating Exchange Rates," *IMF Staff Papers* 9 (November 1962): 369–377; and Robert Mundell, "Capital Mobility and Stabilization Policy Under Fixed and Flexible Exchange Rates," *Canadian Journal of Economics and Political Science* 30 (August 1964): 421–431.

4. John B. Goodman and Louis W. Pauly, "The Obsolescence of Capital Controls? Economic Management in an Age of Global Markets," *World Politics* 46, no. 1 (1993): 50–82.

5. Barry Eichengreen, *Globalizing Capital* (Princeton: Princeton University Press, 1996).

6. This simple description does not do justice to the complexity of international financial flows because it ignores the different levels of risk attached to investments in different currencies. Nonetheless, sophisticated studies taking these factors into account generally conclude that international capital mobility has increased since the 1970s. For a survey, see Jeffrey A. Frankel, "Measuring International Capital Mobility: A Review," *American Economic Review* 87, no. 2 (May 1992): 197–202.

7. From 1973 to 1980, average annual real short-term interest rates were –8.3 percent in Britain, –1.0 percent in France, and –3.6 percent in Italy. From 1981 to 1991, the averages were 4.6 percent in Britain, 4.3 percent in France, and 4.2 percent in Italy. These figures are calculated from data in David M. Andrews, "Capital Mobility and Monetary Adjustment in Western Europe, 1973–1991," *Policy Sciences* 27 (1994): 431–432.

8. Political economy explanations of market exchange rates include Jeffry Frieden, "The Political Economy of European Exchange Rates: An Empirical Assessment," manuscript, Harvard University, August 1998; and Thomas Oatley, *Monetary Politics: Exchange Rate Cooperation in the European Union* (Ann Arbor: University of Michigan Press, 1997).

9. C. Randall Henning, *Currencies and Politics in the United States, Germany, and Japan* (Washington, DC: Institute for International Economics, 1994), 9.

10. Jeffry A. Frieden and Ronald Rogowski, "The Impact of the International Economy on National Policies: An Analytical Overview," in *Internationalization and Domestic Politics*, ed. Robert B. Keohane and Helen Milner (New York: Cambridge University Press, 1996), 25–47.

11. This and the following two paragraphs draw on Jeffry A. Frieden, "Invested Interests: The Politics of National Economic Policies in a World of Global Finance," *International Organization* 45, no. 4 (Autumn 1991): 425–451; and Jeffry A. Frieden, "Exchange-Rate Politics: Contemporary Lessons from American History," *Review of International Political Economy* 1, no. 1 (Spring 1994): 81–103.

12. Paul De Grauwe and Bernard De Bellefroid, "Long-Run Exchange Rate Variability and International Trade," in *Real Financial Linkages Among Open Economies*, ed. S. Arndt and D. Richardson (Cambridge, MA: MIT Press, 1989); and Avinash Dixit, "Hysteresis, Import Penetration, and Exchange Rate Pass-Through," *Quarterly Journal of Economics* 104, no. 2 (1989): 205–227.

13. Jeffry A. Frieden, "The Impact of Goods and Capital Market Integration on European Monetary Politics," *Comparative Political Studies* 29, no. 2 (April 1996): 193–222.

14. Douglass C. North, *Institutions, Institutional Change, and Economic Performance* (New York: Cambridge University Press, 1990); and Kenneth A. Shepsle, "Institutional Arrangements and Equilibrium in Multi-Dimensional Voting Models," *American Journal of Political Science* 23 (1979): 27–59. An application to European monetary integration is James I. Walsh, "International Constraints and Domestic Choices: Economic Convergence and Exchange-Rate Policy in France and Italy," *Political Studies* 42, no. 2 (June 1994): 243–258.

15. Recent works in this tradition include Matthew Evangelista, "Stalin's Revenge: Institutional Barriers to Internationalization in the Soviet Union," and Geoffrey Garrett and Peter Lange, "Internationalization, Institutions, and Political Change," both in *Internationalization and Domestic Politics*, ed. Robert O. Keohane and Helen V. Milner (New York: Cambridge University Press, 1996); Peter Hall, *Governing the Economy* (New York: Oxford University Press, 1986); Peter A. Hall and Rosemary C. R. Taylor, "Political Science and the Four New Institutionalisms," paper prepared for the Annual Meeting of the American Political Science Association, New York, September 1994; Ellen M. Immergut, "The Theoretical Core of the New Institutionalism," *Politics and Society* 26, no. 1 (March 1998): 5–34; James G. March and Johan P. Olsen, "The New Institutionalism: Organizational Factors in Political Life," *American Political Science Review* 78, no. 3 (September 1984): 734–749; and Kathleen Thelen and Sven Steinmo, "Historical Institutionalism in Comparative Politics," in *Structuring Politics: Historical Institutionalism in Comparative Perspective*, ed. Sven Steinmo, Kathleen Thelen, and Frank Longstreth (New York: Cambridge University Press, 1992), 1–32.

16. Henning, *Currencies and Politics*.

17. Henning, *Currencies and Politics*, 23–26.

18. Henning, *Currencies and Politics*, 30–31; quotation from p. 30.

19. Employment in manufacturing industry as a percentage of gross domestic product also was quite similar in the three countries. Organization for Economic Cooperation and Development, *Historical Statistics 1960–1993* (Paris: OECD, 1995), 42, 43, 57, 66.

20. From 1979 to 1992, foreign assets as a percentage of the money supply averaged 194 percent in Britain, 31 percent in France, and 12 percent in Italy. Calculated from annual data in country tables in International Monetary Fund, *International Financial Statistics Yearbook 1993* (Washington, DC: International Monetary Fund, 1993). Foreign assets are defined as foreign assets of deposit money banks (line 21); money supply is from line 351 and is defined as money (line 34) plus quasi-money (line 35).

21. George S. Tavlas, *On the International Use of Currencies: The Case of the Deutsche Mark*, Princeton Essays in International Finance No. 181 (Princeton: International Finance Section, Department of Economics, Princeton University, March 1991), Table 9; and George S. Tavlas and Yuzuru Ozeki, *The Internationalization of Currencies: An Appraisal of the Japanese Yen*, IMF

Occasional Paper No. 90 (Washington, DC: International Monetary Fund, January 1992), Table 23.

22. See data in Bank for International Settlements, *62nd Annual Report* (Basel: Bank for International Settlements, 1992), 62.

23. The classic analysis is Alexander Gerschenkron, *Economic Backwardness in Historical Perspective* (Cambridge, MA: Belknap Press for Harvard University Press, 1962), 1–30; see also Hall, *Governing the Economy;* Anthony Hilton, *City Within a State: A Portrait of Britain's Financial World* (London: I. B. Tauris, 1987); E. J. Hobsbawm, *Industry and Empire: An Economic History of Britain Since 1750* (London: Weidenfeld and Nicolson, 1968); Geoffrey K. Ingham, *Capitalism Divided? The City and Industry in British Social Development* (Basingstoke: Macmillan, 1984); Frank Longstreth, "The City, Industry, and the State," in *State and Economy in Contemporary Capitalism*, ed. Colin Crouch (London: Croom Helm, 1979); and Michael Lisle-Williams, "The State, Finance and Industry in Britain," in *State, Finance and Industry: A Comparative Analysis of Post-war Trends in Six Advanced Industrial Economies*, ed. Andrew Cox (Brighton: Wheatsheaf Books, 1986).

24. On France, see Hall, *Governing the Economy;* Jack Hayward, *The State and the Market Economy: Industrial Patriotism and Economic Intervention in France* (Brighton: Wheatsheaf Books, 1986); Charles Kindleberger, "The Post-War Resurgence of the French Economy," in *In Search of France*, ed. Stanley Hoffmann et al. (New York: Harper and Row, 1963); Richard F. Kuisel, *Capitalism and the State in Modern France: Renovation and Economic Management in the Twentieth Century* (New York: Cambridge University Press, 1981); Yves Mamou, *Une Machine de Pouvoir: La Direction du Trésor* (Paris: Éditions la Découverte, 1988); Pierre Massé, *Le Plan ou L'Anti-Hasard* (Paris: Gallimard, 1965); John Zysman, "The French State in the International Economy," in *Between Power and Plenty*, ed. Peter J. Katzenstein (Madison: University of Wisconsin Press, 1978); and John Zysman, *Governments, Markets, and Growth: Financial Systems and the Politics of Industrial Change* (Ithaca, NY: Cornell University Press, 1983). For Italy, see Mario Caciagli, "Il Resistable Declino del DC," in *Il Sistema Politico Italiano*, ed. Gianfranco Pasquino (Bari: Laterza, 1985); Giuseppe Di Palma, "The Available State: Problems of Reform," *West European Politics* 2, no. 3 (October 1979): 149–165; Paul Furlong, "State, Finance and Industry in Italy," in *State, Finance and Industry: A Comparative Analysis of Post-War Trends in Six Advanced Industrial Economies*, ed. Andrew Cox (Brighton: Wheatsheaf Books, 1986); Paul Ginsborg, *A History of Contemporary Italy: Society and Politics 1943–1988* (London: Penguin, 1990), 141–185; Alan R. Posner, "Italy: Dependence and Political Fragmentation," in *Between Power and Plenty,* ed. Peter J. Katzenstein (Madison: University of Wisconsin Press, 1978); Eugenio Scalfari and Giuseppe Turani, *Razza Padrona* (Milan: Feltrinelli, 1974); and Eugenio Scalfari, ed., *Intervista sul Capitalismo* (Bari: Laterza, 1976).

25. Colin Mayer, "New Issues in Corporate Finance," *European Economic Review* 32 (1988): 1172; and Andrew D. Bain, "Causes of Change and Innovation in the Mix of Financial Instruments: The UK Experience," in *Shifting Frontiers in Financial Markets*, ed. D. E. Fair (Dordrecht: Martinus Nijhoff, 1986), 96.

26. For Britain, see Charles Goodhart, "Structural Changes in the British Capital Markets," in *The Operation and Regulation of Financial Markets*, ed. Charles Goodhart, David Currie, and David T. Llewellyn (London: Macmillan, 1987); David T. Llewellyn, "Competition, Diversification, and Structural Change in the British Financial System," in *Banking Structures in Major Countries*, ed.

George G. Kaufman (Boston: Kluwer Academic Publishers, 1992). For France, see Philip G. Cerny, "The 'Little Big Bang' in Paris: Financial Market Deregulation in a *Dirigiste* System," *European Journal of Political Research* 17 (1989): 180–181; Christian de Boissieu, "Lessons from the French Experience as Compared with Some Other OECD Countries," in *Changing Money: Financial Innovation in Developed Countries*, ed. Marcello de Cecco (New York: Basil Blackwell, 1987); John B. Goodman, "Monetary Policy and Financial Deregulation in France," *French Politics and Society* 10, no. 4 (Fall 1992); Michael Loriaux, "States and Markets: French Financial Interventionism in the Seventies," *Comparative Politics* 20, no. 2 (January 1988); Jacques Mélitz, "Monetary Policy in France," Centre for Economic Policy Research Discussion Paper No. 509 (January 1991). For Italy, see Cesare Caranza and Carlo Cottarelli, "Financial Innovation in Italy: A Lop-Sided Process," in *Changing Money: Financial Innovation in Developed Countries*, ed. Marcello De Cecco (Oxford: Basil Blackwell, 1987); Marcello de Cecco and Giovanni Ferri, "Origini e natura speciale dell'attivitá di banca d'affari in Italia," Banca d'Italia Temi di discussione No. 242 (December 1994); Gerald A. Epstein and Juliet B. Schor, "The Divorce of the Banca d'Italia and the Italian Treasury: A Case Study of Central Bank Independence," in *State, Market, and Social Regulation: New Perspectives on Italy,* ed. Peter Lange and Marino Regini (New York: Cambridge University Press, 1989); and C. Milana, "Introduzione," in *Processi di Accumulazione e Politica Industriale in Italia*, ed. C. Milana (Milan: Franco Angeli, 1992).

27. Bank for International Settlements, *59th Annual Report* (Basel: Bank for International Settlements, 12 June 1989), 87.

28. M. Bianco and S. Trento, "Capitalismi a Confronto: I Modelli di Controllo delle Imprese," *Stato e Mercato* 43 (April 1995): 65–93; and Vivien A. Schmidt, *From State to Market? The Transformation of French Business and Government* (New York: Cambridge University Press, 1996), 157–162, 372.

29. Oran Young, *International Cooperation* (Ithaca, NY: Cornell University Press, 1989), 12–13.

30. Key works include Andreas Hasenclever, Peter Mayer, and Volker Rittberger, *Theories of International Regimes* (New York: Cambridge University Press, 1997); Robert Keohane, *After Hegemony* (Princeton: Princeton University Press, 1984); Stephen Krasner, ed., *International Regimes* (Ithaca, NY: Cornell University Press, 1983); and Michael C. Webb, *The Political Economy of Policy Coordination* (Ithaca, NY: Cornell University Press, 1995).

31. Geoffrey Garrett, "International Cooperation and Institutional Choice: The European Community's Internal Market," *International Organization* 46, no. 2 (Spring 1992): 533–560; and Stephen Krasner, "Global Communications and National Power: Life on the Pareto Frontier," *World Politics* 43 (April 1991): 336–366.

32. Albert O. Hirschman, *National Power and the Structure of Foreign Trade* (Berkeley: University of California Press, 1945/1980); and Thomas C. Schelling, *The Strategy of Conflict* (Cambridge: Harvard University Press, 1960).

33. Benjamin J. Cohen, *Organizing the World's Money: The Political Economy of International Monetary Relations* (New York: Basic Books, 1977); Robert Gilpin, *The Political Economy of International Relations* (Princeton: Princeton University Press, 1987); 118–170; and Alberto Giovannini, "How Do Fixed-Exchange Rate Regimes Work? Evidence from the Gold Standard, Bretton Woods and the EMS," in *Blueprints for Exchange Rate Management*, ed. Marcus Miller, Barry Eichengreen, and Richard Portes (New York: Academic Press, 1989).

34. This sterilization of capital inflows is not quite as easy as this sentence implies. Indeed, one reason advanced for German membership in the EMS is that by making the mark and other EMS assets more similar, the regime spreads capital inflows over a larger number of countries. Nonetheless, Germany has more monetary policy autonomy than other participants. See Jürgen von Hagen, "Monetary Policy Coordination in the European Monetary System," in *Monetary Policy in Developed Economies*, ed. Michele U. Fratianni and Dominick Salvatore (Westport, CT: Greenwood Press, 1993), 538.

35. von Hagen, "Monetary Policy Coordination in the European Monetary System," 541; see also Charles Wyplosz, "Asymmetry in the EMS: Intentional or Systemic?" *European Economic Review* 33 (1989): 310–320.

36. Paul De Grauwe, "The Political Economy of Monetary Union in Europe," *The World Economy* 16, no. 6 (November 1993): 653–661; Geoffrey Garrett, "The Politics of Maastricht," *Economics and Politics* 5, no. 2 (July 1993): 105–123; Joseph M. Grieco, "The Maastricht Treaty, Economic and Monetary Union, and the Neo-Realist Research Programme," *Review of International Studies* 21 (1995): 21–40; Matthias Kaelberer, "Money and Power in Europe," manuscript, Iowa State University, n.d.; Andrew Moravcsik, *The Choice for Europe: Social Purpose and State Power from Messina to Maastricht* (Ithaca, NY: Cornell University Press, 1998); and Louis W. Pauly, "The Politics of European Monetary Union: National Strategies, International Implications," *International Journal* (Winter 1991–1992): 93–111.

37. Henning, *Currencies and Politics*.

38. Karl Kaltenthaler, *Germany and the Politics of Europe's Money* (Durham, NC: Duke University Press, 1998); and Oatley, *Monetary Politics*.

39. Key works include Jeffrey T. Checkel, "The Constructivist Turn in International Relations Theory," *World Politics* 50, no. 2 (January 1998): 324–348; Martha Finnemore, *National Interests in International Society* (Ithaca, NY: Cornell University Press, 1996); Peter J. Katzenstein, ed., *The Culture of National Security* (New York: Columbia University Press, 1996); Friedrich V. Kratochwil and John Gerard Ruggie, "International Organization: A State of the Art on an Art of the State," *International Organization* 40 (1986): 753–775; and Alexander Wendt, "Collective Identity Formation and the International State," *American Political Science Review* 88, no. 2 (June 1994): 384–397.

40. Works that focus on the role of ideas and learning in international cooperation include Barry Eichengreen and Marc Uzan, "The 1933 World Economic Conference as an Instance of Failed International Cooperation," in *Double-Edged Diplomacy*, ed. Peter B. Evans, Harold K. Jacobson, and Robert D. Putnam (Berkeley: University of California Press, 1993), 171–206; Judith Goldstein and Robert O. Keohane, eds., *Ideas and Foreign Policy: Beliefs, Institutions, and Political Change* (Ithaca, NY: Cornell University Press, 1993); Peter M. Haas and Ernst B. Haas, "Learning to Learn: Improving International Governance," *Global Governance* 1 (1995): 255–285; Christian Joerges and Jürgen Neyer, "Transforming Strategic Interaction into Deliberative Problem-Solving," *Journal of European Public Policy* 4, no. 4 (December 1997): 609–625; Jack S. Levy, "Learning and Foreign Policy: Sweeping a Conceptual Minefield," *International Organization* 48, no. 2 (Spring 1994): 279–312; John Odell, "From London to Bretton Woods," *Journal of Public Policy* 8 (July–December 1988): 287–315; and Dan Reiter, *Crucible of Beliefs: Learning, Alliances, and World Wars* (Ithaca, NY: Cornell University Press, 1996).

41. Arthur T. Denzau and Douglass C. North, "Shared Mental Models:

Ideologies and Institutions," *Kyklos* 47 (1994): 3–31; Geoffrey Garrett and Barry R. Weingast, "Ideas, Interests, and Institutions: Constructing the European Community's Internal Market," in *Ideas and Foreign Policy*, ed. Robert Keohane and Judith Goldstein (Ithaca, NY: Cornell University Press, 1993); David Kreps, "Corporate Culture and Economic Theory," in *Perspectives on Positive Political Economy*, ed. James E. Alt and Kenneth A. Shepsle (New York: Cambridge University Press, 1990); and Barry R. Weingast, "A Rational Choice Perspective on the Role of Ideas," *Politics and Society* 23, no. 4 (December 1995): 449–464.

42. Examples include Garrett and Weingast, "Ideas, Interests and Institutions"; Ernst B. Haas, *The Uniting of Europe: Political, Social, and Economic Forces, 1950–1957* (Stanford: Stanford University Press, 1958); Leon N. Lindberg, *The Political Dynamics of European Economic Integration* (Stanford: Stanford University Press, 1963); and Wayne Sandholtz and John Zysman, "1992: Recasting the European Bargain," *World Politics* 42, no. 3 (October 1989): 95–128.

43. Kathleen R. McNamara, *The Currency of Ideas* (Ithaca, NY: Cornell University Press, 1998); see also David R. Cameron, "Transnational Relations and the Development of European Economic and Monetary Union," in *Bringing Transnational Relations Back In: Non-State Actors, Domestic Structures and International Institutions*, ed. Thomas Risse-Kappen (New York: Cambridge University Press, 1995); Kenneth Dyson, Kevin Featherstone, and George Michalopoulos, "Strapped to the Mast: EC Central Bankers Between Global Financial Markets and Regional Integration," *Journal of European Public Policy* 2, no. 3 (September 1995): 465–487; Wayne Sandholtz, "Choosing Union: Monetary Politics and Maastricht," *International Organization* 47, no. 1 (Winter 1993): 1–39; and Wayne Sandholtz, "Monetary Bargains: The Treaty on EMU," in *The State of the European Community: The Maastricht Debates and Beyond*, ed. Alan W. Cafruny and Glenda G. Rosenthal (Boulder: Lynne Rienner, 1995), 125–142.

44. On complex learning, see Joseph Nye, "Nuclear Learning in U.S.-Soviet Security Regimes," *International Organization* 41 (Summer 1987): 371–402.

45. Cameron, "Transnational Relations"; and McNamara, *Currency of Ideas*, 69, 154–156.

46. Dyson, Featherstone, and Michalopoulos, "Strapped to the Mast."

47. A criticism made by Checkel, "Constructivist Turn," 332; Paul Kowert and Jeffrey Legro, "Norms, Identity, and Their Limits: A Theoretical Reprise," in *The Culture of National Security*, ed. Peter J. Katzenstein (New York: Columbia University Press, 1996); and John Mearsheimer, "The False Promise of International Institutions," *International Security* 19, no. 3 (1994–1995): 42.

48. Alexander L. George and Timothy J. McKeown, "Case Studies and Theories of Organizational Decision Making," *Advances in Information Processing in Organizations* 2 (1985): 29–41.

49. George and McKeown, "Case Studies and Theories of Organizational Decision Making," 34.

2

Negotiating the European Monetary System

After the breakdown of the Bretton Woods regime of fixed exchange rates in the early 1970s, European governments constructed a regional arrangement, commonly called the "snake," to coordinate their monetary policies. The snake soon collapsed into a small group of countries dominated by Germany after Britain, France, and Italy withdrew and allowed their currencies to float. Governments in these three countries were unwilling to tighten monetary policy and risk recession in order to stabilize their currencies against the appreciating German mark. Instead they experimented with new frameworks for monetary policy that included deliberate currency depreciation and expansionary macroeconomic policies to promote growth and employment.

European governments did create a durable institution in 1978, the European Monetary System (EMS), to replace the snake. Yet the rules of the snake and the EMS were quite similar regarding approval of parity changes, balance-of-payments financing, requirements for policy adjustment, and other issues. Why would European governments agree to a new institution in 1978 so similar to the one that had failed to stabilize exchange rates just a few years earlier? Two answers to this question exist in the literature. The learning explanation holds that British, French, and Italian experiments with floating exchange rates and macroeconomic expansion outside the snake produced currency instability and high inflation but had little appreciable influence on growth and employment. By 1978 authorities had a better understanding of the advantages of keeping inflation low and preventing currency depreciation, making them more willing to agree to a new institution with rules likely to encourage such policies and outcomes.[1] The distributional bargaining explanation acknowledges that sharp depreciation and high inflation did give governments reasons to adopt policies more oriented toward price stability. But this change in preferences occurred at the margin and did not involve learning about and adopting new economic policy models and priorities. Governments did not commit themselves to Germany's mix of currency appreciation, monetary targeting, and central bank independence, which was intended to keep inflation low. Therefore, British, French, and Italian negotiators advocated rules for the EMS that differed from those of the snake. They preferred that the new institution provide them with greater external support for policies aimed at maintaining growth and employment and include rules that might require Germany to adjust its economic policy. Germany had little incentive to agree to such changes since it was reasonably satisfied with the status quo of floating exchange rates that allowed it to gear policy toward its primary goal of domestic price stability. This position gave German negotiators the power to insist on rules for the EMS that would allow the Bundesbank to focus on keeping inflation low when doing so conflicted with exchange-rate stabilization.[2]

In this chapter, I evaluate these explanations by examining the negotiation of the EMS in detail. I begin with a brief overview of the snake, demonstrating that by 1978 British, French, and Italian governments had some incentives to stabilize their exchange rates in a regional institution. The second section summarizes the EMS negotiations from the autumn of 1977 to the spring of 1979 and explains the origins of the German government's newfound interest in monetary policy cooperation. The rest of the chapter describes the fate of the EMS proposal in Britain, France, and Italy. For each country I describe government preferences regarding the rules of the EMS and their willingness or unwillingness to challenge domestic political opponents of the new institution. In the final section I conclude that most of the evidence supports the distributional bargaining rather than the learning explanation of the rules of the EMS.

The Snake

All the European countries were members of the Bretton Woods system of fixed exchange rates centered around the U.S. dollar, which was established after World War II. Tensions developed in the system in the 1960s and culminated in the U.S. unilateral devaluation in 1971. The Smithsonian Agreement of December 1971 ratified this devaluation and widened participating currencies' fluctuation bands from ±1 percent to ±2.25 percent against the dollar. This had the effect of greatly increasing the permissible exchange-rate fluctuations among European currencies. If one European currency was at the top of its fluctuation band against the dollar and another was at the bottom of its band, the two currencies would diverge from each other by 9 percent. To prevent such large fluctuations, European governments in March 1972 implemented an agreement to limit bilateral fluctuations to ±2.25 percent, supported by coordinated foreign exchange market intervention and credit lines among central banks. The system of narrower European bands came to be known as the "snake" (technically the Narrower Margins Agreement), which moved within the "tunnel" of wider dollar fluctuation bands established in the Smithsonian Agreement. When European countries stopped defending their currencies' parities against the dollar in March 1973, the "tunnel" disappeared and the European currencies floated jointly against the dollar.

The snake failed to become the basis for sustained monetary cooperation in Europe. Britain withdrew and floated sterling in June 1972, and Italy and France followed in February 1973 and January 1974, respectively (France rejoined from July 1975 to March 1976). The snake failed because German authorities pursued restrictive monetary policies that encouraged appreciation of the mark, but British, French, and Italian governments were unwilling to follow Germany's lead and implemented expansionary monetary policies to encourage growth and employment.[3]

Governments in all three countries soon became disenchanted with floating currencies. Between withdrawal from the snake and the negotiation of the EMS, each country experienced episodes of rapid currency depreciation and high inflation during a worldwide recession. The Heath government in Britain responded in the early 1970s with a Keynesian strategy of using fiscal and monetary policies to stimulate the economy. The Labour government elected in 1974 under Harold Wilson continued these expansionist policies, and by early 1975 inflation was increasing at an annual rate of 25 percent. A serious sterling crisis in 1976 led the new Labour prime minister, James Callaghan, to turn to the International Monetary Fund for a standby loan and to reduce the growth of government spending, tighten monetary policy, and introduce targets for the rate of growth of the money supply.[4]

French governments maintained an accommodating monetary policy to promote economic recovery in the early 1970s. This placed downward pressure on the franc in the foreign exchange markets, and the authorities chose to withdraw from the snake in 1974 rather than to raise interest rates to stabilize the currency. After winning the presidential election in 1974, Valéry Giscard d'Estaing increased taxes and tightened credit controls to reduce the double-digit inflation rate. Combined with slower growth overseas, these measures led to a recession by the end of the year but did allow the franc to rejoin the snake in July 1975. Despite some evidence that the recession was coming to an end, Prime Minister Jacques Chirac loosened fiscal policy in September 1975. The resulting increase in domestic demand pushed the current account from surplus to deficit in 1976, depreciated the franc, and led the government to withdraw from the snake again to avoid having to disinflate. This second withdrawal from the snake resulted in a 20 percent depreciation of the franc, and the new government under Prime Minister Raymond Barre, who was appointed in August 1976, adopted an austerity program to reduce inflation, stabilize the franc, and restore profitability to French firms. The government was willing to accept high levels of unemployment to achieve these goals, especially after the victory of the right-wing parties in the 1978 parliamentary elections.[5]

The Italian lira depreciated by 15 percent after its withdrawal from the snake in February 1973. Combined with accommodating fiscal and monetary policies, the depreciation created high inflation and rapid economic growth. The rise in world oil prices in the autumn of 1973 pushed the current account into deficit and further increased inflation. In early 1974, the government began discussions with the International Monetary Fund over a standby loan, eventually agreeing on a program to reduce the current account deficit and inflation by tightening monetary and credit policies. This program was more effective than expected, and by late 1974 economic growth had slowed dramatically. The authorities quickly loosened monetary policy, again increasing inflation and output and pushing the current account into deficit. A low level of central bank foreign currency reserves, combined with the recent collapse of a coalition government, fueled speculation against the lira. The central bank stopped supporting the currency in January 1976 and closed the foreign exchange market for two months after nearly exhausting its reserves. In June, Prime Minister Giulio Andreotti assembled a minority government informally supported by all the major parties, including the opposition Communist Party (the Partito Comunista Italiano [PCI]). Hoping to increase its credibility with voters, the PCI backed austerity measures when the lira came under speculative attack again in September, supported another agreement with the International Monetary Fund, and encouraged attempts to restrain wage growth. These measures, combined with the depreciation of the lira, led to slower growth but rapid improvement in the current account balance in 1977 and 1978.[6]

British, French, and Italian governments all had disappointing experiences with floating exchange rates. Each country went through at least one severe currency crisis, and both Britain and Italy turned to the International Monetary Fund for assistance. Many officials and observers concluded that deficit spending and accommodating monetary policies not only aggravated these currency crises but also were ineffective levers over domestic inflation, output, and employment. Thus governments throughout Europe had reasons to view favorably a new attempt to coordinate monetary and exchange-rate policies. Germany's response to the economic problems of the 1970s provided them with an alternative model for policy. German institutions and practices, such as targeting the rate of growth of the money supply and entrusting monetary policy to an independent central bank, produced lower inflation, higher employment, and currency appreciation. Macroeconomic stabilization plans implemented in Britain, France, and Italy from 1976 to 1978 incorporated some elements of German policy.

In the next section, I explain Germany's interest in exchange-rate cooperation and summarize the negotiations that created the European Monetary System in 1978. In the remainder of this chapter, I explore the links between these changes in policy goals and instruments and negotiating positions regarding the design of European monetary institutions.

Overview of the Negotiations

In October 1977, European Commission president Roy Jenkins called for closer coordination of monetary and economic policies within the European Economic Community and initiated discussions of these issues among foreign ministers.[7] His proposals attracted little attention until West German chancellor Helmut Schmidt proposed the creation of a "zone of monetary stability" in Western Europe at the meeting of the European Council of heads of state and government in Copenhagen in April 1978. Schmidt had initiated secret discussions with Giscard on this matter, and they agreed to cooperate in creating a new European monetary institution.[8] In addition to coordinating monetary policies, Schmidt envisioned creating a European Monetary Fund (EMF) to take over existing credit lines among central banks, pooling some official reserves, using European currencies rather than the dollar for foreign exchange market intervention, and encouraging use of the European unit of account (the predecessor to the European currency unit [ECU]) as a composite reserve asset.[9]

Schmidt hoped that a new European monetary institution might stop the depreciation of the dollar and a number of European currencies against the mark that threatened the competitiveness of German industry. Formal monetary policy cooperation might stabilize mark exchange rates and limit Germany's exposure to U.S. policy.[10] The Bundesbank was a reluctant participant in the negotiations, fearing that a new European institution would undermine its independence by requiring changes in interest rates and foreign exchange market intervention to stabilize the mark. These concerns led German negotiators to prefer rules that gave each member state the right to request changes in currencies' bilateral parities, limited requirements for intervention, and minimized any direct multilateral control of monetary policy.[11]

Schmidt's initiative coincided with useful developments in the foreign exchange markets. Sterling, the franc, and the lira all depreciated significantly in the mid-1970s. By 1977, this process had eliminated most of their real overvaluation, especially against the dollar. In 1978, these currencies depreciated in nominal terms against the mark, although sterling depreciated less than the franc and lira and did experience modest real appreciation. There was some speculative selling of the three currencies in October and November 1978, which stopped quickly when central banks raised interest rates. But in comparison to 1975 and 1976, the foreign exchange markets were relatively calm, making contemplation of a new monetary institution much easier. Also by 1978, inflation rates in the three countries had begun to converge; the annual percentage change in consumer prices in 1978 stood at 8.1 percent in Britain, 9.7 percent in France, and 12.1 percent in Italy. And during the preceding two years, governments in each country had made reducing inflation an important goal of economic policy.

After the Copenhagen summit, the next major step came at the European Council meeting in early July 1978 in Bremen, where Schmidt and Giscard persuaded the other leaders to consider establishing a new monetary institution by the end of the year. The essential elements of their proposal involved establishing currency fluctuation bands of ±2.25 percent around central parities to be supported by convergence of macroeconomic policies; subjecting realignments of parities (i.e., devaluation or revaluation) to mutual consent; establishing a new unit of account, the ECU, for settlement of credit lines among central banks; and creating an EMF within two years. At the Bremen meeting, Callaghan and Andreotti demanded that the EMS include significant resource transfers to poorer member states to offset their reduced monetary policy autonomy. Technical advisers discussed the exact structures and functions of the EMS during the summer and fall of 1978. During these discussions, the French, British, and Italians pressed for a system in which responsibilities for policy changes and foreign exchange market intervention would be based on a divergence indicator rather than a parity grid. Under the divergence indicator, countries whose exchange rates were diverging from the EMS average would adjust macroeconomic policy, regardless of whether the currency was appreciating or depreciating. Germany and the Netherlands favored a parity grid to determine policy changes, which in effect would require countries with depreciating currencies to adjust policy. The so-called Belgian Compromise of autumn 1978 held that the EMS would incorporate both the divergence indicator and parity grid. However, the divergence indicator would not *require* policy changes by countries with appreciating currencies and spoke only of a "presumption of action" on their part.[12]

Callaghan decided by October 1978 against taking sterling into the new institution. Over the next two months, he would negotiate a compromise under which Britain would become a member of the EMS, but sterling would continue to float and would not participate in the core of the system, the exchange-rate mechanism (ERM), which established parities among participating currencies. During final negotiations at the European Council meeting in December 1978, Giscard threatened to scuttle the EMS unless provisions dealing with agricultural trade were changed, and Andreotti briefly threatened not to participate because of insufficient resource transfers. These difficulties were resolved in late 1978 and early 1979, and the EMS began operation on 13 March 1979, with France, Italy, Germany, and five other countries joining the ERM and Britain opting not to participate in the ERM.[13]

The final agreement created a system of fixed-but-adjustable exchange rates with changes in parities agreed on by mutual consent. Each currency had a parity expressed in ECU, from which bilateral central exchange rates were calculated to form the parity grid. Market exchange rates were permitted to fluctuate within ±2.25 percent of these central rates (the fluctuation band for the Italian lira was ±6 percent). When a currency reached the margins of its fluctuation band against the ECU, states participating in the ERM were required to undertake "marginal intervention" in the foreign exchange markets to maintain the parity, preferably by intervening with EMS currencies rather than with the dollar. Central banks could intervene before their currency reached its fluctuation margin (so-called intramarginal intervention) if they secured the approval of the central bank whose currency was being bought or sold. If a currency crossed the divergence indicator, which was set at 75 percent of the currency's fluctuation band, the authorities were "presumed," in the language of the agreement, to take measures to maintain the parity. The agreement also increased currency swaps among participating central banks to finance intervention and to prevent balance-of-payments disequilibria. These consisted of the very-short-term financing facility (VSTF) to finance (required) marginal intervention, short-term financial support (STFS) to finance immediate balance-of-payments problems, and medium-term financial assistance (MTFA) for longer-term financing. Because marginal intervention was required for countries whose currencies reached their bilateral fluctuation margins, credit under the VSTF was automatic, unlimited, and initially repayable within forty-five days; the repayment period could be extended up to three months. Borrowing countries repaid half the credit in the borrowed currency and half in ECU. Finally, all countries, including Britain, contributed 20 percent of their foreign exchange reserves to the European Monetary Cooperation Fund but maintained control over the use of these reserves, and an EMF was to be created within two years to further institutionalize monetary policy coordination.[14]

European governments had incentives to create a new monetary institution in the late 1970s to replace the snake. The German government hoped that the EMS could restrain the appreciation of the mark that reduced industry's competitiveness. British, French, and Italian governments favored a new European institution that might prevent speculative attacks on their exchange rate and could support their attempts to reduce inflation. But this possibility of joint gains does not tell us much about the specific rules that each state preferred. In the following three sections, I examine British, French, and Italian preferences regarding the rules of the EMS to see if policy failure during the snake period led them to favor Germany's proposals or if their preferences remained substantially different from those of Germany.

Britain: The Primacy of Domestic Politics

James Callaghan was chancellor during the devaluation of 1967 and prime minister during the sterling crisis of 1976. These experiences had "made him sensitive to the difficulties facing sterling and much more aware of the problems which exchange-rate fluctuations and large flows of capital from one reserve asset to another could cause."[15] The 1976 crisis also jarred the Treasury, which "was disenchanted with floating exchange rates and naturally saw the immense advantages of currency stability as correspondingly more attractive."[16] In its EMS Green Paper, the government acknowledged that depreciation alone would not solve Britain's economic problems and that participation in the EMS might quell short-term speculation.[17]

The British nonetheless had serious reservations about the EMS proposal during early negotiations. Callaghan and Chancellor Denis Healey feared that participation could repeat the experience of the snake, in which currencies fixed to the mark that did not devalue or withdraw experienced real appreciation and high interest rates. This result could increase unemployment and trade union opposition to the Labour government.[18] Shortly before the Bremen summit in July 1978, Callaghan expressed doubts about a fixed exchange-rate regime that did not include significant resource transfers and stated that he would not unequivocally support the Franco-German plan for the EMS.[19] These concerns led the British to push during the summer of 1978 for greater resource transfers, a more symmetrical distribution of policy adjustment requirements among countries with appreciating and depreciating currencies, and an emphasis on economic growth over currency stability.[20] In addition, Callaghan earlier had proposed policy coordination within the Group of Seven (G-7) countries with the aim of persuading Germany to reinflate its economy. The G-7 had an advantage over European fora because it would allow Britain to ally with the United States and increase pressure on Germany.[21]

British officials analyzed the pros and cons of membership in the EMS during summer and autumn 1978. The Bank of England and the Treasury pointed out that some form of participation could stabilize expectations about future monetary policy and reduce both speculation against sterling and inflationary wage demands. In the end, this argument did not carry much weight with Callaghan and Healey, who, for example, rejected an Italian proposal that both the lira and sterling enter the EMS with wide fluctuation bands.[22] The Department of Industry concluded that participation in the EMS might make it easier to maintain a competitive exchange rate by stabilizing expectations, reducing the effects of future North Sea oil exports on the exchange rate, and providing Britain with access to balance-of-payments financing:

> The Department concluded that, provided satisfactory arrangements could be negotiated, there could be net benefits to British industry in joining the EMS. The main requirements were flexibility to adjust exchange rates, a commitment by the strong countries to expansion or upward adjustment of their exchange rates, and access to the EMF on reasonable terms.[23]

This analysis also did not influence the thinking of Callaghan and Healey because they felt it made unrealistic assumptions about possible German concessions.

Opposition from parts of the Labour Party to higher interest rates and sterling appreciation contributed to the government's reluctance to participate in the EMS. Callaghan decided in September to delay the next general election until the last possible moment in spring 1979. Since the government did not have a Labour majority in Parliament, it not only had to hold marginal seats but also had to win seats from the Conservatives and Liberals. Polls published at the time showed the Conservatives with a small lead, and Callaghan did not wish to risk an election in this environment.[24] His decision to delay the general election made him a captive of intra–Labour Party conflicts over the EMS and other issues. The government received a number of signals that any attempt to join the EMS would provoke rebellion among Labour members of Parliament and threaten the government's position in the House of Commons.

Labour's annual conference in October 1978 revealed strong opposition to the EMS proposal from the left wing of the party, which felt that participation would lead to higher interest rates and sterling appreciation. At the meeting of the Labour Party's National Executive Committee on 1 October 1978 to consider motions for the upcoming party conference, a proposal "denouncing and rejecting the EMS" passed by a vote of sixteen to nine.[25] Opponents of the EMS failed to force a vote on this motion at the conference, but their efforts revealed enough hostility to the EMS to persuade Callaghan that he could not count on the party's support.[26] In mid-November 1978, over half of backbench Labour members of Parliament signed a motion opposing "any attempt by the [European Economic Community], its institutions or its member states to assume control of domestic policies through a new monetary system for the Community." The sponsors of the motion claimed that many more Labour parliamentarians and half of the noncabinet members of the government supported their position. In late October, the Trade Unions Congress informed Callaghan and Healey that it opposed participation in the EMS as well.[27] The prime minister avoided formal cabinet discussions of the EMS until November 1978 because of this opposition. When the cabinet discussed the issue, a clear majority, including Healey, opposed British participation on the grounds that it would require higher interest rates and a reduction in monetary policy autonomy.[28]

In his memoirs, Callaghan wrote that he was "sympathetic to the general proposal" of the EMS, but was worried about the political consequences of full participation.

> I favored the general idea as likely to bring more order into the currency markets of Europe and the world, but quite apart from my technical concerns I could not travel fast. Many people in the Labour Party remained suspicious of what they thought was too close an entanglement with Europe, and this, coupled with my own and the Treasury's belief that sterling was standing too high to make our entry advantageous, led me . . . to tell Schmidt and Giscard that we could not enter the European monetary scheme at the outset. On the other hand, I publicly welcomed the scheme in principle, and when it was finally set up the Cabinet agreed to a number of steps to associate Britain with the development of a European Currency Unit (ECU).[29]

The British government was not enthusiastic about Schmidt's EMS proposal, and its weak political position in the House of Commons and strong opposition within the Labour Party further reduced government interest in participation. Callaghan feared that the domestic political consequences of British participation would outweigh any advantages in terms of stabilizing sterling but also wanted to prevent Britain from being locked out of future European and international monetary initiatives. Thus in late November the British negotiators successfully proposed separating participation in the ERM, the system of fixed but adjustable parities among participating currencies, from membership in the EMS. This would allow Britain to have a flexible exchange rate and some input into the development of the EMS.[30]

France: A Preoccupation with Economic Power

French president Giscard strongly believed that French economic and political power should match that of West Germany; this was "a theme to which he [returned] constantly, almost obsessively, in his speeches."[31] France, Giscard stated, must be the equal of Germany to secure its influence over

European politics. As he put it in an interview in October 1978, "Why do I talk so much about Germany. . . ? Because it would not be a good idea for Europe to be dominated by one country. . . . What I want France to achieve is to make sure that there are in Europe at least two countries of comparable influence, . . . Germany and France."[32] He emphasized that doing so required that France increase exports, especially of high-value-added goods; improve the competitiveness of French industry; and reduce inflation. These goals, along with stable agricultural prices, could be achieved with the creation of a new European monetary institution that would stabilize currencies, increase exports, and strengthen the government's credibility in the financial markets.[33]

Giscard expressed interest in Jenkins's proposals in the fall of 1977 but was hesitant about participating in a new institution that resembled the snake, from which he had withdrawn the franc on two occasions.[34] Instead, he preferred an institution with rules that not only would stabilize European currencies but also would give France greater resources to avoid disinflationary policies.[35] From this perspective, the initial EMS proposal had a number of advantages over the snake, including rules requiring that realignments be approved by mutual consent, which could reduce the necessity of choosing between withdrawal or sharp disinflation; the possibility of using the divergence indicator, which could limit the appreciation of the mark and the policy autonomy of the Bundesbank; and extensive balance-of-payments financing.[36]

By early 1978 the French were committed to a new monetary institution in western Europe. The government faced an early constraint on its economic policies and approach to the EMS in the form of parliamentary elections scheduled for March 1978. Following setbacks in local elections in the mid-1970s, it was widely expected that the ruling coalition of the Rassemblement pour la République (RPR), led by Jacques Chirac, and the Union pour la Démocratie Française (UDF), affiliated with Giscard, would lose the election to the alliance of the Socialist and Communist parties.[37] As events turned out, the RPR-UDF alliance won a majority of eighty-nine seats in the National Assembly. What was more significant was the distribution of seats within the right-wing alliance. The RPR remained the largest party in the legislature but lost twenty seats, whereas the UDF made significant advances. As a consequence, the government gained a certain amount of legitimacy to continue its moderately disinflationary policies and greater freedom to begin serious negotiations on the EMS. The victory of the right, and in particular of the UDF, also was important in persuading Schmidt to proceed with the negotiations.[38]

Serious negotiations over the EMS began soon after the French legislative elections, culminating in the agreement reached at the Bremen summit in July 1978. An important turning point was the Franco-German summit in

Aachen on 14–15 September. The French and Germans agreed that the EMS should encourage the convergence of member states' economic policies, decided to base intervention obligations on the parity grid rather than the divergence indicator, and delayed indefinitely the creation of an EMF. This agreement marked a substantial retreat from French preferences for rules that differed from those of the snake. Although Giscard and his officials pushed hard for such changes, it appears that technical considerations and clear signals from the Bundesbank led them to conclude that Schmidt was not in a position to make many concessions.[39]

Giscard still faced one domestic challenge before the EMS could come into existence—the impact of the EMS on French farmers, who feared that participation would raise the price of French agricultural goods within the Common Agricultural Policy (CAP). The RPR scheduled a debate on this issue in the National Assembly in mid-December 1978, hoping to exploit the discontent of farmers. In response, the government took a hard stand within the European Council, threatening to abandon the EMS project and eventually delaying its implementation by over two months. Although Barre apparently denied in a meeting with Jenkins in December 1978 that the government had suddenly lost interest in the EMS,[40] he and Giscard pressed hard in private and public for changes to the CAP that would compensate French farmers.[41]

Italy: A Complicated Political Puzzle

Like their counterparts in Britain and France, Italian authorities were dissatisfied with floating exchange rates that failed to insulate domestic economic policy from international developments. The rapid and uncontrolled depreciation of the lira in 1976 had increased inflation, undermined the credibility of monetary policy, and led Italy to turn to the International Monetary Fund for assistance. Paolo Baffi, governor of the Banca d'Italia, wrote that "in the conditions prevailing in Italy the effectiveness of exchange-rate changes as a balancing force is limited in both degree and duration; after a small initial gain, the rapid adjustment of domestic prices to the new exchange rate tends to cause a shift to a higher rate of inflation."[42] Italian participation in the EMS could limit the depreciation and instability of the lira's exchange rate and help control inflation. There was also the concern that failure to participate in the EMS would weaken Italy's international position. As Renato Ruggiero, the foreign ministry official charged with oversight of EMS negotiations, put it: "If we did not participate in the EMS, this would show that we are unwilling to accept the challenge . . . of being a fully European country."[43]

Although decisionmakers' general attitude toward the EMS was positive, they preferred that the new institution differ from the snake by not imposing too great an external constraint on economic policy. As early as July 1978, the government pushed for a more symmetrical system in which obligations to intervene in the foreign exchange market and to adjust economic policy would be shared between countries with appreciating and depreciating currencies. Specific proposals included replacing the parity grid with the divergence indicator, strengthening mechanisms for extending credit among central banks, and instituting wider currency fluctuation bands that could be changed more easily.[44] In addition, the Italian negotiators pressed for an increase in the European Economic Community budget to finance regional policy and a reform of the CAP to provide more assistance to Mediterranean farmers.[45]

Most of these demands were not met during the negotiations. The Belgian Compromise, accepted by France and Germany in September, effectively ruled out using the divergence indicator to determine obligations for economic policy adjustment and foreign exchange market intervention. On 14 November 1978, European Economic Community central bankers granted Italy a larger ±6 percent fluctuation band in the EMS but refused to widen the system's bands beyond ±2.25 percent and expressed little interest in the more flexible system advocated by the Italians. Treasury minister Filippo Maria Pandolfi pressed for an increased community budget, more regional funds, and reform of the CAP at a meeting of economics and finance ministers on 21 November, but his counterparts gave him little support.[46] At the Brussels summit in December, a dissatisfied Andreotti announced a week-long "pause for reflection" regarding participation in the EMS, but on 12 December he declared before the Chamber of Deputies in Rome that Italy would join in the EMS without securing further concessions.[47]

Andreotti's "pause for reflection" reflected not only dissatisfaction with the structure of the EMS but also a complex political situation in Italy. He headed a loose coalition of centrist and leftist parties, including the PCI, that had pledged to support the government, although only members of Andreotti's party, Democrazia Christiana (DC), held cabinet positions. Divisions arose in 1978 within both the PCI and the DC over the usefulness of this alliance. Right-wing elements of the DC wished to end the agreement with the PCI and saw divisions over the EMS as a good way to achieve this goal. Many PCI members demanded that the party withdraw support for the government unless it was granted a formal position in the cabinet. However, PCI leaders were reluctant to move too quickly against Andreotti and risk elections because of their poor performance in earlier local elections.[48]

The PCI, although internally divided and unwilling to reveal its hand too early, by late November was critical of immediate entry into the EMS.

The party leadership argued that the EMS would place Italy under German hegemony and create higher unemployment and that it included insufficient side payments in the form of greater regional and agricultural aid. Party leaders proposed renegotiating the terms of the EMS and postponing entry into the system until domestic inflation was lower.[49] The PCI's public criticisms of the EMS were seen as an attempt to tie the hands of Andreotti and to demonstrate the PCI's influence both to its supporters and to other parties. But the PCI was not willing to go so far as to cause a government crisis over the issue.[50]

The DC leadership formally endorsed EMS entry in early December 1978, although it too was divided on the issue. Many members of the party, particularly those opposed to working with the PCI, "tended to view the EMS issue as a trial of strength with the Communists, or to transform it into one," and wanted to "dispel the impression" that Andreotti's pause for reflection was inspired by PCI opposition. These party officials felt that joining the EMS would isolate and humiliate the PCI and perhaps lead it to withdraw support for the government. Shortly after the Brussels summit, DC foreign minister Arnaldo Forlani stated in an interview that the issue of Italian participation in the EMS could cause a government crisis.[51]

The small but politically important Partito Repubblicano Italiano (PRI) supported EMS entry. In response to Andreotti's announcement of the "pause for reflection" at the Brussels summit in December, it threatened to withdraw support from the government if Italy did not enter the EMS in January. Another small party, the Partito Socialista Democratico Italiano (PSDI), did not support the EMS as strongly as did the PRI, but by early December 1978 the PSDI argued that the government had secured enough concessions to participate in the system.[52] The Partito Socialista Italiano (PSI) expressed some fears that EMS participation would create too stringent an external anchor for economic policy, forcing the government to pursue disinflationary policies harmful to the PSI's supporters. More importantly, the right wing of the party, led by secretary Bettino Craxi, foresaw PCI opposition and viewed the EMS as a useful tool for replacing the PCI as the DC's major ally. Shortly after the Brussels summit, the PSI proposed to the PCI that Italy join the EMS in six months to soften the disinflationary impact of the system. If successful, this proposal would burnish the image of the PSI as a "responsible" party able to reconcile the much larger PCI and DC. Andreotti, however, decided to enter immediately. His pause for reflection at the Brussels summit was an attempt to avoid isolating the PCI by forcing it into openly opposing the EMS while also avoiding being seen as capitulating to its demands. When this failed, he announced his decision to the Chamber of Deputies in early December 1978. He allowed the PSI to make its proposal to embarrass Craxi and to increase his own support within the DC. Prior to the vote on the EMS in the legislature on 13 December, Andreotti attempted to win the support of the PSI and the abstention of the PCI for immediate entry into the EMS but was unsuccessful. The PSI abstained, in part out of anger at Andreotti's duplicitous behavior, and the PCI voted against the section calling for immediate entry and abstained on the remainder.[53]

Comparisons and Conclusions

By 1978, many in Britain, France, and Italy were disenchanted with both floating exchange rates and the rules of the snake. Floating exchange rates had led to widespread and seemingly uncontrollable speculation and currency depreciation. German chancellor Schmidt also favored a new institution to limit further appreciation of the mark, partly because the United States was not interested in more comprehensive international monetary reform. In what follows I assess the extent to which these experiences led governments to learn about and adopt a new model for European monetary institutions and why the negotiations produced the specific rules of the EMS.

Preferences

Table 2.1 summarizes governments' preferences regarding the design of the EMS and indicates that little convergence occurred during the 1970s. German preferences mirrored those exhibited during the snake period. Schmidt played an important role in launching the EMS proposal, but pressure from the Bundesbank led him to press for rules similar to those of the

Table 2.1 National Preferences Regarding the Rules of the European Monetary System, 1970s

Preferences	Germany	Britain	France	Italy
Favored initial proposal	Yes	No	Yes	Yes
Symmetrical intervention rules	No	Yes	Yes	Yes
Balance-of-payments financing	Limited	Yes	Yes	Yes
Significant resource transfers	No	Yes	No	Yes
Size of fluctuation bands	Narrow	?	Narrow	Wide
Future development of system	Limited	No	Yes	Yes

snake that would allow Germany to pursue domestic monetary policies aimed at keeping inflation low if this conflicted with the goal of currency stabilization. This position led German negotiators to oppose using the divergence indicator as a guide for policy since it could require Bundesbank intervention on foreign exchange markets to support other ERM currencies, to prefer limited balance-of-payments financing and resource transfers, and to keep statements about the future development of the institution vague.

French and Italian officials were enthusiastic about creating the EMS once Schmidt began circulating his proposals in the first half of 1978. But they preferred that the new institution include significant balance-of-payment financing and more symmetrical policy obligations among countries with appreciating and depreciating currencies. In addition, they wanted a clear indicator that the institution would gain more authority over national monetary and exchange-rate policies in the future. In contrast, Callaghan was quite hesitant about the EMS proposal as early as the Copenhagen summit. The British government's priority was coordinated reflation that could increase growth, employment, and domestic political support, and it was unwilling to contemplate fixing sterling if doing so would threaten these goals. Before deciding not to participate in the ERM, British negotiators favored a regime that would be more symmetrical than the snake, one that used a divergence indicator rather than a parity grid to determine policy obligations and included significant balance-of-payments financing and resource transfers. The British articulated few clear ideas about the preferred size of the system's fluctuation bands (and thus its constraint on domestic monetary policy) and did not support its future development.

These differences indicate that policy learning had a weak effect on national preferences regarding the rules of the EMS. The learning approach expects a convergence of preferences toward those of Germany for rules resembling the snake. But governments in the countries that experienced policy failure—Britain, France, and Italy—preferred that the rules of the EMS distribute the burden of adjustment more equally than did the rules of the snake. In particular, they wanted the EMS to have more symmetrical obligations for policy changes, extensive balance-of-payments financing on generous terms, and (for France and Italy) a commitment that the institution would evolve in a more symmetrical fashion in the future. Domestic political considerations drove these preferences; leaders in each country feared that another institution that too closely resembled the snake would force them to choose between withdrawal or disinflation. The importance of this conclusion should not be overstated. Governments only had a few years experience of floating exchange rates and policy failure when they negotiated the EMS, and this may not have been sufficient time for them to absorb fully the advantages of the German model of economic policy and monetary coordination. A more reasonable test of the learning approach is presented in Chapter 4, which analyzes the negotiations a decade later over creating a monetary union.

Outcomes

Both the learning and distributional bargaining approaches expect that the final outcome of the negotiations would create an institution that reflected German preferences. In many respects, the rules of the EMS closely resemble those of the snake. The requirements under the EMS for foreign exchange market intervention and policy changes were to be determined by the parity grid rather than the divergence indicator. This meant that countries with appreciating currencies, such as Germany, would come under less pressure to relax monetary policy to accommodate countries with depreciating currencies. The EMS did include more balance-of-payments financing than the snake, such as unlimited lending by countries with appreciating currencies to finance intervention at the margins of bilateral fluctuation bands. But the extent of this financing was limited by two factors. First, borrowing by countries with depreciating currencies ultimately was limited by their ability to repay by accumulating foreign exchange reserves. Second, in 1978 the Bundesbank won a promise from the German government that it would release the central bank from its intervention obligations if these threatened domestic price stability.[54]

German negotiators did make some concessions to other member states on less important issues. They agreed to call the new unit of account the ECU, which was both an English-language acronym for European currency unit and the name of an ancient French coin. They also permitted the inclusion of the divergence indicator, which could have created greater obligations for German intervention and policy changes but ensured that the language of the agreement made it clear that the parity grid was the principal rule for determining the timing and extent of such obligations. German negotiators acquiesced to unlimited financing for intervention but insisted that it applied only to marginal interventions, when countries with depreciating currencies already were in a weak position, rather than intramarginal interventions. And they signed off on a vague promise to reconsider the rules of the EMS within a few years but kept specifics to a minimum.

Notes

1. Kathleen R. McNamara, *The Currency of Ideas: Monetary Politics in the European Union* (Ithaca, NY: Cornell University Press, 1998), 128–135.

2. Matthias Kaelberer, "Money and Power in Europe" (manuscript, Iowa State University, n.d.); Andrew Moravcsik, *The Choice for Europe: Social Purpose and State Power from Messina to Maastricht* (Ithaca, NY: Cornell University Press, 1998); and Thomas Oatley, *Monetary Politics: Exchange Rate Cooperation in the European Union* (Ann Arbor: University of Michigan Press, 1997).

3. Loukas Tsoukalis, *The Politics and Economics of European Monetary Integration* (London: George Allen and Unwin, 1977).

4. Kathleen Burk and Alec Cairncross, *"Goodbye, Great Britain": The 1976 IMF Crisis* (New Haven, CT: Yale University Press, 1992); and Martin Holmes, *The Labour Government, 1974–79: Political Aims and Economic Reality* (London: Macmillan, 1985).

5. John B. Goodman, *Monetary Sovereignty: The Politics of Central Banking in Western Europe* (Ithaca, NY: Cornell University Press, 1992), 112–118; and Jacques Mélitz, "Monetary Policy in France," Centre for Economic Policy Research Discussion Paper No. 509 (December 1991), 7.

6. Goodman, *Monetary Sovereignty*, 146–162; Norman Kogan, *A Political History of Italy: The Postwar Years* (New York: Praeger, 1983), 283–304; and Luigi Spaventa, "Two Letters of Intent: External Crises and Stabilization Policy, Italy, 1973–1977," in *IMF Conditionality*, ed. John Williamson (Washington, DC: Institute for International Economics, 1983).

7. Jenkins's initial speech is reprinted as "Europe's Present Challenge and Future Opportunity," *Bulletin of the European Communities*, Supplement 10 (1977): 6–14; see also Roy Jenkins, *A Life at the Center* (London: Collins, 1989), 432.

8. Peter Ludlow, *The Making of the European Monetary System: A Case Study of the Politics of the European Community* (London: Butterworth Scientific, 1982), 63.

9. *Le Monde,* 11 April 1978, 5.

10. Jonathan Carr, *Helmut Schmidt: Helmsman of Germany* (London: Weidenfeld and Nicolson, 1985), 139–140; Ellen Kennedy, *The Bundesbank: Germany's Central Bank in the International Monetary System* (New York: Council on Foreign Relations Press, 1991), 60–63; Helmut Schmidt, *Men and Powers: A Political Retrospective*, trans. Ruth Hein (New York: Random House, 1989), 265–256; and Jonathan Story, "The Launching of the EMS: An Analysis of Change in Foreign Economic Policy," *Political Studies* 36 (1988): 397–412.

11. C. Randall Henning, *Currencies and Politics in the United States, Germany, and Japan* (Washington, DC: Institute for International Economics, 1994), 185–189.

12. Ludlow, *The Making of the European Monetary System*, 239; and Jacques van Ypersele and Jean-Claude Koeune, *The European Monetary System: Origins, Operation, and Outlook* (Luxemburg: Commission of the European Communities, 1985), 48–49. Van Ypersele was the Belgian representative to the European Economic Community's Monetary Committee and the author of the Belgian Compromise. More technical discussions of these issues include L. Spaventa, "Algebraic Properties and Economic Improprieties of the 'Indicator of Divergence' in the European Monetary System," and J. J. Rey, "The Indicator of Divergence of the European Monetary System: A Sobering View," both in "Seminar on the Indicator of Divergence in the European Monetary System," *Discussion Papers on International Economics and Finance* 1 (Rome: Research Department, Banca d'Italia, 3 July 1981).

13. The EMS is the product of the resolution of the European Council of 5 December 1978, not of a treaty, and thus did not require parliamentary approval. The EMS was not incorporated into the Treaty of Rome until the ratification of the

Treaty on European Union in 1993, although the Single European Act of 1987 referred to the system. The Council's resolution is reprinted in *European Economy* 3 (July 1979), 95–97. The operating procedures of the EMS were established in the "Agreement Between the Central Banks of the Member States of the European Economic Community Laying Down the Operating Procedures for the European Monetary System," reprinted in *European Economy* 3 (July 1979), 102–106.

14. Horst Ungerer, "The European Monetary System: The Experience, 1979–82," International Monetary Fund Occasional Paper No. 19 (Washington, DC: International Monetary Fund, May 1983).

15. Joycelyn Statler, "The European Monetary System: From Conception to Birth," *International Affairs* 55, no. 2 (April 1979): 208; see also Callaghan's remarks to the House of Commons in *Hansard*, 10 April 1978, col. 986.

16. K. Johnson and C. Painter, "British Governments and the EMS," *The Political Quarterly* 51, no. 3 (July–September 1980): 321; see also Chancellor Denis Healey's remarks in *Hansard*, 29 November 1978, col. 464.

17. Denis Healey, *The Time of My Life* (London: Michael Joseph, 1989), 450; and Johnson and Painter, "British Governments and the EMS," 321.

18. Healey, *Time of My Life*, 439; and Ludlow, *The Making of the European Monetary System*, 111.

19. *Guardian*, 7 July 1978.

20. See, for example, *Times*, 27 June 1978, 21, and *Times*, 6 July 1978, 16; a good overview is Edmund Dell, "Britain and the Origins of the European Monetary System," *Contemporary European History* 3, no. 1 (1994): 1–60.

21. See Ludlow, *The Making of the European Monetary System*, 109–110; and *Times*, 17 April 1978, 19.

22. Ludlow, *The Making of the European Monetary System*, 151–152; and interview with former Bank of England official.

23. Dell, "Britain and the Origins of the European Monetary System," 48.

24. Martin Holmes, *The Labour Government, 1974–79: Political Aims and Economic Reality* (London: Macmillan, 1984), 129–134.

25. See Tony Benn, *Conflicts of Interest: Diaries 1977–80* (London: Hutchinson, 1990), 353–354; and *Times*, 2 October 1978, 2. In later meetings with the government, the National Executive Committee reiterated its opposition; see *Times*, 25 October 1978, 2, and *Times*, 28 October 1978, 2.

26. *Times*, 7 October 1978, 2.

27. Quoted in Ludlow, *The Making of the European Monetary System*, 220–221; for details on conflicts within the cabinet, see Benn, *Conflicts of Interest*, 376, 384; *Times*, 24 October 1978, 1, and *Times*, 31 October 1978, 1.

28. Ludlow, *The Making of the European Monetary System*, 219; *Times*, 3 November 1978, 25, and *Times*, 4 November 1978, 1.

29. James Callaghan, *Time and Chance* (London: Collins, 1987), 492–493; see also Johnson and Painter, "British Governments and the EMS," 325; and Statler, "The European Monetary System," 224.

30. Dell, "Britain and the Origins of the European Monetary System," 52; Ludlow, *The Making of the European Monetary System*, 224, 246; and David Owen, *Personally Speaking to Kenneth Harris* (London: Weidenfeld and Nicolson, 1987), 116–118.

31. J. R. Frears, *France in the Giscard Presidency* (London: George Allen and Unwin, 1981), 106.

32. Quoted in Peter Ludlow, *The Making of the European Monetary System*, 200.

33. Valéry Giscard d'Estaing, *Démocratie Française* (Paris: Fayard, 1976),

123–124, 128–129; Valéry Giscard d'Estaing, *Le Pouvoir et la Vie* (Paris: Compagnie 12, 1988), 137; Goodman, *Monetary Sovereignty*, 126; Ludlow, *The Making of the European Monetary System*, 200; and Kathleen McNamara, "Common Markets, Uncommon Currencies," in *Coping with Complexity in the International System*, ed. Jack Snyder and Robert Jervis (Boulder, CO: Westview Press, 1992).

34. Statler, "The European Monetary System," 214–215.

35. Giscard d'Estaing, *Le Pouvoir et la Vie*, 141–143.

36. Ibid.; Michael Loriaux, *France After Hegemony: International Change and Financial Reform* (Ithaca, NY: Cornell University Press, 1991), 251; and Statler, "The European Monetary System," 214–215.

37. Goodman, *Monetary Sovereignty*, 123; see also Ludlow, *The Making of the European Monetary System*, 82–84; and Story, "The Launching of the EMS," 401.

38. Ludlow, *The Making of the European Monetary System*, 84–85.

39. Ibid., 180–185.

40. For Jenkins's account of this meeting, see Roy Jenkins, *European Diary 1977–81* (London: Collins, 1989), 380.

41. R. Formesyn, "Europeanisation and the Pursuit of National Interests," in *Continuity and Change in France*, ed. Vincent Wright (London: George Allen and Unwin, 1984), 226.

42. See Banca d'Italia, *Report for the Year 1977* (Rome: Printing Office of the Banca d'Italia, 1978), 138–139.

43. Quoted in Luigi Spaventa, *Italy Joins the EMS: A Political History*, Johns Hopkins University Bologna Center Occasional Paper 32 (June 1980), 69. Andreotti later wrote that both Giscard and Schmidt telephoned him in early December 1978, urging Italian participation for similar reasons, as well as to prevent the government from being seen as giving in to pressure from the Communist Party. See Giulio Andreotti, *Diari 1976 1979: Gli Anni della Solidarietá* (Milan: Rizzoli, 1981), 287–288.

44. See Ludlow, *The Making of the European Monetary System*, 148–151; and Spaventa, *Italy Joins the EMS*, 72–73, 77–79.

45. Ludlow, *The Making of the European Monetary System*, 187; and Spaventa, *Italy Joins the EMS*, 80–81.

46. Spaventa, *Italy Joins the EMS*, 80–81.

47. The exception was the credit facilities to be available under the EMS, most of which were designated for short-term support of foreign exchange market intervention with settlement within forty-five days. See Spaventa, *Italy Joins the EMS*, 84.

48. Stephen Hellman, *Italian Communism in Transition* (New York: Oxford University Press, 1988), 93; James Ruscoe, *On the Threshold of Government: The Italian Communist Party, 1976–81* (New York: St. Martin's Press, 1982), 171–172; and Douglas A. Wertman, "The Christian Democrats: Masters of Survival," in *Italy at the Polls, 1979,* ed. Howard R. Penniman (Washington, DC: American Enterprise Institute for Public Policy Research, 1981).

49. *Il Corriere della Sera*, 9 December 1978, 1; and Spaventa, *Italy Joins the EMS*, 83.

50. After the PRI threatened to leave the government over the EMS, senior leaders of the PCI, PSI, and DC separately published articles in party newspapers calling on the party to consider the consequences of a government crisis. See *Il Corriere della Sera*, 7 December 1978, 1.

51. *Il Corriere della Sera*, 8 December 1978, 1; Spaventa, *Italy Joins the*

EMS, 87. See also Ludlow, *The Making of the European Monetary System*, 207–209; and Ruscoe, *On the Threshold of Government*, 172–174. Their concerns were heightened in the fall of 1978, when Andreotti dismissed his right-wing DC minister of industry, Carlo Donat-Cattin, and helped settle a wave of strikes. See *Il Corriere della Sera*, 3 November 1978, 1. Andreotti clearly did not want to be seen as a "slave" to the PCI; see Andreotti, *Diari 1976 1979*, 287–288.

52. *Il Corriere della Sera*, 7 December 1978, 1; *Il Corriere della Sera*, 9 December 1978, 1; and Ludlow, *The Making of the European Monetary System*, 212.

53. *Il Corriere della Sera*, 9 December 1978, 1; *Il Corriere della Sera*, 10 December 1978, 1, *Il Corriere della Sera*, 12 December 1978, 1; *Il Corriere della Sera*, 14 December 1978, 1; Ludlow, *The Making of the European Monetary System*, 212–217, 273; and Spaventa, *Italy Joins the EMS*, 68, 91.

54. Henning, *Currencies and Politics*, 97, 188–189; and Ludlow, *The Making of the European Monetary System*, 284.

3

Exchange-Rate Politics, 1979–1988

This chapter compares British, French, and Italian exchange-rate politics and policies from 1979 until 1988. Governments dealt with the problems of slow economic growth, high inflation, and an unstable international monetary environment during this period in quite different ways. After 1978 the British government kept sterling out of the exchange-rate mechanism (ERM) of the European Monetary System (EMS) and reduced inflation quickly by raising interest rates and encouraging real currency appreciation. Once sterling began depreciating from a high level in 1982, the government raised interest rates but was unwilling to take more comprehensive steps to stabilize the currency. French and Italian governments also tightened monetary policy in the early 1980s but discouraged currency appreciation by devaluing in the ERM.

Why did governments respond to common challenges with different policies? Chapter 1 outlined two explanations. The openness approach explains policy choices as a function of the political conflicts generated by the degree of dependence on international trade and investment. Producers of tradable goods, such as industrial firms, prefer policies that stabilize the exchange rate at a competitive level and become more influential as they are exposed to greater overseas competition and investment opportunities. Based on investment data summarized in Chapter 1, the openness explanation leads one to expect that British authorities would be quite interested in exchange-rate competitiveness and stability during the 1980s. The institutional approach focuses on differences in bank-industry ties to explain policy choices. British banks had weak ties to industry; as a consequence, banks and other financial firms should have preferred policies that would reduce inflation quickly, whereas industry preferred policies that would stabilize sterling at a competitive level. Banks and industry had stronger ties in France and Italy during this period; thus bankers, industrialists, and government officials in those countries would be expected to demonstrate stronger preferences for stabilizing the franc and lira at competitive levels than for reducing inflation quickly.

I find that the institutional approach does a better job of explaining exchange-rate policy choice for two reasons. First, actual policy choices during the 1980s accorded more closely with its predictions. Second, close examination of domestic groups' preferences and lobbying activities demonstrates that British banks and financial firms were more interested in keeping inflation low, regardless of the effects on the exchange rate and industrial competitiveness, than their counterparts in France and Italy.

This chapter is structured as follows. The next section describes changes in inflation and exchange rates to identify periods of currency instability and appreciation that activated the preferences of domestic groups. The following three sections trace the preferences of banks and industry and the policy choices in each country. The concluding section draws on this evidence to compare the relationships between openness, bank-industry ties, preferences, and policy choices.

The Economic Environment

Rapid increases in the prices of petroleum and other commodities in 1979, combined with upward pressure on domestic prices, increased inflation in most industrialized countries (see Table 3.1). Large inflation differentials among the members of the ERM placed continual strains on the stability of exchange rates in the early 1980s. From 1979 to 1984, the annual percentage change in consumer prices averaged 11.1 percent in France and 16.2 percent in Italy but only 4.5 percent in Germany. This more rapid loss of purchasing power in France and Italy led the franc and lira to depreciate in nominal terms against the mark (Figure 3.1). But the fluctuation bands of the ERM kept the franc and lira from depreciating enough to offset real exchange-rate appreciation produced by high French and Italian inflation. French and Italian governments responded by negotiating frequent devaluations within the ERM to maintain competitiveness. Between 1979 and 1987, the franc and lira effectively were devalued six and eight times, respectively, against the mark (see Table 3.2). This strategy helped prevent significant real appreciation of the franc and lira (Figure 3.2). In contrast, sterling appreciated in nominal terms from 1979 to 1981 against the mark. Since Britain's inflation rate was quite high during this period, sterling appreciated strongly in real terms in 1979–1981. Thereafter, sterling depreciated in both nominal and real terms from this high level.

Table 3.1 Annual Percentage Changes in Consumer Prices, 1979–1987

	Britain	France	Italy	Germany
1979	13.4	10.8	15.7	4.1
1980	18.0	13.6	21.1	5.5
1981	11.9	13.4	18.7	6.3
1982	8.6	11.8	16.3	5.3
1983	4.6	9.6	15.0	3.3
1984	5.0	7.4	10.6	2.4
1985	6.1	5.8	8.6	2.2
1986	3.4	2.7	6.1	-0.1
1987	4.1	3.1	4.6	0.2

Source: Organization for Economic Cooperation and Development, *OECD Economic Outlook* 54 (December 1993): 140.

Table 3.2 Percentage Realignments of Central Parities

	French Franc	Italian Lira	German Mark
24 September 1979			+2.00
22 March 1981		-6.00	
5 October 1981	-3.00	-3.00	+5.50
14 June 1982	-5.75	-2.75	+4.25
21 March 1983	-2.50	-2.50	+5.50
22 July 1985	+2.00	-6.00	+2.00
7 April 1986	-3.00		+3.00
12 January 1987			+3.00

Source: Stefan Collignon et al., *Europe's Monetary Future* (Rutherford: Fairleigh Dickinson University Press, 1994), 26.

Note: A minus sign indicates devaluation against currencies whose bilateral parities remained unchanged; a plus sign indicates a revaluation.

Figure 3.1 Index of Monthly Mark Exchange Rates, 1979–1987 (January 1979 = 100)

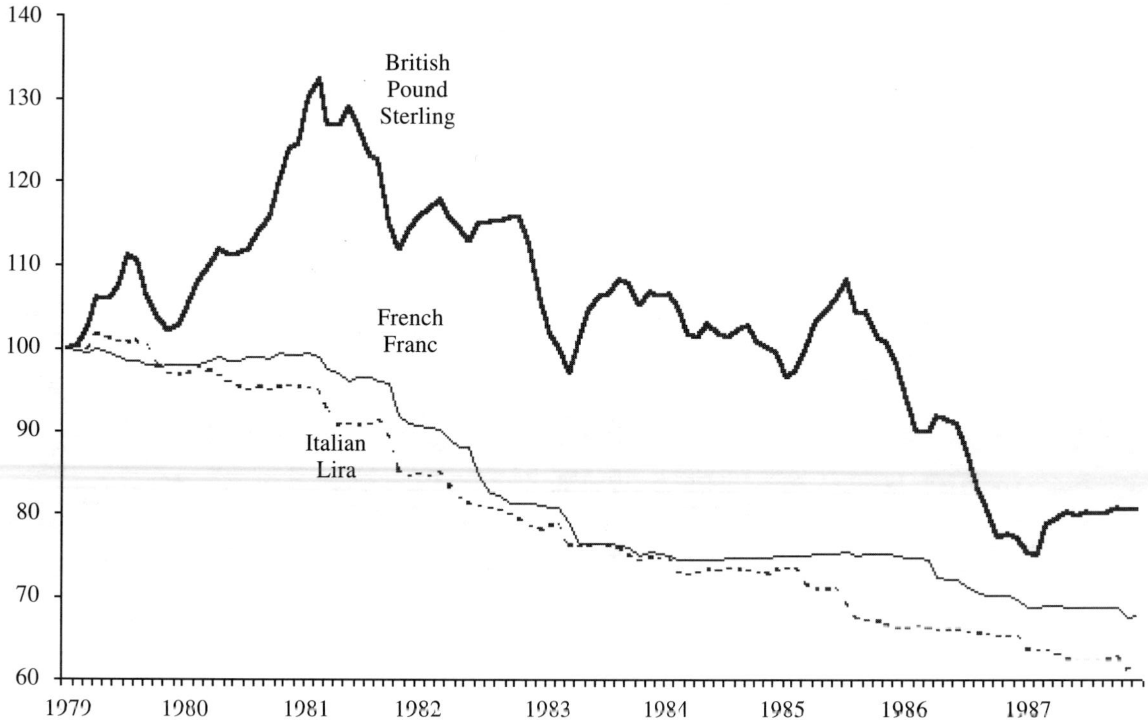

Source: Calculated from *Federal Reserve Economic Database*

Figure 3.2 Annual Percentage Change in Real Effective Exchange Rates, 1979–1987 (based on relative normalized unit labor costs)

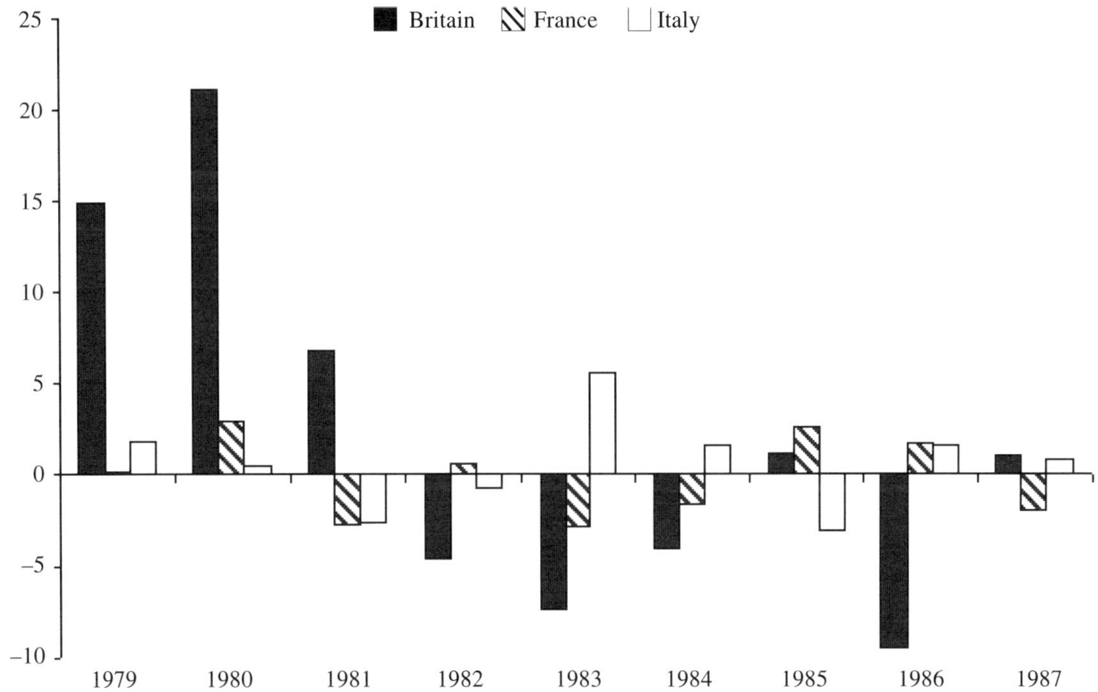

Source: Calculated from International Monetary Fund, *International Financial Statistics,* various years.

Britain: Political Conflict and Exchange-Rate Appreciation

British exchange-rate policy went through four distinct phases during the 1980s. Monetary policy tightening in 1979 led to sharp appreciation of sterling until late 1981. The second phase began after sterling reached its peak in late 1981 and began to depreciate from this overvalued level until 1986. The government accepted this as consistent with economic fundamentals, but when necessary raised interest rates to prevent a sharp depreciation. The third phase occurred during 1984–1986, when depreciation, combined with technical difficulties with the implementation of domestic monetary policy, led some to express greater interest in stabilizing the exchange rate by bringing sterling into the ERM. In the fourth phase, the authorities informally "shadowed" (pegged sterling to) the mark outside the ERM in 1986–1987 but abandoned this tactic when they concluded that sterling needed to appreciate to reduce domestic inflation.

Sterling Appreciation, 1979–1981

After taking office in the spring of 1979, the Conservative government under Prime Minister Margaret Thatcher decided against bringing sterling into the ERM.[1] Thereafter, officials stated that Britain would join the ERM when "the time was right" but did not spell out any explicit conditions for entry. The background to this decision was a domestically oriented monetary policy framework developed before taking office. *The Right Approach to the Economy,* the Conservative election manifesto published in late 1977, called for a "virtuous circle" of low inflation brought about by sterling appreciation and North Sea oil income and stated that "we reject the simplistic argument that a depreciating currency is required to maintain competitiveness. Internal inflation is the real enemy. . . . A falling exchange rate makes internal inflation worse."[2] The new government's immediate priority was to eliminate Britain's system of capital controls by the end of the year. The motivations for dismantling controls were to force British industrial firms to compete for funds with overseas companies and to reinforce the international position of City banks and financial firms.[3]

Investors' confidence in the new government and recent increases in the price of petroleum appreciated sterling during the summer of 1979. This accelerated after Chancellor Geoffrey Howe raised interest rates by 3 percent to the unprecedented level of 17 percent on 15 November. Ministers encouraged appreciation to reduce domestic inflation. Under the government's macroeconomic framework, which after the 1980 budget came to be known as the medium-term financial strategy (MTFS), interest-rate policy was determined by the rate of growth of the monetary aggregate M3 and was not influenced by exchange-rate considerations. This commitment to domestic stabilization went so far that government officials vetted Bank of England press releases announcing changes in interest rates to ensure that they contained no references to the exchange rate.[4] Senior ministers recognized and accepted that currency appreciation was not only the natural consequence of higher interest rates but that it also helped lower inflation by inducing a sharp recession, reducing the prices of imports, and lowering employment and wage demands.[5] Although the government publicly placed the blame for sterling appreciation on petroleum exports, it did not support this argument with significant intervention on the foreign exchange markets and ignored the fact that other petroleum-exporting countries, such as the Netherlands, did not see their currencies appreciate as significantly. Economists estimated that North Sea oil caused only about 10 percent of sterling's appreciation.[6]

The sharp real appreciation of sterling (see Figure 3.3) soon led to public complaints from industrialists. In the spring of 1980, the president of the Confederation of British Industry (CBI), John Greenborough, attacked high interest rates as damaging to British industry. Thatcher replied disdainfully that many firms' management was "patchy" and "found it convenient to be regulated by government and saved by subsidies." Ministers were quite clear that their goal was to use a tight monetary policy and currency appreciation, as well as reductions in subsidies to nationalized industries, to force firms to cut costs, shed labor, and become more competitive.[7]

In the autumn of 1980, British industrialists mounted a sustained but ineffective campaign against the government's monetary policy. Many of the prime minister's friends in industry told her that interest rates and sterling were too high, and in an unprecedented move Maurice Hodgson, chair of ICI, visited Thatcher privately to inform her of the company's first quarterly loss. In November the CBI annual conference approved a motion criticizing the government's interest-rate and exchange-rate policies and advocating an active policy to depreciate sterling. The CBI's director-general, Terence Beckett of Ford, emphasized the devastating effects of rapid sterling appreciation on British manufacturing firms. Michael Edwardes, chair of British Leyland, argued that if North Sea oil were the cause of sterling appreciation, he would prefer to "leave the bloody stuff in the ground."[8] In contrast, most representatives of the City as well as the Institute of Directors supported the government's priority of reducing inflation quickly. Members of the Treasury's panel of academic and City economists consistently expressed more concern about a premature loosening of monetary policy than did the CBI. Financial firms as well as some prominent economic journalists were strong and early supporters of monetarist ideas and

Figure 3.3 Index of Real Effective Exchange Rate of Sterling, 1978–1988 (1990 = 100)

Source: International Monetary Fund, *International Financial Statistics*, various years.

used their positions to convince investors that adherence to monetary targets should be an important part of their assessments of government policy.[9]

The effects of sterling appreciation on British industry concerned moderate Conservatives, but they had little influence on cabinet discussions and never were able to come up with a viable alternative to the monetarist program of Thatcher, Howe, and their advisers. British industry lacked a "champion" in the cabinet, since the first minister for industry, Keith Joseph, was fundamentally opposed to government intervention and wedded to the MTFS. His successor, Patrick Jenkin, was afraid of being too outspoken on industry's behalf for fear of seeing his influence reduced. The government took only modest steps to mitigate the effects of currency appreciation in 1980. For example, the Bank of England created a small team to analyze the "distress borrowing" by industrial firms during the recession and to serve as an honest broker between the firms and their bankers to restructure short-term liabilities. The focus was on avoiding short-term, strictly financial crises, and the Bank of England never advanced credit to these firms or their bankers.[10]

Sterling Depreciation, 1982–1986

Monetary targeting and higher interest rates were effective in stopping inflation, albeit at the cost of a deep recession. But technical problems made monetary targeting an inaccurate policy guide beginning in 1981, which led ministers to give more weight to the exchange rate when making monetary policy decisions. From late 1980 to September 1981, the government reduced interest rates gradually and saw sterling's effective exchange rate depreciate gently by about 10 percent. It also acquiesced in the overshooting of its money supply targets, which many blamed on unpredictable changes in the velocity of money produced by the elimination of restrictions on bank lending. But this modest shift in the government's monetarist strategy did not reduce its commitment to keeping inflation low. The Bank of England and Treasury became concerned about inflation when depreciation accelerated in September, and they responded by raising interest rates to 16 percent. Until this point, policy had been dictated (with decreasing effectiveness) by the behavior of monetary aggregates, and sterling appreciation was either ignored or encouraged. But now the authorities would raise interest rates when the still overvalued currency threatened to depreciate precipitously, although they did not adopt an explicit exchange-rate target.[11]

Dissatisfaction with monetary targeting and large exchange-rate swings led ministers to discuss but reject the possibility of bringing sterling into the ERM in late 1981 and early 1982. Thatcher emphasized that the

ERM offered no positive advantages since currencies were subject to frequent realignments. Nigel Lawson at the Treasury, Governor Gordon Richardson of the Bank of England, and Foreign Secretary Peter Carrington expressed interest in the ERM. But Chancellor Howe had serious reservations, arguing that such a dramatic shift in policy would reduce the government's credibility with the financial markets. He and Thatcher were particularly concerned that predictions of a Labour victory in the run-up to an election could lead to sterling depreciation and force them to raise interest rates to defend the currency at a politically sensitive time.[12]

January 1985 marked the effective end of using monetary targets for setting monetary policy. Hereafter, interest rate changes were dictated almost exclusively by the exchange rate: the government would cut interest rates when sterling was stable or appreciating and would raise them when sterling depreciated and fed domestic inflation. In early January, Thatcher's press secretary, Bernard Ingham, told journalists off the record that an increase in interest rates the previous July to support sterling's exchange rate was now considered a mistake and would not be repeated. Nigel Lawson, now chancellor, raised interest rates from 9.5 percent to 10.5 percent to ward off sales of sterling when news services reported Ingham's comments. Later the same day, Ingham gave reporters the impression that Thatcher preferred a hands-off exchange-rate policy. When this story appeared in the Sunday newspapers on 13 January, Lawson feared that sterling would come under severe selling pressure. He persuaded Thatcher to raise interest rates a further 1.5 percent as well as to agree to foreign exchange market intervention coordinated with other industrialized countries. Unpredictable episodes of sterling depreciation such as these threatened to fuel domestic inflation and convinced many in the government, Lawson in particular, of the advantages of a more activist exchange-rate policy.[13]

The Debate over the Exchange-Rate Mechanism

The end of targeting the rate of growth of the money supply led Chancellor Lawson, Bank of England governor Robin Leigh-Pemberton, and Geoffrey Howe, now the foreign secretary, to support ERM entry.[14] In his Mansion House speech in October 1984, Lawson noted the importance of the exchange rate as an indicator of monetary tightness. The same month Leigh-Pemberton pointed to some of the disadvantages of relying on monetary targets and the potential utility of entering the ERM.[15] Another reason for new interest in the ERM was a weakening in industry's demands for depreciation and more calls to stabilize the exchange rate. After depreciation of sterling from late 1981 to 1984 and some evidence of an increase in domestic demand as the recession began to moderate, industrialists muted their criticisms of government policy. Eight months earlier the CBI had launched a concerted attack on the government's "crazy" interest-rate policy and called for sterling depreciation, but by late 1982 industrialists were reluctant to criticize the Conservative government in the run-up to an election campaign. At its annual conference, CBI members formally voted nearly two-to-one against a resolution calling on the government to "adopt an exchange-rate policy that will encourage manufacturing industry," although procedural problems masked the fact that a larger number probably favored depreciation.[16] Some in the CBI also called for consideration of entering the ERM to stabilize sterling.[17]

In February 1985, Lawson raised the issue of ERM entry with Thatcher. He argued that monetary discipline was available by targeting either monetary aggregates or the exchange rate and that the choice between the two came down to political and technical factors that favored the latter course. The sterling crisis of January 1985 had revealed that the government could not ignore rapid depreciation, and participation in the ERM might make such incidents less likely. Lawson thought that since the majority of Conservative members of Parliament and business leaders favored ERM entry, the discipline of a fixed exchange rate would be useful when it came time to persuade them to accept tight monetary and fiscal policies. Thatcher was not persuaded by his arguments, and they agreed that any immediate moves were not feasible because of continued turbulence in the foreign exchange market.[18]

Support for ERM entry increased within the government in the spring of 1985. Senior Treasury officials supported ERM entry on "hard" terms (i.e., at a high level for sterling) so as to maintain downward pressure against inflation. Changing economic fundamentals in 1985 also encouraged interest in the ERM. A fall in the price of oil from about $30 per barrel to about $20 per barrel led sterling to depreciate further, wiping out much of the accumulated overvaluation of the currency. The fall in oil prices greatly undercut the argument that Britain could not enter the ERM because of its "petro-currency" status, and the CBI, Association of British Chambers of Commerce, and Institute of Directors came out in support of entry to stabilize the exchange rate.[19]

But Thatcher remained opposed to joining the ERM. In August 1985, Lawson again brought up the issue, and Thatcher reluctantly agreed to hold another meeting of senior advisers the next month. Lawson emphasized that entry would bolster the government's anti-inflationary credentials by making "it clear to industry that they could not look to exchange-rate depreciation to solve their difficulties." Thatcher was not prepared to support British participation in the ERM, arguing that it would increase the volatility of interest rates and eliminate the government's monetary policy autonomy. Lawson replied that, based on recent experience, the exchange rate already had a strong influence on interest-rate policy and that after the fall in the price of oil earlier in the year, the markets no longer considered sterling a petro-currency. Thatcher vetoed immediate entry until she could hold another meeting with a wider circle of advisers. At the ministerial meeting to discuss ERM entry on 13 November, Lawson, supported by all but one of the ministers present, reiterated his reasons for advocating ERM entry. Leon Brittan of the Department of Trade and Industry said that industrial firms were pressing for entry, and the party chairman, Norman Tebbitt, and the chief whip, John Wakeham, told the prime minister that she could expect support for entering the ERM from Conservative members of Parliament. Thatcher still disagreed and refused to join the ERM.[20]

"Shadowing" the Mark, 1986–1988

Events in 1986 further strengthened Lawson's support of ERM entry. A minor sterling crisis in January, brought about by another fall in oil prices, forced him to raise interest rates until March to prevent a run on sterling. Between June and September 1986, sterling depreciated continuously, threatening to fall below 3.00 marks. This process provided further encouragement to industry to support ERM entry since sterling was now at a more competitive level (much of the appreciation of the early 1980s had been reversed—see Figure 3.3), and the CBI and others were concerned about limiting its volatility.[21] At the same time, some opposition to entry appeared in the City and among economists based on fears that the current exchange rate was too inflationary.[22]

By early 1987 at the latest, Lawson decided to "shadow the mark," keeping the sterling-mark exchange rate within a secret fluctuation band. Shadowing would be a first step toward entry into the ERM after the general election expected for 1987 and would prevent any inflationary depreciation of sterling now that oil prices had stabilized. Lawson also thought that successful foreign exchange market intervention coordinated with the Bundesbank in October 1986 and in the Group of Seven in early 1987 could provide support for his informal exchange-rate target. After having the Treasury consult with industrialists about a competitive level for sterling, Lawson decided that 2.90 marks was a good medium-term target, with 3.00 marks as sterling's ceiling.[23] As the election in June approached, predictions of another Conservative victory led sterling to rise toward 3.00 marks, and Lawson authorized foreign exchange market intervention and cut interest rates to prevent further appreciation.[24]

Increases in domestic inflation led Lawson to stop shadowing the mark in 1988. In August 1987, Lawson raised interest rates from 9 percent to 10 percent to offset the inflationary effects of sterling depreciation and expected that future changes in interest rates would be in the same direction. This projection was temporarily proven false in the wake of the worldwide stock market crashes of October 1987, after which the government cut interest rates as part of coordinated monetary policy changes among the Group of Seven countries. This coordination was successful and reversed sterling's earlier depreciation. Although Lawson emphasized that these interest-rate cuts were aimed at restoring confidence to financial markets and stopping depreciation of the dollar, they also accorded with his informal exchange-rate policy. Reducing interest rates allowed Lawson to ease upward pressure against his secret 3.00-mark ceiling on sterling as the currency appreciated.[25] These interest-rate cuts, as well as heavy foreign exchange market intervention, began to arouse concerns about inflation in the government and Bank of England in late 1987 and early 1988.[26] On 17 December 1987, Lawson decided that intervention and interest-rate cuts could not continue for much longer and that an informal "revaluation" of sterling might be necessary to reduce inflation. By early March, the Bank of England was intervening on a massive scale to restrain the appreciating currency, and on the advice of bank and Treasury officials Thatcher ordered Lawson to let sterling appreciate above 3.00 marks.[27]

Summary

The exchange rate was a contentious issue in British politics in the 1980s. Sharp appreciation from 1979 to 1982 led to an intense lobbying campaign from industry and trade unions against the Thatcher government's policy of reducing inflation with high interest rates. But this policy mix pleased many banks and financial firms because it maintained the value of their assets and restored London's role as a leading international financial center. British authorities chose to treat the exchange rate as the residual of domestic macroeconomic policy throughout the 1980s. The goal of the policy choices of the Conservative government from 1979 to late 1981—pursuing monetary targets and encouraging currency appreciation—was to reduce inflation as quickly as possible. Once sterling peaked in late 1981, the authorities tried to prevent rapid depreciation that threatened to increase inflation. Two factors led authorities to consider more comprehensive exchange-rate arrangements, such as bringing sterling into the ERM, in the mid-1980s. First, monetary targeting became an unreliable policy guide, leading some to see the exchange rate as a natural nominal anchor for stabilizing investors' expectations. Second, economic fundamentals—the over-appreciation of 1979–1981, along with decreases in the price of oil in 1982, 1985, and 1986—led to a secular decline in the value of sterling, and some believed that entry into the ERM could reduce the likelihood and severity of currency crises. This belief did not mark a shift to a competitiveness-oriented exchange-rate policy; rather, ERM entry was interpreted as a way to stabilize expectations, discourage depreciation, and increase the government's credibility in the financial markets. Thatcher opposed ERM entry because it would reduce the government's ability to implement an autonomous monetary policy but consistently authorized short-term increases in interest rates to support sterling. Although there was not a consensus on ERM entry, there was a consensus on preventing rapid depreciation or levels of interest rates that could fuel domestic inflation. For example, when ministers, with the exception of Lawson, concluded that the exchange rate in mid-1987 was inflationary, the consensus in favor of ERM membership weakened, and the Treasury stopped "shadowing" the mark.

France: Devaluation and Competitiveness

Like their British counterparts, French authorities in the 1980s tightened monetary policy and attached greater importance to reducing inflation, but they implemented these policies in ways that mitigated exchange-rate pressures on French industry. After instituting an expansionary fiscal policy in 1981, the government tightened macroeconomic policy in 1982 and 1983 but accompanied this with devaluations in the ERM to prevent real appreciation of the franc. Further real appreciation in the mid-1980s also was countered with devaluations in 1986 and 1987.

Reflation and the 1981 Devaluation

From late 1979 to early 1981, the mark was one of the weak currencies in the ERM because of German current account deficits and high U.S. interest rates. In late October 1980 and February 1981, the mark closed at its lower band in the ERM, and the Banque de France had to sell francs in the foreign exchange market to support the German currency.[28] This period of mark weakness and franc strength ended in early 1981. One reason was that the franc was overvalued by perhaps 10 percent because of relatively high inflation in France (see Table 3.1). Another was investors' worries about Valéry Giscard d'Estaing's chances of retaining office in the May 1981 presidential election. When the candidate of the Parti Socialiste (PS) and the Parti Communiste Français (PCF), François Mitterrand, began performing well during the election campaign, many investors began selling the franc even though Mitterrand's macroeconomic platform was quite conventional in many respects.[29]

The depreciation of the franc accelerated after Mitterrand won the second round of the presidential election on 10 May 1981. The next day the franc fell to the floor of its fluctuation band in the ERM for the first time, and during the next two weeks the Banque de France intervened on the foreign exchange market to support the currency. Although he would not be inaugurated until 21 May, Mitterrand immediately began receiving contrasting advice on the problem of the exchange rate. Many senior advisers favored either a large devaluation of 10–15 percent or withdrawing from the ERM and allowing the franc to depreciate in order to boost competitiveness; others advocated defending the franc's ERM parity. On the day of his inauguration, Mitterrand and the new prime minister, Pierre Mauroy, discussed the issue. Mauroy conveyed the opinions for and against devaluing or withdrawing from the ERM and stated that he favored a devaluation. Mitterrand objected that devaluation would ruin the PS's credibility with voters in the forthcoming legislative elections. That evening Mauroy, Finance Minister Jacques Delors, and senior advisers from the Treasury and Banque de France agreed to raise interest rates, tighten capital controls, and limit import credits to stabilize the franc.[30]

The debate over exchange-rate policy continued into the summer of 1981. Many business leaders expressed concern about the overvalued franc and the high interest rates necessary to support it, and ministers Jean-Pierre Chevènement and Michel Rocard both advised withdrawing from the ERM because French firms faced strong competition from imports. Mitterrand refused to devalue or withdraw, hoping that the pressure on French industry would ease during a recovery in the domestic and international economy in early 1982. He decided to implement his electoral promises to promote growth and employment through deficit spending, and in July 1981 the government announced a 1982 fiscal deficit of 90 billion francs.[31] This prompted heavy selling of the franc; for the next two months the Banque de France had to intervene regularly on the foreign exchange market to stabilize the exchange rate, and in late September the authorities raised interest rates and further tightened capital controls.[32]

Delors and senior Treasury and Banque de France officials concluded from this continual downward pressure on the exchange rate that a devaluation was inevitable, although they opposed withdrawing from the ERM. Delors hoped to negotiate a devaluation of about 12–15 percent to offset the overvaluation of the franc but was willing to accept a smaller parity change.[33] At the meeting of European Economic Community economics and finance ministers on 4 October, Delors secured revaluations of the mark and Dutch guilder of 5.5 percent and devaluation of the franc by 3 percent. The result was an overall devaluation of the franc by 8.5 percent against the mark. To accompany the devaluation, Delors proposed a six-month wage and price freeze, cuts in the 1982 budget deficit of 20 billion francs, and fiscal measures to increase investment. Mitterrand, Mauroy, and Budget Minister Laurent Fabius rejected this plan at the cabinet meeting on

7 October, although they did agree to reduce the 1982 budget deficit by 10 billion francs and to limited price controls to prevent Delors from resigning.[34]

Austerity and the 1982 Devaluation

In early 1982, the franc hovered near the bottom of its fluctuation band in the ERM despite frequent Banque de France intervention in the foreign exchange market. Two camps of political and business leaders organized to influence Mitterrand's response. The first camp advocated policies aimed at helping French industry, including a large devaluation within or withdrawal from the ERM, an expansionary fiscal policy, and more controls on capital movements and imports. Early in 1982, Mitterrand began inviting informal advisers to the Élysée to inform him of this perspective. These *visiteurs du soir* included Jean Riboud, the head of the multinational firm Schlumberger; Mitterrand's chief of staff Pierre Bérégovoy; cabinet ministers Pierre Jobert, Chevènement, and Fabius; and Georges Plescoff, the head of the financial group Suez. Riboud warned the president that French industry could not tolerate indefinitely stabilizing the franc in the ERM. Jobert and Chevènement advocated in private that the president consider withdrawing from the ERM. In May 1982, three of Mitterrand's closest friends outside the government, Riboud, Plescoff, and Jean-Jacques Servan-Schreiber, told him that macroeconomic austerity was not consistent with the electoral mandate and ideological aims of the PS and advocated leaving the ERM, placing strict controls on wages to promote noninflationary growth, and requiring import deposits.[35]

The second camp concluded that the current macroeconomic policy mix was unsustainable due to slow growth overseas. Price and wage increases as well as the trade deficit outstripped projections. Many large private and nationalized firms announced poor results. The steel industry was expected to, and did, lose large amounts of money in 1981, but so did many supposedly healthy firms, including Pechiney, Rhone-Poulenc, CII-Honeywell-Bull, Peugeot, and Renault.[36] Mauroy and Delors led this camp in advocating tighter monetary and fiscal policies. Advisers began preparing a detailed set of austerity measures but kept their work secret from the Élysée and the *visiteurs du soir* so as not to arouse immediate opposition. Their proposals for devaluation, wage and price controls, and limiting the budget deficit to 3 percent of gross domestic product were ready in late March. Mauroy presented the plan to Mitterrand and advocated a devaluation of 10 percent but opposed withdrawing from the ERM on the grounds that this would reduce the government's credibility in the European Economic Community and the financial markets.[37]

Mitterrand hoped that at the Group of Seven summit in Versailles in

June he could secure significant reforms of the international monetary system, including persuading the United States to reduce interest rates in order to promote recovery. This would stabilize the franc in the ERM, allow the Banque de France to cut French interest rates, and reduce the cost of France's dollar-denominated imports.[38] The summit did not produce the changes Mitterrand advocated, and in the second week of June, depreciation of the franc intensified. Mauroy told Mitterrand that the Banque de France's reserves had fallen 60 percent in 1982 and that the franc's ERM parity could not be sustained with central bank intervention for much longer. Mitterrand acquiesced, and Delors was sent to negotiate a franc devaluation of 5.75 percent and a mark revaluation of 4.25 percent in the ERM. In exchange for the effective 10 percent devaluation, Delors promised the German negotiators that he would tighten macroeconomic policy, an issue that they had discussed in secret for two weeks.[39]

This time devaluation was accompanied by significant changes in economic policy aimed at reducing inflation. Approved by the president and cabinet on 16 June 1982, these included placing a six-month freeze on wages and prices, basing the wage-indexing arrangements on the government's inflation forecasts, reducing the 1983 budget deficit, and securing a 28-billion-franc loan from international banks and the Saudi government to replenish the Banque de France's reserves.[40] Mitterrand was not happy about approving these measures. At the cabinet meeting, he said that if the austerity program did not work, he would consider withdrawing the franc from the ERM, an implicit encouragement to the *visiteurs du soir*. In August 1982, Mitterrand told Mauroy that he would find a new prime minister unless the economy improved by the end of the year. The next month Mitterrand approved a tightening of fiscal policy in 1983 but argued that the real problem was the high levels of indebtedness of French firms, a theme he repeated in a speech to business leaders later in the month.[41]

Austerity and the 1983 Devaluation

Between September and December, France ran large monthly trade deficits, the franc depreciated within its ERM fluctuation band, and central bank reserves dropped. This convinced Mauroy and Delors of the need for another devaluation and further tightening of macroeconomic policy. Mitterrand rejected austerity and admitted he was considering withdrawing the franc from the ERM, raising trade barriers, and taking steps to promote domestic demand.[42]

During the winter and spring of 1983, supporters and opponents of macroeconomic austerity again mobilized to influence Mitterrand. The president was still of two minds about economic policy. Although he recognized that France could not pursue macroeconomic policies greatly different from those of other major economies, he was intensely concerned about the competitiveness of French firms. The *visiteurs du soir*, including ministers, presidential advisers, economists, and the heads of large firms and banks, continued to meet with the president; as Mauroy put it, "during the day, Mitterrand worked with a government implementing the policy decided in June 1982. During the evening, he received a concubine who proposed another policy." Three frequent *visiteurs*, Riboud, Bérégovoy, and Fabius, supported by Chevènement and Interior Minister Gaston Deffere, began quietly mobilizing support within the PS for their *autre politique*. They argued that French industry was handicapped by the franc's continual real appreciation and that withdrawing from the ERM or securing a sizable devaluation would increase firms' profits.[43] Riboud of Schlumberger, Plescoff of Suez, and Jean Deflassieux of the commercial bank Crédit Lyonnais argued that indebted French firms were being suffocated by the high interest rates necessary to stabilize the franc in the ERM. They also pointed out that under Presidents Pompidou and Giscard this burden was eased by occasional devaluation. Regular memos from two of Mitterrand's economic policy advisers, Charles Salzmann and Alain Boublil, emphasized the financial weakness of French firms when interest rates were so high.[44]

Although speculation against the franc's ERM parity mounted in early 1983, Mitterrand delayed a decision on economic policy until after the March municipal elections. This allowed supporters of austerity to begin to counter the advice of the *visiteurs du soir* by generating a stream of memos and analyses emphasizing the negative consequences of withdrawing from the ERM. Led by presidential adviser Jacques Attali and others in the Élysée, they emphasized that it would be possible to reinforce the competitiveness and profitability of French industry by devaluing *within* the ERM. In late January and early February, Attali emphasized to Mitterrand that a devaluation was a necessary part of an austerity package and that if Germany objected, France could threaten to implement import safeguard clauses in the Treaty of Rome. In late February, presidential adviser Élisabeth Guigou emphasized the negative consequences of withdrawing from the ERM, including depreciation against the dollar, an increased trade deficit, higher foreign debt costs, and the possibility of having to turn to the European Economic Community or International Monetary Fund for assistance.[45]

With setbacks for the PS in the first round of municipal elections on 6 March 1983 and the recent electoral victory of the conservative coalition in Germany, the depreciation of the franc accelerated and forced a decision.[46] On the morning of 14 March, Mitterrand told Mauroy that he wished to retain him as prime minister but as head of a reshuffled "war cabinet" including *visiteurs du soir* Jean Riboud as head of a new superministry of industry and international trade, Fabius at finance, and Bérégovoy at social affairs. Mitterrand said that the franc should be withdrawn from the ERM and that the government should protect French industry from imports, a solution advocated by his "best experts," presumably a reference to the *visiteurs du soir*.[47] Mauroy objected, stating that remaining in the ERM would allow France to secure assistance from other European Economic Community countries and that France had to adjust to a difficult international environment by tightening monetary and fiscal policies. Mauroy threatened to resign rather than oversee the franc's withdrawal from the ERM.[48] The next day Delors told Mitterrand that withdrawing from the ERM would cause the franc to depreciate by 20–30 percent, and that any positive effect on exports would be wiped out within six months by higher inflation. He also said that the Banque de France's reserves were almost exhausted, standing at only 30 billion francs. Disturbed by this news, Mitterrand asked Fabius to check Delors's figures.[49] Fabius contacted Michel Camdessus, the director of the Treasury, who confirmed Delors's reserves figures and analysis of the effects of withdrawing from the ERM. This convinced Fabius and Bérégovoy that the costs of their *autre politique* would be higher than remaining in the ERM, and they persuaded Mitterrand to abandon the idea of withdrawing.[50]

Mitterrand told Delors to begin talks with his German counterpart about an ERM realignment. The German finance minister, Gerhard Stoltenberg, initially agreed to a mark revaluation of 5 percent, but this was not large enough to correct the accumulated inflation differential between Germany and France. Although Mitterrand already had decided to remain in the ERM, to obtain a negotiating advantage he pretended to be considering withdrawal of the franc.[51] Mitterrand instructed Delors to secure a parity change of between 7 and 9 percent. Delors's opening proposal was for a 3 percent devaluation of the franc and an 8–12 percent revaluation of the mark. He argued that without a sizable devaluation, the "protectionists" would take over the French government. Stoltenberg countered with an offer of a total adjustment of 6 percent, along with widening the ERM fluctuation margins from ±2.25 percent to ±4 percent. They agreed on a mark revaluation of 5.5 percent and a franc devaluation of 2.5 percent (for an effective franc devaluation of 8 percent), accompanied by guarantees of a tightening of French economic policy.[52]

Mitterrand's decision to remain in the ERM strengthened the political positions of Mauroy and Delors. In a March government reshuffle, Mauroy remained as prime minister, Delors took control of the budget from Fabius, and Chevènement and Jobert resigned. To ensure that Delors could not dominate economic policy completely, Mitterrand reappointed Bérégovoy as minister for social affairs and moved Fabius from the budget portfolio to the ministry of industry and research.[53] Delors's first act was to tighten fiscal policy. He cut the budget deficit by 20 billion francs, reduced financial assistance to nationalized firms, raised taxes on energy and transport, increased social security and health care charges, and limited the amount of currency French citizens could take overseas.[54]

The Devaluations of 1986 and 1987

The franc was stable in the ERM from the devaluation in March 1983 through 1985, but French inflation remained relatively high. It dropped from 9.6 percent in 1983 to 5.8 percent in 1985, whereas German inflation fell from 3.3 percent to 2.2 percent. This inflation differential, combined with the depreciation of the dollar beginning in early 1985, led the franc to appreciate in real terms. Individuals in the PS and the Banque de France advocated a "preventive devaluation" of the franc within the ERM to offset this loss of competitiveness and to prevent foreign exchange market turbulence before the 1986 legislative elections. This issue came to a head in July 1985 when the Italian government requested a devaluation of the lira. Mitterrand and Bérégovoy, recently appointed as finance minister, rejected this advice and declined to accompany Italy in devaluing.[55]

Depreciation before the parliamentary elections of 16 March 1986 forced the Banque de France to intervene on the foreign exchange market to defend the franc's ERM parity. The Socialist government opposed devaluation for fear that it would play into the hands of the opposition shortly before the election. But the conservative parties that won the election were quick to devalue and to restore competitiveness to French firms.[56] Instead of waiting for downward pressure against the franc to build in the foreign exchange market, the Banque de France announced on 4 April that it would no longer intervene to defend the franc's ERM parity, and the new finance minister, Edouard Balladur, called a meeting of economics and finance ministers to negotiate a realignment. Other governments were upset with these tactics, which forced them to agree to a devaluation or risk a rapid decline in the value of the franc requiring coordinated foreign exchange market intervention under the rules of the EMS. They rejected the request of Prime Minister Jacques Chirac and Balladur for a devaluation of 8 percent, limiting the parity change to only 3 percent.[57]

Mark appreciation and dollar depreciation in late 1986 and early 1987 threatened the stability of ERM parities. In September 1986, the Chirac government raised interest rates and delayed a promised relaxation of capital controls to defend the franc's parity. Four months later Chirac and Balladur began campaigning for a revaluation of the mark and reform of the rules of the EMS. The Banque de France again refused to support the franc above the floor of its ERM fluctuation band in an attempt to pressure the Bundesbank either to intervene by buying francs, to cut interest rates, or to revalue the mark; on 12 January Germany agreed to revalue by 3 percent against other ERM currencies. The 1986 and 1987 devaluations wiped out most of the franc's real appreciation against the mark accumulated since 1983.[58]

Summary

High French inflation meant that the franc appreciated in real terms during the early 1980s. Governments sought devaluations within the ERM every year after 1981, except 1984 and 1985, to restore competitiveness to French industry. Another goal of French authorities was to stabilize the exchange rate with capital controls, foreign exchange market intervention, and brief increases in short-term interest rates. These policy choices were consistent with the preferences of financial and industrial firms for devaluation or withdrawal from the ERM. In sharp contrast with the British experience, no state-owned or private firms in France preferred to reduce inflation with currency appreciation. Almost all senior members of the French government supported devaluation to maintain growth and industrial competitiveness, but most British ministers favored appreciation of sterling to reduce inflation. The primary conflicts among French authorities were not over the desirability of devaluations but over their size and the severity of accompanying austerity measures. The switch in French economic policy in 1983 toward tighter monetary and fiscal policies took place in the context of a limited set of policy options, all of which included devaluation.

Italy

Italy experienced high inflation and continual real appreciation of the lira during the 1980s. The authorities took two steps to prevent this from undermining the competitiveness of Italian industry. First, they secured frequent devaluations of the lira within the ERM. Second, they utilized the lira's wider ERM fluctuation band to allow the currency to depreciate on the foreign exchange market between devaluations. As in France, the government tightened monetary policy to reduce inflation but did so later and did not seek to reduce large budget deficits.

Attempted Austerity and Devaluation, 1979–1981

Italian authorities understood that joining the ERM with a high inflation rate would lead to real appreciation of the lira. The Banca d'Italia intervened on the foreign exchange markets in early 1979 to depreciate the lira and offset any loss of industrial competitiveness. The central bank's subsequent strategy was to "pilot" the lira down against the mark in a controlled, gradual depreciation, thus improving competitiveness against other ERM currencies while keeping the lira stable against the appreciating dollar to stabilize import prices. When the Bundesbank began increasing interest rates in 1981, the mark strengthened against most European currencies, and Italian authorities began raising interest rates and devaluing to maintain competitiveness.[59]

In the first half of 1980, the Italian economy boomed, with output growing at an annual rate of 6 percent and inflation approaching 20 percent. Rapid growth increased imports, and high inflation led to real exchange rate appreciation and shifted the current account from surplus to deficit. Senior bankers at Credito Italiano and well-known industrialists such as Carlo de Benedetti of Olivetti and Giovanni Agnelli of FIAT advocated a devaluation within the ERM and measures to reduce labor costs to offset these developments. Officials in the Treasury and the Banca d'Italia, including Treasury Minister Filippo Maria Pandolfi and bank Governor Carlo Azeglio Ciampi, allied with each other to resist these demands. They countered that Italian industry could not rely on devaluation to restore competitiveness lost through high inflation and that it needed to devote more attention to controlling costs.[60] The Cossiga government split the difference between these proposals. Beginning in June 1980, it had the Banca d'Italia raise interest rates to restrain the unsustainable rate of growth and intervene on the foreign exchange market to bring about a controlled depreciation of the lira within its fluctuation band.[61] Although Ciampi advocated reducing public spending and increasing the flexibility of the labor market, the government focused instead on implementing payroll deductions to finance investment and export subsidies and refused to consider widely demanded reforms to the wage indexation system, the *scala mobile*.[62]

These measures did little to stop rumors of a devaluation, which intensified in late September 1980 when Cossiga resigned as prime minister because of the failure to secure agreement on his government's medium-term economic plan. The Banca d'Italia attempted to stabilize the lira by raising interest rates to 16.5 percent, tightening capital controls, and intervening on the foreign exchange markets.[63] But political pressures for devaluation grew stronger, and by early 1981 many industrial associations and a sizable number of cabinet ministers insisted that it was the only way to restore the competitiveness of Italian manufacturing.[64] The Italian authorities secured a devaluation of 6 percent effective 22 March after telephone consultations among European Economic Community economics and finance ministers.[65]

After the devaluation, the Banca d'Italia raised interest rates by 2.5 percent to 19 percent (before this real interest rates were negative, with price increases for the coming year predicted to be 17–19 percent). Budget Minister Giorgio La Malfa of the Partito Repubblicano Italiano (PRI) and Treasury Minister Beniamino Andreatta of Democrazia Christiana (DC) proposed cutting public spending and freezing public-sector wages to accompany the devaluation. Andreatta argued that without these measures, another devaluation would be inevitable in the near future, a position that his opponents in the government seemed to acknowledge. But the minister for state holdings, Gianni De Michelis of the Partito Socialista Italiano (PSI), successfully mobilized opposition within the government to significant spending cuts or wage reforms.[66]

The next devaluation of the lira—widely foreshadowed by ministers' comments to the press—occurred on 4 October 1981. A Franco-German agreement to devalue the franc dictated the timing. The French and Germans asked the Italian delegation in Brussels to devalue the lira. Although the Italian negotiators were somewhat upset about this fait accompli and demanded minor changes in rates of currencies' parity changes, they quickly secured approval from political authorities in Rome for an effective devaluation of the lira of 8 percent against the mark. Andreatta emphasized that the reductions in the budget deficit foreseen in the government's medium-term economic policy document should accompany the devaluation, but ministers took no real action on this front.[67]

Attempted Austerity and Devaluation, 1981–1983

Despite these devaluations, the employers' confederation, Confindustria, argued that the high interest rates necessary to stabilize the lira damaged heavily indebted firms. Vittorio Merloni, president of Confindustria, said that the two devaluations of 1981 had allowed Italian firms to regain competitiveness within Europe but that their position had eroded quickly without another devaluation or other policy measures. The organization's vice president, Walter Mandelli, argued that "when the inflation differential between Italy and another European Community country touches 10 percent there is no alternative: one either increases productivity by 10 percent or must devalue."[68] Francesco Cingano, director of the Banca Commerciale Italiano, joined in by arguing that it was unlikely that competitiveness would be restored through a "very rigorous economic policy," although he preferred this to a devaluation. Ministers from the PSI and elements of the DC as well as the opposition Partito Comunista Italiano (PCI) pressed the Spadolini government to reduce interest rates and to relax quantitative controls on bank lending in late 1981.[69] The minister for industry, Giovanni Marcora, said that there would have to be a devaluation in the near future, although he thought it could be delayed until after the summer tourist season's influx of currency reserves. Andreatta at the Treasury and Ciampi at the Banca d'Italia continued to campaign against devaluation.[70]

The authorities responded by negotiating an effective 7 percent devaluation of the lira against the mark at the general realignment of ERM parities in June 1982. Andreatta again called for austerity measures similar to those implemented in France, including wage and price controls and budget cuts. But the government failed to produce a concrete plan of action because the PSI wanted to loosen monetary policy. Andreatta was forced to announce a series of "fantasy" austerity measures in Brussels that were never implemented. He did succeed in limiting the size of the devaluation so that it did not overly compensate for the accumulated inflation differential between Italy and other ERM currencies. Ciampi supported Andreatta, having complained recently that previous devaluations had been accompanied by empty promises to reduce the government deficit. Without a correction, fiscal policy would crowd out the funds available for private investment and increase interest rates and inflation by stimulating domestic demand.[71]

In early 1983, further conflict erupted between those in favor of a relaxation of monetary policy and those preferring to stabilize the lira. The PSI minister for state holdings, De Michelis, called for reducing unemployment rather than inflation; coordinating international monetary policy to stabilize exchange rates and lower real interest rates; and finding "new ways" to finance public spending, including a reduction in the autonomy of the Banca d'Italia from the Treasury.[72] Other PSI ministers claimed that interest rates could be reduced by 4 percent immediately with little effect on inflation. Although DC treasury minister Giovanni Goria was committed to reducing inflation by cutting interest rates gradually, others in his party, as well as Confindustria, also favored a more rapid reduction of interest rates.[73] The solution to this conflict was to reduce interest rates and to devalue along with the French franc in the ERM realignment of March 1983, despite the fact that the lira was in the upper half of its fluctuation band until early March. Ciampi claimed that these "successful tactics" improved competitiveness only in the short run; longer-term improvements would depend on Italian inflation and fiscal policy converging with those of the other members of the ERM.[74]

The Shift Toward Austerity, 1984–1985

Prime Minister Bettino Craxi of the PSI introduced a certain amount of political stability to Italian politics by retaining office from 1983 until 1987. His government implemented a shift toward austerity in August 1983 by tightening monetary policy and liberalizing international capital movements.[75] Craxi also was determined to change the *scala mobile* wage-indexing system over the opposition of the PCI and the party's allies in the union movement. Some government leaders hoped that the promise of lower interest rates would persuade the labor union confederations and PCI to agree to reforms that would reduce wage costs and inflation. In early February 1984, the three main union confederations, Confindustria, and the government negotiated a provisional set of changes to the *scala mobile* that the Communist-affiliated union federation and the PCI then decided to oppose. The Craxi government announced that it would implement these changes with a temporary decree that both houses of parliament passed into law in June. The PCI mobilized a referendum to overturn the law, which it lost in June 1985. By weakening the opposition PCI and delivering a personal political victory to Craxi, the referendum result further strengthened the hands of those supporting a more restrictive monetary policy.[76]

The 1985 Devaluation

The policy of the Banca d'Italia during 1984 and early 1985 was to pilot the lira down against other ERM currencies within the currency's wide fluctuation band. By late 1984, industrialists, Confindustria, and officials of FIAT and the state-owned holding company IRI complained about the real appreciation of the lira this policy produced because of high Italian inflation. They argued that a devaluation soon would be necessary without further reforms to state spending or labor markets.[77] The Craxi government and the Banca d'Italia were willing to devalue by early 1985, but they decided to wait until the end of the Italian presidency of the European Economic Community in June.[78]

In early July 1985, the secretaries of the five parties forming the government, along with Treasury Minister Giovanni Goria and Labor Minister Gianni De Michelis, agreed to secure a lira devaluation over the weekend. Their plan was to engineer a surprise devaluation during a period of market calm and avoid having to sell reserves to defend the lira's ERM parity. But a problem broke out on Friday, 19 July, when the state-owned energy firm ENI either guessed that a devaluation was being arranged or had inside information about the government's plans and attempted to purchase a large amount of dollars. This sparked a market panic that caused the lira to depreciate 19 percent against the dollar, leading the Treasury to close the foreign exchange market for the remainder of the day. The lira regained much of the ground lost against the dollar after authorities secured an 8 percent devaluation against the lira's ERM parity over the weekend.[79]

Mark Appreciation, 1986–1987

The dollar depreciated against most European currencies in early 1986, causing tensions in the ERM between strong currencies such as the mark and weak currencies such as the franc and the lira. On 16 January the

Italian government reimposed quantitative limits on bank lending for six months, reintroduced some capital controls, and intervened intramarginally to defend what it termed a "realistic and appropriate" exchange rate.[80] But Italian authorities were quick to agree to a 3 percent devaluation against the mark when the French government requested a realignment in April 1986. The only criticism this move attracted from the private sector, including Confindustria and some senior bankers, was that, like many previous devaluations, it was not accompanied by a credible plan to reduce the budget deficit. Critics also noted that since Italian inflation had fallen from the high levels of the early 1980s, the challenge was to persuade countries with large balance-of-payments surpluses to implement more expansionary fiscal and monetary policies, thereby reducing interest rates in Italy and cutting the cost to firms of servicing their bank debts.[81] Depreciation of the franc against the mark in late 1986 spread to the lira, and the authorities agreed to a 3 percent revaluation of the mark in early 1987 so as not to lose competitiveness.[82]

Summary

Italian and French exchange-rate politics shared important characteristics in the 1980s. Beginning in 1980, Italian authorities moderately tightened monetary policy and attached greater importance to reducing inflation. They chose to reach this goal gradually, which meant that Italian inflation remained persistently high and that the lira appreciated in real terms. To offset the effect of currency appreciation on industry, Italian governments acquiesced to frequent depreciation and devaluation of the lira—the currency was devalued against the mark on eight occasions between 1979 and 1987. The Banca d'Italia also made full use of the wider fluctuation band during this period, allowing the lira to depreciate toward the bottom of the band before requesting devaluation. This strategy was supported by Confindustria, which frequently called for devaluations, and most of the leaders of the governing parties. Some policymakers—Pandolfi and Andreatta at the Treasury and Ciampi at the Banca d'Italia—favored a tighter monetary policy stance, but they were unable to muster the necessary political support. They also called for more comprehensive reforms to macroeconomic policy, including reducing the large budget deficit, but saw little success there as well.

Comparisons and Conclusions

British, French, and Italian governments pursued different exchange-rate policies during the 1980s. To explain these differences, I first compare the policy preferences articulated by domestic groups regarding currency instability and real appreciation with the expectations of the openness and institutional approaches. I then analyze the congruence between exchange-rate changes, groups' preferences, and policy choices. The bulk of the evidence supports the conclusion that the institutional approach is a superior explanation of groups' preferences and their influence on policy choice. I conclude by discussing the reasons that, on a few occasions, governments did not accede to the preferences of powerful domestic groups.

Industry opposed real exchange-rate appreciation in all three countries, as both the openness and institutional explanations predict. Although quite sympathetic to the Conservative government in Britain, the CBI and individual firms complained loudly and publicly about the policy of encouraging sterling appreciation in the early 1980s. Leaders of nationalized and private firms in France articulated similar preferences. Many worked behind the scenes with ministers, advisers, and the president to devise alternatives to macroeconomic austerity and to press for devaluation of the franc. Individual Italian managers, as well as the employers' association Confindustria, regularly advocated devaluation to maintain competitiveness. Although Confindustria called for changes to fiscal and labor market policies as well, industry viewed devaluation as the best way to maintain its competitive position in the short term. The intensity of industry's preference for a competitive real exchange rate varied over the business cycle. With high inflation, low economic growth, and exchange-rate appreciation in the early 1980s, industry saw currency devaluation or depreciation as an efficient policy tool for boosting domestic and international demand for its products. An increase in growth and lower inflation by the mid-1980s in France and Italy and somewhat earlier in Britain led industry to reduce its focus on currency questions. Industry in all three countries also favored currency stability, which was partially achieved in France and Italy through participation in the ERM. After 1984 British industry advocated entry of sterling into the ERM to prevent unpredictable changes in the exchange rate.

As predicted by the institutionalist approach, banks and financial firms in France and Italy shared industry's opposition to exchange-rate appreciation and instability. Despite its greater openness to international transactions, the preferences of the financial community in Britain varied with the inflation rate rather than the exchange rate. When inflation was high or rising, British bankers and financiers preferred immediate increases in interest rates regardless of the level of sterling. ERM entry attracted little support in the early 1980s, on the grounds that it could undermine the domestic orientation of targeting the rate of growth of the money supply (which was quite popular among City economists) and lead to a more gradual reduction in inflation. Similar concerns emerged again in 1987 when inflation began to increase, although after the technical failures of monetary targeting, some supported "hard" ERM entry at a high exchange rate as a credible anti-inflation device. In contrast, French and Italian bankers did not oppose ERM membership but expressed concern that participation not lead to over-valued currencies that would threaten the profitability of industrial firms carrying high levels of debt. Because of these ties with industry, French bankers and industrialists in the state-owned and private sectors lobbied together and had greater influence on policy deliberations than their British counterparts. Representatives of Italian banks did not advocate a more rapid tightening of monetary policy and exchange-rate appreciation as a way to reduce domestic demand and joined industry's calls for devaluation, lower budget deficits, and labor market reforms.

Further evidence in support of the institutionalist explanation is found in Table 3.3, which summarizes the congruence between changes in exchange rates and policy choices. Weak bank-industry ties in Britain were associated with policy choices that accorded little priority to stabilizing sterling at a competitive level. The Thatcher government adopted the domestically oriented strategy of targeting the money supply and an ideological position favoring a floating exchange rate that contradicted the preferences of industry. The government removed capital controls, increased interest rates, and encouraged a sharp appreciation to reduce inflation. Beginning in 1982, the concern was to prevent depreciation from fueling inflation and reducing the credibility of the government's monetary policy targets, despite the fact that sterling remained overvalued (see Figure 3.3). Increasing credibility, rather that stabilizing sterling's external value *per se*, was the key reason for growing interest in ERM from 1984 to 1986. Chancellor Lawson and others saw ERM membership as a useful discipline on macroeconomic policy but were overruled by Thatcher's political concerns about the consequences of losing control over interest rates. The Treasury informally fixed sterling to the mark beginning in late 1986 but abandoned this policy in early 1988 by raising interest rates and allowing the currency to appreciate in order to bear down on inflation.

Unlike the Thatcher government, the French and Italian authorities chose to participate in the ERM. They tightened monetary policy to reduce inflation in the early 1980s but sought frequent devaluations to offset the loss of competitiveness caused by real appreciation. After the election of Mitterrand to the presidency in 1981, French authorities focused on increasing domestic demand by running larger budget deficits and increasing social spending. They were unwilling to countenance the impact of real appreciation on growth and competitiveness and secured a large devaluation in October 1981. When the domestic and international economies failed to recover and inflation remained high in 1982 and 1983, the French responded by tightening monetary policy and devaluing in both years.

Table 3.3 Changes in Exchange Rates and Policy Choices, 1979–1988

Britain		France		Italy	
Changes in Exchange Rate	Policy Choices	Changes in Exchange Rate	Policy Choices	Changes in Exchange Rate	Policy Choices
Real appreciation 1979–1981	Encouraged appreciation	Real appreciation 1979–1981	Devalued in 1981	Real appreciation 1980–1981	Devalued twice in 1981
Sterling depreciation 1982–1986	Discouraged depreciation	Real appreciation 1982–1983	Tightened monetary and fiscal policies, devalued in 1982 and 1983	Real appreciation 1982–1983	Devalued in 1982 and 1983
ERM entry 1984–1986	Refused entry	Real appreciation 1983–1985	Resisted devaluation	Real appreciation 1984–1985	Tightened monetary policy, devalued in 1985
Shadowing the mark 1986–1988	Abandoned to reduce inflation	Mark appreciation 1986–1987	Devalued in 1986 and 1987	Mark appreciation 1986–1987	Devalued in 1986 and 1987

French officials refused a further devaluation in 1985, but the conservative government elected in 1986 did devalue shortly after taking office and again in early 1987 as the mark appreciated. Italian policy followed a similar pattern of devaluing to keep the lira at a competitive level, although these devaluations were not accompanied by as sharp a tightening of macroeconomic policy.[83] High inflation and real appreciation of the lira between 1981 and 1983 led governments to devalue on four occasions. Further devaluations were delayed until July 1985, resulting in some real appreciation that reduced competitiveness. The Italians followed the French in devaluing in 1986 and 1987 when the mark began appreciating.

French and Italian authorities did share some of their British counterparts' perceptions of exchange-rate policy. Mitterrand, for example, vetoed politically sensitive devaluations before elections in 1981, 1983, and 1986 but was quick to approve them shortly afterward. Conversely, British officials on one occasion saw the advantages of exchange-rate stability and a competitive value for sterling. The decision to shadow the mark was influenced by the opinions of industry. But British authorities saw the primary advantages of an exchange-rate commitment as providing a visible and anti-inflationary anchor for monetary policy. Consequently, Thatcher insisted on "uncapping" sterling from its informal mark parity once it became clear that inflation was increasing.

Notes

1. Geoffrey Howe, *Conflict of Loyalty* (London: Macmillan, 1994), 111; and Margaret Thatcher, *The Downing Street Years* (New York: HarperCollins, 1993), 691–693.

2. Cited in William Keegan, *Mrs. Thatcher's Economic Experiment* (London: Allen Lane, 1984), 101–102.

3. *Economist*, 12 May 1978, 58; Howe, *Conflict of Loyalty*, 140–143; Christopher Johnson, *The Grand Experiment: Mrs. Thatcher's Revolution and How It Spread* (Boulder, CO: Westview Press, 1991), 37; and Nigel Lawson, *The View from No. 11: Memoirs of a Tory Radical* (New York and London: Doubleday, 1993), 39–41.

4. Many officials in the Treasury and the Bank of England thought that the government's explicit rejection of any exchange-rate targets was "doctrinaire" and "theoretical." But few advocated ERM entry, especially as the Bank of England director responsible for domestic monetary policy gained influence at the expense of the overseas directors. Interviews with former Bank of England officials.

5. Lawson, *The View from No. 11*, 59; Peter Riddell, *The Thatcher Era and Its Legacy* (Oxford: Basil Blackwell, 1991), 18–22; and David Smith, *The Rise and Fall of Monetarism* (London: Penguin, 1987), 90.

6. Willem Buiter and Marcus Miller, "The Thatcher Experiment: The First Two Years," *Brookings Papers on Economic Activity* 2 (1981): 315–379; see also Keegan, *Mrs. Thatcher's Economic Experiment*, 148.

7. Interview with former minister; quotations from Martin Holmes, *The First Thatcher Government 1979–1983: Contemporary Conservatism and Economic Change* (Boulder, CO: Westview Press, 1985), 155–156.

8. Quoted in David Smith, *From Boom to Bust: Trial and Error in British Economic Policy* (London: Penguin Books, 1992), 91.

9. Peter Hall, "Policy Paradigms, Social Learning, and the State," *Comparative Politics* 26 (1993): 286; Holmes, *The First Thatcher Government*, 157–158; and interview with former minister.

10. Keegan, *Mrs. Thatcher's Economic Experiment*, 165–166; and interview with former Bank of England official.

11. The March 1982 budget statement indicated less concern about meeting the monetary targets due to changes in the financial system and stated that the exchange rate would be an indicator of the tightness of monetary policy but not a policy target. Howe, *Conflict of Loyalty*, 226–227; Smith, *The Rise and Fall of Monetarism;* and interviews with former minister and former director of the Bank of England.

12. Smith, *From Boom to Bust*, 48; Thatcher, *The Downing Street Years*, 693; and interview with former minister.

13. Bernard Ingham, *Kill the Messenger* (London: HarperCollins, 1991), 339; Lawson, *The View from No. 11*, 468–469; Smith, *From Boom to Bust*, 50–51; and Thatcher, *The Downing Street Years*, 694.

14. Howe, *Conflict of Loyalty*, 276; and Lawson, *The View from No. 11*, 486.

15. Johnson, *The Grand Experiment*, 51; Lawson, *The View from No. 11*, 461–463, 465; and Smith, *The Rise and Fall of Monetarism.*

16. *Financial Times*, 13 July 1982, 6; *Financial Times*, 5 November 1982, 16; and Holmes, *The First Thatcher Government*, 159–160.

17. See the letter by J. P. M. Denny of the CBI in *Financial Times*, 6 November 1982, 14, which also called for depreciation of sterling against the mark.

18. Lawson, *The View from No. 11*, 485–489; and Thatcher, *The Downing Street Years*, 694–695.

19. William Keegan, *Mr. Lawson's Gamble* (London: Hodeer and Stoughton, 1989), 183–186; Lawson, *The View from No. 11*, 647–648, 651–652; and Smith, *From Boom to Bust*, 51–52.

20. The memorandum Lawson prepared for this meeting is reprinted in Lawson, *The View from No. 11*, 1055–1059; see also Howe, *Conflict of Loyalty*, 449–450; Lawson, *The View from No. 11*, 497–500; and Thatcher, *The Downing Street Years*, 697–698, and interview with a former minister. Thatcher's comments about interest rates are reprinted in *Financial Times*, 1 June 1986, 12.

In early December, Treasury and Bank of England officials, without Thatcher's knowledge, met their German counterparts to discuss operational aspects of the ERM and potential exchange rates at which sterling could enter the mechanism and to arrange a swap arrangement with the Bundesbank. Bundesbank officials, including Karl Otto Pöhl and Hans Tietmeyer, warned that Britain could only enter near the prevailing market exchange rate and strongly supported British entry in part because they saw the "Bonn-Paris axis" as threatening their autonomy. Lawson, *The View from No. 11*, 500–501; and interview with former Bank of England official.

21. See the letter favoring ERM entry to reduce exchange rate volatility by J. T. Caff, director of economic affairs at the CBI, in *Financial Times*, 5 February 1985, 17. Later in the month, the CBI council approved a motion advocating ERM entry for similar reasons. See *Financial Times*, 27 February 1986, 10. In September,

the Bow Group, a club of parliamentarians and businessmen in the Conservative party, also called for ERM membership. See *Reuters North European Service*, 19 September 1986.

22. *Reuters Money Report*, 7 July 1987.

23. Keegan, *Mr. Lawson's Gamble*, 194; Lawson, *The View from No. 11*, 731–732, 783; and Smith, *From Boom to Bust*, 100–101, 103; and interview with former director of the Bank of England.

24. Lawson, *The View from No. 11*, 682–683.

25. Lawson, *The View from No. 11*, 732, 748–749; and Smith, *From Boom to Bust*, 108, 118–119.

26. Interview with former director of the Bank of England.

27. Lawson, *The View from No. 11*, 794–795; Smith, *From Boom to Bust*, 133, 135–137; and Thatcher, *The Downing Street Years*, 702–705.

28. *Economist*, 29 September 1979, 77; and C. Randall Henning, *Currencies and Politics in the United States, Germany, and Japan* (Washington, DC: Institute for International Economics, 1994), 189–194.

29. Investors seem to have focused on Mitterrand's promise to nationalize many large banks and firms. For example, while presidential candidate Jacques Chirac called for reflationary economic policies to bring about economic growth of 6 percent and George Marchais of the PCF called for growth of 4.5 percent, Mitterrand saw 3 percent as a more realistic figure. Mitterrand's platform also focused on raising the income of the poor and of pensioners and was offset by tax increases. See Thomas R. Christofferson, *The French Socialists in Power, 1981–1986: From Autogestion to Cohabitation* (Newark: University of Delaware Press, 1991), 25.

30. David Cameron, "Exchange Rate Politics in France, 1981–1983: The Regime-Defining Choices of the Mitterrand Presidency" (manuscript, Yale University, n.d.), 13–14; Franz-Olivier Giesbert, *Le Président* (Paris: Seuil, 1990), 87–88; and Pierre Mauroy, *C'est Ici le Chemin* (Paris: Flammarion, 1982), 19–25.

31. Philippe Bauchard, *La Guerre des Deux Roses* (Paris: Grasset, 1986), 33–34; Pierre Favier and Michel Martin-Roland, *La Décennie Mitterrand: 1: Les Ruptures (1981–1984)* (Paris: Éditions du Seuil, 1990), 403; Solange Gras and Christian Gras, *Histoire de la Première République Mitterrandienne* (Paris: Robert Laffont, 1991), 69.

32. *Reuters*, 20 September 1981.

33. See his comments reported in *Reuters*, 4 October 1981.

34. Bauchard, *La Guerre des Deux Roses*, 55–60; Christofferson, *The French Socialists in Power*, 69–70; Favier and Martin-Roland, *La Décennie Mitterrand*, 405–407; and Giesbert, *Le Président*, 108–110.

35. Bauchard, *La Guerre des Deux Roses*, 91; Favier and Martin-Roland, *La Décennie Mitterrand*, 415; and Giesbert, *Le Président*, 163.

36. Christofferson, *The French Socialists in Power*, 100–101.

37. Favier and Martin-Roland, *La Décennie Mitterrand*, 412–415; Gras and Gras, *Histoire de la Première République Mitterrandienne*, 101; and Catherine Nay, *Les Sept Mitterrand* (Paris: Bernard Grasset, 1988), 86.

38. Stéphane Denis, *La Leçon D'Automne: Jeux et Enjeux de François Mitterrand* (Paris: Albin Michel, 1983), 64–66.

39. Bauchard, *La Guerre des Deux Roses*, 89; Cameron, "Exchange Rate Politics in France," 23–24; Christofferson, *The French Socialists in Power*, 102–105; and Giesbert, *Le Président*, 150–154.

40. Gras and Gras, *Histoire de la Première République Mitterrandienne*, 105–107.

41. Favier and Martin-Roland, *La Décennie Mitterrand*, 444–446; Serge July, *Les Années Mitterrand: Histoire Baroque d'une Normalisation Inachevée* (Paris: Grasset, 1986), 84; and Nay, *Les Sept Mitterrand*, 81.

42. Christofferson, *The French Socialists in Power*, 112–114; Giesbert, *Le Président*, 167–168; Gras and Gras, *Histoire de la Première République Mitterrandienne*, 112–113; and Nay, *Les Sept Mitterrand*, 85.

43. Quotation from Favier and Martin-Roland, *La Décennie Mitterrand*, 441; see also Robert Elgie, *The Role of the Prime Minister in France, 1981–1991* (London: St. Martin's Press, 1993), 131–132; and Giesbert, *Le Président*, 174.

44. Favier and Martin-Roland, *La Décennie Mitterrand*, 441–442.

45. Ibid., 460–463.

46. The first round of elections indicated a landslide victory for the right, but the left recovered somewhat in the second round on 13 March, during which the right-wing parties won 53 percent of the vote, and the left lost control of 31 municipal governments.

47. The same day, Mitterrand asked Fabius, Bérégovoy, and Riboud for a concrete plan of action to implement their economic policies. See Favier and Martin-Roland, *La Décennie Mitterrand*, 467–468.

48. Bauchard, *La Guerre des Deux Roses*, 141; Favier and Martin-Roland, *La Décennie Mitterrand*, 466–467; Giesbert, *Le Président*, 169–173; and July, *Les Années Mitterrand*, 90.

49. Apparently, asking Fabius was the idea of Attali and Delors, who hoped to persuade one of the president's closest advisers to support their position. Elgie, *The Role of the Prime Minister in France*, 127–128.

50. Bauchard, *La Guerre des Deux Roses*, 144–145; Favier and Martin-Roland, *La Décennie Mitterrand*, 471; Giesbert, *Le Président*, 176–179; and Nay, *Les Sept Mitterrand*, 100–101.

51. Favier and Martin-Roland, *La Décennie Mitterrand*, 472.

52. Bauchard, *La Guerre des Deux Roses*, 146–147; Favier and Martin-Roland, *La Décennie Mitterrand*, 472–474; July, *Les Années Mitterrand*, 95; and Nay, *Les Sept Mitterrand*, 102.

53. Christofferson, *The French Socialists in Power*, 122.

54. *Financial Times*, 20 July 1984, 20; and Giesbert, *Le Président*, 215–216; and Nay, *Les Sept Mitterrand*, 110.

55. Favier and Martin-Roland, *La Décennie Mitterrand*, 393.

56. *Economist*, 8 February 1986, 58; and interview with Banque de France official.

57. Favier and Martin-Roland, *La Décennie Mitterrand*, 504–505; *Reuters North European Service*, 5 April 1986; and *Reuters North European Service*, 23 August 1986.

58. Favier and Martin-Roland, *La Décennie Mitterrand*, 556; *Financial Times*, 7 January 1987, 1; *Financial Times*, 10 January 1987, 1; and interview with former Banque de France official.

59. Rainer S. Masera, *L'Unificazione Monetaria e lo Sme: L'Esperienza dei Primi Otto Anni* (Bologna: Il Mulino, 1987), 146; see also the remarks of the governor of the central bank in Banca d'Italia, *Assemblea Generale Ordinaria dei Participanti* (Rome: Banca d'Italia, 1982), 393–394.

60. Cesare Romiti, *Questi Anni alla FIAT* (Milan: Rizzoli, 1988), 107–112; John B. Goodman, *Monetary Sovereignty: The Politics of Central Banking in Western Europe* (Ithaca, NY: Cornell University Press, 1992), 165; *Reuters*, 27 May 1980; and interview with former Banca d'Italia official. Most complaints about the competitiveness of the lira came from large industries and banks; pressure from

small and medium-sized industries was muted by their higher productivity growth; see *Il Mondo Economico*, 5 July 1980, 6–7.

61. "La Lira Non Svaluta; Si Deprezza Lentamente," *Bancaria* (June 1980): 622–625; and *Il Mondo Economico*, 5 July 1980, 6–7.

62. Carlo A. Ciampi, "La Condizione Esterna della Lira: Bilanci e Prospettive," *Bancaria* (August 1980): 794; see also Ciampi's remarks to the annual meeting of the Banca d'Italia, reprinted in Banca d'Italia, *Assemblea Generale Ordinaria dei Participanti* (Rome: Banca d'Italia, 1981), 366–368; and the comments by Treasury Minister Filippo Maria Pandolfi, reprinted in "Quadro Economico Internazionale, Scelte di Politica Economica Italiana e Sistema Bancario," *Bancaria* (April 1980): 354–357.

63. Claudio De Vincenti, "Congiuntura in Italia," *Politica ed Economia* 11, no. 4 (December 1980): 74; and *Il Mondo Economico* 4 October 1980, 6–7.

64. See the comments by the president of Confindustria that Italian competitiveness had declined by 5 percent in 1980, in *Il Mondo Economico*, 27 December 1980, 11–13; and *Il Mondo Economico*, 1 April 1981, 6–7.

65. Masera, *L'Unificazione Monetaria e lo Sme*, 148–149; and Niels Thygesen, "Exchange-Rate Policies and Monetary Targets in the EMS Countries," in *Europe's Money: Problems of European Monetary Co-ordination and Integration*, ed. Rainer S. Masera and Robert Triffin (Oxford: Clarendon, 1984), 268.

66. "La Svalutazione Rischia di Risultare una Pura Misura Defensiva," *Bancaria* 1 (1981): 68–78; see also Nino Andreatta, "Linee Essenziali della Politica Finanziaria e Monetaria," *Bancaria* 4 (1981): 348–353; *Il Corriere della Sera*, 1 February 1981, 1; *Reuters*, 22 March 1981; and *Reuters*, 24 March 1981.

67. *Il Mondo Economico*, 14 October 1981, 6–8, 17–8; *Il Mondo Economico*, 21 October 1981, 8–10; and Thygesen, "Exchange-Rate Policies and Monetary Targets in the EMS Countries," 269.

68. *Il Mondo Economico*, 8 December 1982, 9–10, my translation.

69. Paolo Forcellini, "L'Economia tra il Partito del 'Rilancio' e Quello della 'Persistenza,'" *Politica ed Economia* 13, no. 3 (March 1982): 3–4; *Il Mondo Economico*, 13 January 1982, 6–8; and *Il Mondo Economico*, 27 January 1982, 6–9.

70. "Perché Parlare de Svalutazione?" *Bancaria* 2 (February 1982): 193–203; the quotation is from 198 and is my translation.

71. Carlo Azeglio Ciampi, "Tempo di Decisioni per l'Economia Italiana," text of speech delivered before the annual meeting of the Banca d'Italia, 31 May 1982; the reference to "fantasy" austerity measures is in "Svalutazione Senza Deprezzamento," *Bancaria* (March 1982): 311–319.

72. *Il Mondo Economico*, 9 February 1983, 6–9.

73. *Il Mondo Economico*, 2 March 1983, 6–7; and *Il Mondo Economico*, 16 March 1983, 11–12.

74. *Il Mondo Economico*, 23 March 1983, 9–11; and Carlo Azeglio Ciampi, "Le Scelte da Compiere per una Represa nella Stabilità," text of speech delivered to the annual meeting of the Banca d'Italia, 31 May 1983.

75. *Il Mondo Economico*, 7 September 1983, 5–8; *Il Mondo Economico*, 4 October 1984, 14–16; and *Il Mondo Economico*, 10 January 1985, 6–8.

76. Peter Lange, "The End of an Era: The Wage Indexation Referendum of 1985," in *Italian Politics*, vol. 1, ed. Robert Leonardi and Raffaella Nanetti (London: Francis Pinter, 1986).

77. *Il Mondo Economico*, 15 July 1985, 22–24; and Livio Magnani, "Il Riallineamento della Lira," *Bancaria* (July 1985): 690–699.

78. *Il Mondo Economico,* 15 July 1985, 22–24; and Istituto Affari Internazionali, *L'Italia Nella Politica Internazionale: Anno Tredicesimo 1984–1985* (Rome: Franco Angeli, 1986), 294–297; and *Il Mondo Economico*, 15 March 1984, 16–18.

79. *Financial Times*, 24 July 1985, 1; Magnani, "Il Riallineamento della Lira"; Gianluigi Mengarelli, "Due Punti de Solidarietá nella Svalutazione della Lira," *Politica ed Economia* 16, no. 9 (September 1985), 13–14; and *Il Mondo Economico*, 5 August 1985, 18–20; see also Carlo A. Ciampi, "Il Quadro Istituzionale e gli Orientamenti della Politica Valutaria nell'Economia Italiana," address to the 28th National Congress of the Forex Club Italiano, 26 October 1985.

80. Banca d'Italia, *Assemblea Generale Ordinaria dei Participanti* (Rome: Banca d'Italia, 1986), 39–41; *Financial Times*, 17 January 1986, 1; and *Financial Times*, 21 January 1986, 2.

81. Istituto Affari Internazionali, *L'Italia Nella Politica Internazionale: Anno Quattordicesimo 1985–1986* (Rome: Franco Angeli, 1988), 260–261; Livio Magnani, "La Lira: Qualche Conto Dopo il Riallineamento dello SME," *Bancaria* (May 1986): 21–23; *Il Mondo Economico*, 21 April 1986, 34; and *Il Mondo Economico*, 14 July 1986, 29.

82. Istituto Affari Internazionali, *L'Italia Nella Politica Internazionale: Anno Quindicesimo 1986–1987* (Rome: Franco Angeli, 1989), 234–237; and "Tassi, Cambio e Liberalizzazione," *Bancaria* (March 1987): 48–49.

83. James I. Walsh, "International Constraints and Domestic Choices: Economic Convergence and Exchange Rate Policy in France and Italy," *Political Studies* 42, no. 2 (June 1994): 243–258.

4

Negotiating Monetary Union

Meeting in the Dutch town of Maastricht in late 1991, political leaders from the European Community finalized the Treaty on European Union, a detailed plan to create full economic and monetary union by the end of the decade. The treaty proposed a much more ambitious venture than the exchange-rate policy coordination carried out in the European Monetary System (EMS). Monetary union would replace national currencies with a single European currency, centralize authority over monetary policy in a European Central Bank independent of political influence, and impose supranational controls over national fiscal policies.

Why were the member states able to agree on such an ambitious and far-reaching plan for monetary unification? Any why did they agree on the specific rules and procedures included in the Maastricht Treaty rather than other, equally viable rules? In this chapter I examine the negotiations culminating in the Maastricht Treaty to determine whether distributional bargaining among states with different preferences or failure-induced policy learning provide superior answers to these questions. Both explanations predict that the outcome of the negotiations would reflect the preferences of the German government and central bank, but they differ in their understanding of the preferences of other member states.

The distributional bargaining approach holds that French and Italian governments were interested in monetary union to reduce the asymmetrical functioning of the exchange-rate mechanism (ERM) of the EMS. The rules of the ERM allowed the Bundesbank to set its monetary and interest-rate policies to maintain low domestic inflation. Other participants in the ERM, including France and Italy, had to match German monetary policy if they wished to stabilize their currencies against the mark. But since inflation was higher in these countries than in Germany, exchange-rate stabilization led to real appreciation of the franc and lira. This result was offset by occasional realignments of ERM parities, which undermined the goal of exchange-rate stabilization. From the perspective of the French and Italians, monetary union would eliminate the need for realignments and give them some influence over a pan-European monetary policy that took into account their domestic economic conditions. The Bundesbank and the German government were lukewarm about monetary union precisely because it would require abandoning the ability to implement an autonomous monetary policy. German negotiators therefore bargained hard for a treaty that would create a monetary union managed by a European Central Bank as independent as the Bundesbank and that would extend membership only to those states with low inflation and small budget deficits.[1]

The learning explanation places more emphasis on how policy failure and repeated interaction and communication in European institutions led governments to redefine their preferences in mutually beneficial ways. According to this approach, the observation that tight monetary, exchange-rate, and fiscal policies produced superior outcomes in Germany led French and Italian governments to see the advantages of German ideas about the proper conduct of economic policy. During the 1980s, this process of learning and interaction produced a consensus that European monetary institutions should give priority to keeping inflation low, delegate policy responsibility to independent central banks, and limit member states' ability to run up large budget deficits.[2]

The evidence indicates that distributional bargaining had a larger influence than learning did in negotiations over European monetary institutions. Germany's negotiating power, in particular its greater willingness to accept the status quo over most proposed changes, rather than the persuasiveness of its economic ideas determined the outcome of negotiations during the 1980s and 1990s. In the next section, I show that governments' preferences regarding reforms of the rules of the EMS did not change very much during the 1980s, contrary to the expectations of the learning approach. France and Italy consistently pressed for changes that would have the effect of reducing Germany's power in the EMS, despite the fact that their macroeconomic policies failed to produce low inflation and high employment. Germany always opposed these changes, and the British remained uninterested in monetary cooperation. Then I examine the work of the Delors Committee, which was charged in 1988 with preparing a plan for the development of full monetary union. There is some evidence in support of both learning and distributional bargaining here. Most of the committee members were technical experts or central bankers who could agree on the desirability of low inflation, central bank independence, and rules that would limit budget deficits. But important members of the committee, including central bank governors from Germany, France, and Britain, worked hard to ensure that the committee's report reflected deep-seated national preferences regarding the rules of European monetary institutions. I then consider the negotiations from 1989 to 1991 that turned the Delors Committee report into the Maastricht Treaty's plan for monetary union. Negotiators tried to ensure that the final treaty accorded as closely as possible with national preferences; agreement on even technical details was characterized by hard bargaining rather than a consensus among like-minded experts.

The European Monetary System, 1979–1988

The European Council resolution of 5 December 1978 establishing the EMS called for the consolidation of the system's "initial phase" within two years, including the full use of the ECU as a reserve asset and means of settlement among central banks and the creation of a European Monetary Fund to finance foreign exchange market intervention. The European Commission, the Committee of Central Bank Governors, and the Monetary Committee worked on various proposals for reducing the asymmetry of the EMS in the 1980s but did not make much progress. The failure to carry through with the 1978 commitment to strengthen the EMS is consistent with the emphasis of the distributional bargaining approach on bargaining power and different national preferences. French and Italian governments did not share Germany's priorities of low inflation and economic convergence, but the EMS required them to tighten monetary policy or sacrifice exchange-rate stability by devaluing their ERM parities. The solution preferred by French and Italian authorities was for Germany also to adjust economic policy by lowering interest rates. Therefore, they favored reforms to the EMS that would identify Germany as the country pursuing divergent economic policies and that would lead the Bundesbank to adjust its monetary policy to stabilize the ERM.

German central bankers and political authorities feared precisely this outcome and took a number of steps to prevent it. German negotiators ensured that, in the EMS agreement, foreign exchange market intervention and changes in monetary policy were guided by the parity grid rather than the divergence indicator. As discussed in Chapter 2, the parity grid effectively placed the burden of policy changes on countries with depreciating currencies, although the divergence indicator could have required policy changes from countries with appreciating currencies, such as Germany. Especially after 1983, the French and Italian central banks intervened on foreign exchange markets "intramarginally," before their currencies reached the limits of their fluctuation bands, to prevent currency crises. But the Bundesbank refused to intervene or to extend intramarginal credits, forcing most of the intervention burden onto other members of the ERM.

Instead, the Bundesbank concentrated its foreign exchange market intervention on the dollar exchange rate. And German negotiators insisted on greater convergence of economic outcomes—especially inflation rates—before agreeing to reforms of the EMS.[3]

In March 1982, the French and Belgian finance ministers proposed increased exchange-rate policy consultations with the United States and Japan, multilateral surveillance of macroeconomic policies in the EMS, and greater financing of central bank intervention. The Bundesbank and the German government opposed these ideas, fearing that more political consultations and increased requirements for intervention could undermine German monetary policy autonomy.[4] A proposal by the European Commission in early 1984, supported by the French and Italian finance ministers, that the European Monetary Fund be created by unanimity among a minority of member states also met opposition from the German finance ministry and Bundesbank officials.[5] In December 1985, governments did agree to incorporate references to the EMS into the Treaty of Rome through the Single European Act. But German and British demands limited the references to the system's current operating mechanisms and required that further development toward monetary union could occur only through the lengthy process of revising and ratifying the treaty.[6]

There was agreement on limited changes to the EMS in 1987, known as the Basel-Nyborg accords. This nonbinding understanding, named after the towns in Switzerland and Denmark where central bank governors and finance ministers negotiated it, was introduced by the French government. The aim was to stabilize currencies by strengthening the coordination of monetary and interest-rate policies and by modestly reducing the asymmetry of intervention rules. Specific measures of the Basel-Nyborg accords included increasing short-term credits among central banks for financing intervention, extending the initial credit repayment period to three-and-one-half months, and allowing repayment of credits in European currency units (ECUs) rather than in national currencies. The accords encouraged central banks to intervene on the foreign exchange markets before their currencies reached the limits of their fluctuation margins and to rely on interest rates rather than capital controls to stabilize exchange rates. In exchange for these concessions, the German government won a promise that the French and Italians would remove all capital controls by the end of the decade.[7]

In late 1987, the French and German governments began negotiations over a Franco-German Economic Council composed of finance and economics ministers and central bank governors. The French hoped that the Council would undercut the Bundesbank's focus on low inflation when this conflicted with exchange-rate stability in the ERM. Late in the negotiations, the French proposed that the treaty creating the Council have the status of binding international law. This change greatly concerned the Bundesbank, which feared that such a commitment might require it to lower interest rates or to engage in foreign exchange market intervention. Strong protests from the central bank persuaded Chancellor Helmut Kohl to declare before the Bundestag that the treaty would not undercut the Bundesbank's independence.[8]

French finance minister Edouard Balladur recognized that the Basel-Nyborg accords actually might increase the asymmetry of the EMS. Restrictive German monetary policies would be transmitted quickly to the rest of Europe with the removal of capital controls and greater reliance on interest-rate policy to stabilize exchange rates. This possibility convinced many to advocate a coordinated monetary expansion led by Germany.[9] In early 1988 Balladur circulated a memorandum to the Economics and Finance Council (Ecofin) of the European Community criticizing the asymmetry of the EMS and arguing that "the rapid pursuit of the monetary construction of Europe is the only possible solution."[10] He also sent a personal letter to his German counterpart, Gerhard Stoltenberg, outlining some preliminary ideas for European monetary reform and stated that he was worried that German monetary policy was restraining growth in Europe. French prime minister Jacques Chirac supported reforming the EMS and criticized the Bundesbank's intervention policies, stating that "it is not right that the Bundesbank only intervenes against one currency [the dollar] and refuses to do so against any other currency." In late January, Balladur proposed strengthening the EMS by bringing all Community currencies into the narrow band of the ERM, strengthening multilateral coordination of macroeconomic policies, and creating a European central bank and common currency. These proposals became the basis for the negotiations that culminated in the 1991 Maastricht Treaty.[11]

Distributional bargaining drove the institutional development of the EMS until 1988. French and Italian governments preferred to reduce the asymmetry of the EMS, as well as their need to adjust through devaluation, by strengthening multilateral surveillance of economic policy, increasing central bank credits to finance foreign exchange market intervention, and creating a European Monetary Fund. They hoped that such changes would reduce the need for currency realignments and give them more power to persuade the Bundesbank to loosen monetary policy. But German negotiators vetoed their attempts to change the EMS. They favored limiting the regime's evolution until economic outcomes converged on their preferences for low inflation, and domestic opposition from the Bundesbank as well as a strong balance-of-payments position gave them the power to resist changes to the status quo of the EMS.

Negotiating Maastricht

Given this failure to agree on substantial reforms to the EMS, it is remarkable that in December 1991 governments agreed to the Maastricht Treaty's plan to create a full monetary union with a single currency and the European Central Bank by 1999. In this section I analyze the bargaining over monetary union from 1988 to 1991. I first focus on the negotiations and discussions that took place among central bankers in the Delors Committee, which was appointed in 1988 to propose concrete steps toward monetary union. I describe the Delors Committee's recommendations and evaluate the extent to which this group of experts reached an ideational rather than political consensus on major issues involved in creating a full monetary union. I then turn to tracing national preferences and outcomes regarding the rules of monetary union shortly before and during the intergovernmental negotiations that took place in 1990 and 1991.[12]

The Delors Committee

By late 1987, French prime minister Jacques Chirac and Finance Minister Edouard Balladur were dissatisfied with the functioning of the EMS. French inflation had fallen since the early 1980s, but German interest rates continued to set the floor for other participants in the ERM. This dissatisfaction motivated Balladur's call in early 1988 for a jointly managed European Central Bank and a common currency. Balladur's plan was vague on other issues that would later dominate the discussions, such as central bank independence and the distinctions between a single and common currency. His proposal was essentially a somewhat more ambitious call for greater symmetry and intergovernmental cooperation than the French had issued in the past.[13]

Surprisingly, given their earlier opposition to reforming the EMS, German chancellor Helmut Kohl and foreign minister Hans-Dietrich Genscher put monetary reform on the agenda of the European Council meeting of heads of state and government in Hanover in June. In February, Genscher put forward his own plan for monetary union, which included an independent European Central Bank with the goal of price stability. The Hanover European Council in turn established the Delors Committee, chaired by European Commission president Jacques Delors and including the twelve European Community central bank governors, another member of the Commission, and three experts, all acting in their "personal" rather than official capacities. The Council charged the Committee with proposing "concrete steps" toward monetary union before June 1989.[14]

Although the German government supported serious discussion of monetary union, the Bundesbank was "publicly cool and privately hostile" to the concept.[15] As early as February 1988, a director of the Bundesbank observed that Balladur's ideas for reforming the EMS might conflict with the Bundesbank's focus on domestic price stability.[16] During the Delors Committee's deliberations, Bundesbank president Karl-Otto Pöhl was in the difficult position of reconciling the German government's interest in monetary union with the Bundesbank's mandate of price stability. Pöhl could not reject monetary union out of hand; doing so would upset the government and possibly weaken the Bundesbank's position later in the negotiations. Instead, he emphasized that the European Central Bank should be modeled on the independent Bundesbank, that participation in monetary union be limited to member states that had converged on Germany's economic performance, and that monetary union include constraints on national fiscal policies. By September 1990, the Bundesbank advocated creating a European Central Bank with the explicit goal of price stability that would have complete control over foreign exchange market intervention and recommended monetary union only among countries meeting strict convergence criteria covering inflation rates, budget deficits, interest rates, and exchange-rate stability. It also opposed fixed timetables for the transition to monetary union and argued that during the transition, monetary policies should remain under national control.[17]

French officials originally hoped that the Delors Committee's report would propose immediate reforms to the EMS.[18] For example, during the committee's deliberations Jacques de Larosière, governor of the Banque de France, supported by Delors, the Italians, and the Spanish, proposed that EMS participants pool more reserves for foreign exchange market intervention and lay out explicit deadlines for creating new rules to coordinate national monetary policies. This conflicted with the Bundesbank's approach, which held that monetary policy coordination should occur only after economic convergence. French officials later complained that the committee did not incorporate their proposal or in general suggest sufficiently rapid moves toward monetary policy coordination. But they soon recognized that the Bundesbank would require convergence of economic policies prior to implementing substantial reforms to the EMS and supported the Delors Committee's relatively elaborate plan for a lengthy transition to full monetary union.[19]

Italian authorities were also interested in greater monetary cooperation. In a memorandum to Ecofin in early 1988, Treasury Minister Giuliano Amato called for reforms to the EMS to give it more symmetry between strong and weak currency countries so as to control the real depreciation of the mark within the ERM, and stated that full liberalization of capital movements would require some mechanism to recycle payments surpluses from strong to weak currency countries. The governor of the Banca d'Italia, Carlo Azeglio Ciampi, backed this position, and shortly after the release of the Delors Report observed that the EMS had been useful in reducing inflation in the 1980s but that now the problem was to coordinate macroeconomic policies so as to increase growth.[20]

With few exceptions, British policymakers opposed the idea of monetary union. In early cabinet discussions, Prime Minister Margaret Thatcher and Chancellor Nigel Lawson described monetary union as "an unacceptable 'surrender' of national sovereignty," whereas Foreign Secretary Geoffrey Howe "was alone in regarding a single European currency as a desirable medium-term goal."[21] At the Hanover summit in June 1988, Thatcher did not reject out of hand the idea that the Delors Committee could study limited moves in the monetary field such as increased use of the ECU and the pooling of reserves, but she successfully managed to have all mention of a European Central Bank removed from the final communiqué.[22]

In mid-December 1988, Thatcher, Lawson, and Robin Leigh-Pemberton, governor of the Bank of England and member of the Delors Committee, met to discuss the evolution of the committee's work. Thatcher and Lawson did not want the committee's report to conclude that monetary union was a necessary corollary to the European Community's single-market program or to make many specific recommendations. They felt that attracting Pöhl to their camp was critical and that any British alternatives should be shelved for the time being so as not to alienate him. After discussing a draft of the committee's report in February 1989, Thatcher and Lawson urged Leigh-Pemberton to attach an independent statement opposing its conclusions. Leigh-Pemberton refused, preferring to work inside the committee to change some of the wording of the report. He feared that a dissent would destroy his credibility with his European counterparts, although he nonetheless made it clear that the British government was not interested in monetary union.[23]

The committee issued its proposals, known as the Delors Report, in April 1989. The report began by stating that monetary union would require the full convertibility of national currencies, the integration of European capital markets, and irrevocably fixed exchange rates. The member states had already met the first two requirements, and although the third would not require replacing national currencies with a single currency, the committee argued that this would "clearly demonstrate the irreversibility of the . . . union, considerably facilitate the monetary management of the Community and avoid the transactions costs of converting currencies." Monetary union would require a single monetary policy implemented by a supranational European Central Bank, and the committee suggested that this bank "be committed to the objective of price stability." "Binding rules" on fiscal policy would be needed to prevent "uncoordinated and divergent national budgetary policies [that] would undermine monetary stability."[24]

The committee proposed moving to full monetary union in three stages. In the first stage, all currencies would enter the ERM, and governments would coordinate their fiscal policies according to "precise quantitative guidelines." The second stage would see the introduction of rules limiting the size of national budget deficits and the establishment of a European System of Central Banks composed of national central banks. The European System of Central Banks would set "general monetary orientations . . . for the Community as a whole . . . while the ultimate responsibility for monetary policy decisions would remain with national authorities," and realignments in the ERM would be permitted only in exceptional circumstances. The third stage of full monetary union would involve the irrevocable fixing of exchange rates and the creation of a European Central Bank independent of national governments to conduct a single monetary policy for the participating member states.[25]

The details of the Delors Report reflected the concerns of the Bundesbank, whose positions are evident in the explicit focus on price stability, an independent European Central Bank, and the binding coordination of fiscal policies. The Delors Committee's plan accorded more closely with the preferences of the Bundesbank than with the French proposals for an immediate strengthening of policy coordination. It is not clear if the Bundesbank's influence was a function of Germany's greater bargaining power in monetary affairs or the intellectual merits of Pöhl's case in the minds of his fellow central bankers. On the one hand, there is evidence that central bank governors bargained hard for an institutional design that accorded with the preferences of national governments. Jacques de Larosière advanced proposals inspired by Balladur's desire for rapid moves toward monetary union, and Robin Leigh-Pemberton was careful to represent the views of Thatcher and Lawson while also retaining some credibility with other members of the committee.[26] On the other hand, the central bankers who dominated the committee did have a common interest in proposals that would give priority to monetary stability and central bank independence.[27] It is therefore difficult to conclude if the outcome of the Committee's work reflected a process of distributional bargaining or of transnational learning.

The Intergovernmental Negotiations

The Delors Report provided a reasonably detailed blueprint for monetary union but nevertheless left some key issues unresolved. In this section, I describe national bargaining positions and outcomes for six issues discussed during the intergovernmental negotiations and conference that followed publication of the Delors Report: the desirability of a single rather than common currency, member states' ability to "opt out" of participation in monetary union, the independence of the European Central Bank, policy coordination in the second stage, the criteria for participation in full monetary union, and the deadlines for moving through the three stages. The conclusion assesses the degree to which the intergovernmental negotiations were the product of distributional bargaining or learning among national decisionmakers.

A common or a single currency? The British government alone challenged the idea that monetary union and a single currency were desirable goals. After witnessing strong support from other leaders for the Delors Report's conclusions at the Madrid summit in June 1989, Prime Minister Margaret Thatcher instructed Treasury and Foreign Office officials to draw up alternative plans for monetary policy coordination in the hope of delaying further negotiations. The resulting "competing currencies" proposal advocated making all European Community currencies legal tender. This would force national monetary authorities to compete for the best price and exchange-rate performances, and eventually this competition "could evolve into a system of more-or-less fixed exchange rates." Chancellor Nigel Lawson outlined the plan at an Ecofin meeting in September 1989, but it attracted little support from other ministers, many of whom saw it as a delaying tactic. Lawson himself admitted that it would not be accepted immediately as an alternative to the Delors Report.[28]

Michael Butler, former British permanent representative to the European Community, drafted a similar alternative to the Delors Report in 1990, which was published by the British Invisibles Export Council after consultations with the Treasury and was soon picked up by the government. Known as the "hard ECU," it also called for a common, rather than a single, currency that would circulate alongside existing national currencies, as well as the establishment of a European Monetary Fund that would provide ECU on demand in exchange for national currencies. The European Monetary Fund would set its interest rates so that the ECU was never devalued against any Community currency. Chancellor John Major advanced the hard ECU proposal in the summer of 1990, but with the exception of the Spanish finance minister, few other participants took the idea very seriously. Even Thatcher, who in the summer of 1990 promoted the hard ECU as a realistic alternative to the Delors Report, admitted in Parliament after the October 1990 Rome summit that it was unlikely to evolve into a single currency.[29]

Opt-outs. Although it could veto any treaty that would require participation in monetary union, the British government wanted to avoid such a drastic step. Major, who was elected prime minister by Conservative party members of Parliament after Thatcher resigned in November 1990, was convinced that there was no support for the hard ECU, and he began advocating a provision requiring each member state to "opt in" to the third stage of monetary union. Serious consideration of this issue was delayed until mid-1991 as member states sorted out which voting rules they would use to decide to move to the third stage. In the European Commission's draft treaty of December 1990, the European Council would decide by qualified majority when to start the third stage. The Germans proposed unanimity, a position supported by the British since it would give them a veto; the French and Italians opposed a unanimous decision rule that would allow one member state to block full monetary union. In response, in April 1991 the French representative to the intergovernmental conference, Jean-Claude Trichet, proposed three "safeguard clauses" in the treaty. First, no country could stop others meeting the convergence criteria from creating a single currency; to the French and Italians, this meant that Britain or Germany alone could not stop monetary union. Second, no country meeting the criteria could be kept from participating in the single currency; to the Italians, this meant that they could not be excluded arbitrarily. Third, no country could be forced to join; to the British, this meant that they would be able to opt out of the third stage. Around the same time, Delors floated the idea that the treaty include a protocol allowing only Britain to opt out of the third stage. These ideas were received favorably by British chancellor Norman Lamont, and British officials stated that something along these lines probably would be incorporated into the treaty.[30]

The draft treaty prepared by the Dutch presidency of the European Community in September 1991 therefore concerned the British. The Dutch proposed allowing each member state to "opt out" of participation in the third stage. British negotiators opposed being forced to make a public declaration *not* to join monetary union, preferring instead that member states make positive declarations to participate. The French and Italians also opposed the Dutch provision because it would have allowed Germany to decide not to participate.[31] This conflict was resolved at the final meeting of the intergovernmental conference in December 1991. The Danish government, which like the British did not want to pre-commit to participation in full monetary union, agreed to a treaty protocol that would allow only Denmark to choose to opt out of the third stage. This left the British as the only team favoring a general opt-out. The French and Italians were willing to allow the British to opt out but insisted that only Britain and Denmark have this option. The final compromise committed all other member states, including Germany, to move toward full monetary union. If a majority of member states met the convergence criteria in 1996, they could vote by qualified majority to move to the third stage in 1997. If a decision against moving to the third stage was made in 1996, the member states meeting the convergence criteria, except for Britain and Denmark, automatically would move to the third stage in 1999 with no opportunity to opt out.[32]

Central bank independence and exchange-rate policy. It was clear as early as the convening of the Delors Committee that there would be no monetary union including Germany unless it was managed by a central bank independent of political influence and committed to the goal of price stability. Genscher's proposals of early 1988 included an independent European Central Bank, and officials of the German government and the Bundesbank insisted on this provision throughout the negotiations. The French opposed complete independence for the central bank, preferring that it remain subject to political control, although both the French and Italians recognized that within the ERM their monetary policies already were influenced heavily by the independent Bundesbank.[33] Independence was a somewhat secondary issue for the British, given their opposition to participating in a single currency, and the treaty's opt-out protocol allowed Britain not only to stay out of the third stage but also to retain governmental control over the Bank of England.

Although the members of the Delors Committee were quick to endorse the principle of central bank independence, the subsequent intergovernmental negotiations revealed French opposition to such a provision. The French never explicitly opposed the idea of an independent European Central Bank. Instead, their tactics were to reduce the central bank's autonomy at the margin by advocating increased power for Ecofin and delaying the time when national central banks would have to be made independent. In September 1990, French finance minister Pierre Bérégovoy and his German counterpart, Theo Waigel, met in Munich and agreed that the European Central Bank and national central banks should be independent of governments and European institutions and should have price stability as their principal goal. The Rome summit of heads of state and government in October 1990 endorsed this position. The major differences occurred over when national central banks should be made independent. The Germans favored independence before the start of the second stage but at the Rome summit accepted a compromise proposed by the French that "the second stage will start on 1 January 1994 after . . . a process has been set in train to ensure [central bank] independence." In April 1991, the intergovernmental conference defined this as meaning that member states would grant independence to their central banks before the start of the third stage.[34]

The Rome summit also asked the European Community Committee of Central Bank Governors to prepare a draft statute for the European Central Bank. The governors produced a draft by the end of November 1990 that closely resembled the federal structure of the Bundesbank and gave the

European Central Bank independent control over both monetary and exchange-rate policy. In January 1991, Bérégovoy announced that the French cabinet had agreed on monetary union proposals, including a "fully democratic economic government" in the form of a strengthened Ecofin, with the aim of creating a political counterweight to an independent European Central Bank.[35] In particular, the French draft treaty of early 1991 suggested that control over exchange-rate policy and of banks' minimum reserves in the third stage rest with Ecofin acting by qualified majority. The European Central Bank would be independent, have price stability as its mandate, and could not finance government budget deficits. The Bundesbank opposed a strengthened Ecofin (except for fiscal policy) and wanted the European Central Bank to have complete control over external exchange-rate policy and banks' minimum reserves in order to reduce political influence over these monetary policy tools.

The final compromise created an independent European Central Bank in the third stage with an explicit mandate of price stability over other economic policy goals, independent national central banks, a prohibition on central bank financing of government budget deficits, and European Central Bank control over minimum reserves. For external exchange-rate policy, the Maastricht Treaty divided responsibility between the European Central Bank and Ecofin. Acting by a unanimous vote after consulting with the European Central Bank, Ecofin could peg the single currency to foreign currencies such as the dollar or yen in the context of an undefined "exchange-rate system." However, in the absence of such a system, Ecofin was limited to deciding on "general orientations" for exchange-rate policy by a qualified majority, and these must be "without prejudice to the primary objective" of the European Central Bank to maintain price stability. This provision gave the European Central Bank a substantial degree of independence since it would be difficult for the member states to agree to an exchange-rate system or general orientations that interfered with the central banks' operations.[36]

Monetary Policy Coordination in the Second Stage

The Delors Report foresaw the European Central Bank as beginning operations during the second stage in the expectation that it would play a role in strengthening policy coordination prior to the introduction of the single currency. However, the report did not explain how to accomplish this gradual transfer of monetary policy authority from national central banks, and this ambiguity soon led to conflict. The British and Germans (for different reasons) preferred that the European Central Bank have a weak role in coordinating monetary policies during the second stage, whereas the French and Italians wanted to transfer significant powers to the new institution. During the Monetary Committee's discussions in 1990, the Germans argued that the European Central Bank should not be created in the second stage if it would be only an "empty shell" with few real powers. Although at first glance this implies that the Germans favored a strong institution, in fact the opposite was the case. The Germans preferred no new institution to a weak one that might lead to confusion in financial markets about what body had ultimate control over monetary policy. The British opposed creating any institution that had substantial powers, but the French and Italians favored doing so to maintain progress toward full monetary union.[37]

The Rome summit of October 1990 addressed but did not settle this issue. The British opposed creating the European Central Bank in the second stage and dissented from the summit communiqué. Under strong pressure from the French and Italians, Kohl compromised by agreeing that the second stage would begin on 1 January 1994 and would include the creation of the European Central Bank. The summit communiqué declared that "the new Community institution will be established" with the second stage. The drafters of the communiqué explicitly referred to "the," not "a," institution to indicate that this would be the European Central Bank. During the second stage, the European Central Bank would have among its goals "to strengthen the coordination of monetary policies; to develop the instruments and procedures needed for the future conduct of a single monetary policy."[38]

Shortly after the Rome summit, British and German negotiators argued that the new Community institution in the second stage could not be the European Central Bank, since it would not be a fully operational central bank. They proposed that the new institution consist of a council of governors of national central banks with responsibilities and powers similar to those of the existing Committee of Central Bank Governors. The French and Italians, supported by the European Commission, opposed this formula, arguing that the new institution should be the European Central Bank, which "would serve . . . as a sign of the commitment to the final goal [of monetary union] and as a way of giving some teeth to policy coordination."[39]

The draft treaty put forward by the Luxembourg presidency of the European Community in mid-1991 proposed a compromise between these positions by splitting the second stage into two subperiods. In the first subperiod, a board of governors would have a mandate similar to that of the existing Committee of Central Bank Governors, although its coordinating activities would be based explicitly on maintaining price stability. The European Central Bank would become operational in the second subperiod and begin making technical preparations for the third stage. German negotiators opposed even these limited responsibilities for the European Central Bank during the second stage. In July 1991, the Dutch presidency proposed that two institutions be created: the European Monetary Institute in the second stage and the European Central Bank in the third stage. The European Monetary Institute would have few responsibilities and weak power, and monetary policy would remain firmly under the control of national central banks. German negotiators were satisfied with this formula, and member states agreed to incorporate it into the Maastricht Treaty.[40]

Convergence Criteria

One of the most difficult issues during the negotiations was determining the degree of economic convergence member states would have to meet in order to participate in monetary union. In the summer of 1990, both the Monetary Committee and the Commission issued reports that accepted the Delors Report's emphasis on the desirability of economic convergence prior to monetary union. The Monetary Committee's report identified five possible convergence criteria: price stability, no "excessive" budget deficits or monetary financing of budget deficits, stable exchange rates in the narrow band of the ERM, implementation of the single market, and market assessment that convergence would be sustainable. The October 1990 Rome summit debated whether any convergence criteria should apply to participation in the second stage, as the Bundesbank advocated. The French and Italians opposed this idea and persuaded Kohl to agree that member states could participate in the second stage by meeting four relatively easy conditions: by not monetizing fiscal deficits, by not securing financial bailouts from Community institutions or from other member-states, by ratifying the treaty, and by completing the internal market.

The more contentious issue was the criteria that would be used to deny membership in the third stage. The Dutch and Germans feared that a monetary union with countries with large budget deficits such as Italy could create inflationary pressures, and they advocated binding quantitative criteria. The German draft treaty of early 1991 proposed that meeting explicit convergence criteria be a legal requirement for participation in monetary union. The Germans also proposed that in cases of an (undefined) "excessive" fiscal deficit, Ecofin could suggest changes in fiscal policy; if these were ignored, Ecofin could sanction the member state. Confident that they could meet any reasonable convergence criteria, the French backed the German position and issued a draft treaty that also advocated sanctions against member-states with excessive deficits. The Commission and Italians saw convergence criteria as political goals rather than legal requirements and favored "binding procedures rather than binding rules for budget deficits, by accepting the principle that excessive public deficits should be avoided, but . . . using objective criteria only as a yardstick."[41]

In September 1991, the Monetary Committee agreed on three criteria a member state would have to fulfill in the year prior to participating in full monetary union: no excessive budget deficit, an inflation rate within 1.5 percent of that of the two or three member states with the lowest rates, and participation in the ERM without devaluation "on a country's own initiative" and without heavy foreign exchange market intervention. The Germans successfully insisted on including the convergence of long-term interest rates as a criterion that would measure financial markets' perceptions of the degree of convergence that had been achieved, while the British convinced the negotiators to include vague references to indicators of real convergence, such as labor market flexibility.[42]

The negotiators reached a compromise in which the treaty would include explicit and quantitative criteria, as the Germans demanded, but would also have a modest degree of flexibility when it came to interpreting each member state's degree of convergence. The final treaty stated that a member state's budget deficit was excessive if it was greater than 3 percent of gross domestic product (GDP) unless it "has declined substantially and continuously and reached a level that comes close to [this] reference value . . . or the excess is only exceptional and temporary," and the ratio of debt to GDP had to be less than 60 percent "unless the ratio is sufficiently diminishing and approaching the reference value."[43] The negotiators also agreed to some flexibility in the interpretation of quantitative fiscal criteria by having Ecofin vote by qualified majority when deciding if a member state's budget deficit was excessive. The other criteria for participation were that a member state had not devalued on its "own initiative" for two years and had a consumer price inflation rate within 1.5 percent, and long-term interest rates within 2 percent, of the average rates of the three member states with the lowest rates.

Setting Deadlines

An important issue was the timing of the transitions between the three stages. The French and Italians advocated explicit and pre-established deadlines for all three transitions, which would make it difficult to delay moves toward monetary union. The Bundesbank opposed pre-established deadlines, preferring that member states' economic performance converge before proceeding with monetary union. The British opposed all attempts to set deadlines except for the start of the first stage, fearing that deadlines would create expectations of the further unification that they opposed.

At the Madrid summit in June 1989, French president François Mitterrand insisted that the European Council accept the recommendations of the Delors Report in full, agree on a date to open an intergovernmental conference, and set dates for the beginnings of all three stages. Kohl proposed a starting date of 1 July 1990 for the intergovernmental conference, with the Delors Report forming the basis for the negotiations. Thatcher opposed having any intergovernmental conference and using the report as the only basis of negotiation. She agreed to accept participation in the first stage, including bringing sterling into the ERM at some future date under specific conditions, but refused to commit Britain to participation in the second and third stages.[44] The summit's compromise, put forward by Italian prime minister Ciriaco De Mita, was that there should be "complete and adequate preparation" before the beginning of the intergovernmental conference, that the first stage begin on 1 July 1990, and that the issue of starting dates for the remaining stages be decided later. Over the summer, French officials continued to call for an intergovernmental conference as early as possible, and by late October argued that a group of European experts chaired by Mitterrand adviser Élisabeth Guigou had completed the necessary preparations.[45]

The opening of the Berlin Wall in November 1989 led the French to increase their pressure for early moves on monetary union. On 18 November, Mitterrand convened a meeting of the European Council to prevent the Germans or British from using the uncertainty surrounding the situation in East Germany to delay the start of the intergovernmental conference. Shortly before the Strasbourg European Council meeting in December 1989, France and Germany agreed that the intergovernmental conference should start in late 1990, a position supported by Italian prime minister Giulio Andreotti.[46] The European Council agreed on this date for the intergovernmental conference at the Rome summit in October 1990.

Having settled the starting dates for the first stage and the intergovernmental conference, member states turned to the issue of when the second stage should begin. In July 1990 the Monetary Committee, supported by the Bundesbank, suggested that the convergence criteria apply to participation in both the second and third stages.[47] It also suggested that the second stage should be of short duration, implying that only participants in this stage would be among the first group of member states to participate in full monetary union. The Italian negotiators and other member states with large fiscal deficits opposed this formula, preferring that the second stage begin quickly and be of limited duration and that participation have few, if any, conditions.[48]

Heads of state and government resolved the timing of the second stage at the Rome summit in October 1990. Shortly before the summit, Italian finance minister and president of Ecofin Guido Carli suggested three possible solutions: a starting date with no conditions on participation, participation based solely on meeting some convergence criteria, or a combination of a starting date and convergence criteria. Over British objections, the European Council adopted the third, compromise solution. The second stage would begin on 1 January 1994 and would not require that member states meet any quantitative fiscal or monetary targets. In April 1991, the intergovernmental conference agreed on the four criteria regarding monetization, bailouts, treaty ratification, and the completion of the single market.[49]

The final and most important issue was the timing of the third stage. The German draft treaty of early 1991 called for the European Council to make this decision by unanimity only when a majority of member states met the conditions of price stability, no excessive budget deficit, and convergence of long-term interest rates. The Dutch draft treaty issued in the autumn of 1991 called for the European Council to consider the move to the third stage before the end of 1996 and, if it could not agree on a starting date, merely to reconsider the issue periodically. French negotiators opposed both of these ideas since they did not guarantee that full monetary union would ever begin. At the very end of the intergovernmental conference, after consultations between Mitterrand and Andreotti in Maastricht, the French proposed that the European Council first consider moving to the third stage in 1996. If the Council could not agree to move to full monetary union by a vote of a qualified majority of member states meeting the convergence criteria, the third stage would begin automatically on 1 January 1999 and include all states meeting the convergence criteria. This compromise provided "an unambiguous signal" that monetary union would occur while appeasing the German desire for participation only by countries with low inflation rates. Kohl agreed to this formula to signal his government's commitment to monetary union, although his support came as a "complete surprise" to the Bundesbank.[50]

Comparisons

Distributional bargaining among states with different preferences drove reforms to European monetary institutions during the 1980s and early 1990s. The French and Italians were dissatisfied with the functioning of the EMS and first proposed strengthening the regime by creating a European Monetary Fund, instituting mechanisms for coordinating monetary policy and foreign exchange market intervention, and in the French case creating a Franco-German Economic Council. These reforms could have led Germany to adjust by pursuing less restrictive monetary policies, which in turn would have reduced the need for realignments to prevent real appreciation of the franc and lira within the ERM. With the exception of the Basel-Nyborg reforms of intervention obligations, German negotiators opposed reforms that might have required the Bundesbank to pursue monetary policies more attuned to European conditions. They would agree only to a new institution focused on price stability and governed by an independent central bank, with participation limited to member states whose macroeconomic policies already converged. Significant macroeconomic convergence had occurred by 1988, especially between France and Germany, which led officials in the German government to begin serious negotiations over Balladur's proposals for monetary reform.

Preferences

Contrary to the expectations of the learning approach, British, French, and Italian governments continued to hold quite different preferences about the rules of monetary union despite their failure to match Germany's macroeconomic performance in the 1980s (see Table 4.1). British negotiators opposed the entire concept of monetary union, preferring to retain national control over monetary and exchange-rate policies. The two issues that British negotiators put on the agenda—various forms of competing currencies and national opt-outs—were intended to delay or dilute the Delors Report blueprint for monetary union. The competing currencies and hard ECU proposals of 1989 and 1990 challenged the idea that a single currency and the design for monetary union laid out in the Delors Report were desirable goals. When the willingness of the other member states to negotiate along the lines of the Delors Report became clear to British negotiators, they abandoned attempts to construct alternatives and began pushing for a general opt-out that would allow Britain and any other member state to decide not to participate in the third stage. The French and Italians opposed this proposal, seeing in it the possibility that Germany could exercise an opt-out and abandon monetary union. Their opposition led the British to accept a specific opt-out that would allow the country to retain the pound sterling and a dependent central bank.

Unlike the British, the French and Italians participated in the ERM in the 1980s and strongly supported monetary union. Initially, they hoped to institute immediate changes to the rules of the ERM that gave the Bundesbank disproportionate influence over the monetary policies of other participating member states. When it became clear in 1989 that German negotiators would not agree to substantial changes to the ERM, the French and Italians pushed for the rapid creation of a full monetary union.

Most French activity focused on reducing the independence of the European Central Bank at the margin, strengthening coordination in the second stage, and setting deadlines. The French opposed a European Central Bank as independent of political authorities as was the Bundesbank, arguing that a successful monetary union would require an "economic government" that, among other things, would be more responsive to the preferences of political leaders. German officials, particularly in the Bundesbank, opposed the idea of an economic government for mone-

Table 4.1 Monetary Union Preferences and Outcomes

Issue	Germany	Britain	France	Italy	Outcome
Single currency	Favor	Oppose	Favor	Favor	Single currency
Opt-outs	Oppose general opt-out	Prefer general opt-out	Oppose general opt-out	Oppose general opt-out	British opt-out
European Central Bank independence	Complete independence	Opposed creation of European Central Bank	Partial independence	?	Complete monetary policy independence; partial exchange-rate policy independence
Coordination in second stage	Weak	Weak	Strong	Strong	Weak
Convergence criteria	Binding numerical criteria	?	Numerical criteria	Oppose numerical criteria	Numerical criteria; some interpretation allowed
Deadlines for second and third stages	Opposed by Bundesbank; supported by government	Oppose	Support	Support	Deadlines for second and third stages

tary union, preferring to duplicate German arrangements at the European level. On central bank independence, the French succeeded in marginally altering the Bundesbank's demands for complete European Central Bank control over exchange-rate policy and in delaying until the beginning of the third stage the time when national central banks would have to be made independent. The French pushed for a rapid move toward coordinated monetary policies throughout the negotiations and were instrumental in proposing and negotiating deadlines for the beginning of each stage of monetary union.

The Italians shared the French positions regarding coordination in the second stage and setting deadlines. At the Rome summit in October 1990 and at Maastricht in December 1991, Carli and Andreotti played important and active roles in setting deadlines for the beginnings of the second and third stages. Italian negotiators argued long and hard but without success during 1990 and 1991 that the second stage should be centered around a well-developed system of mutual policy coordination and adjustment as a prelude for full monetary union. In addition, Italian officials were very concerned about the definition and implementation of the convergence criteria, given their relatively poor fiscal performance (French negotiators assumed France would have little difficulty meeting the criteria and backed Germany's position during the negotiations). The Italians preferred that convergence be a political process rather than an automatic one based on quantitative convergence criteria. Here they won only modest concessions. Quantitative criteria were included in the treaty, but the Italians were able to secure language that indicated they could participate in the third stage if they were making ambiguously defined "progress" toward meeting the criteria.

Outcomes

German preferences regarding the rules of monetary union were most important in determining the outcome of the negotiations embodied in the Maastricht Treaty. The Bundesbank was able to set the ground rules for the negotiations in the Delors Committee on two important issues. The European Central Bank and national central banks would have to be independent of other Community institutions and national governments, and substantial economic convergence would be required before moving to monetary union. During the subsequent intergovernmental negotiations, the German government made four concessions—implicitly or explicitly opposed by the Bundesbank—to ensure a successful outcome. First, it agreed that Ecofin could have a limited role in exchange-rate policy in the third stage, which might conflict with the European Central Bank's price stability mandate. Second, it opposed British plans for a general "opt-in" provision that would have allowed a future German government to decline to participate in full monetary union. Third, the government rejected the Bundesbank position that convergence, and thus participation in the single currency, be determined only on the basis of quantitative criteria. Although quantitative convergence criteria were written into the treaty, it also outlines a decisionmaking process that could allow member states making substantial progress toward the criteria to participate. Finally, in Rome in

October 1990 and at Maastricht in December 1991, Kohl agreed to deadlines for the transitions to the second and third stages. Each of these concessions covered issues of secondary importance to Germany, and none were likely to undermine the priority of central bank independence and economic convergence.

The evidence presented here does not provide much support for the argument that the Maastricht Treaty was a German concession designed to secure member states' approval for German unification in 1990.[51] The French, German, and Italian governments were interested in monetary union both before and after unification, but the British government was not, despite the fact that senior government officials expressed serious reservations about the security and economic consequences of unification. The German government cooperated with French leaders in opening discussions on monetary union in early 1988, well before German unification was a likely prospect. German support for monetary union led to the creation of the Delors Committee, and at the Madrid summit in June 1989 the government supported the committee's detailed report as a basis for further negotiations. Shortly after the opening of the Berlin Wall in November 1989, Chancellor Kohl outlined a ten-point plan to integrate East and West Germany rapidly. This attracted criticism from British, French, and Italian officials, and in response the German government reassured the other member states that a unified Germany would remain committed to the European Community and the North Atlantic Treaty Organization. German monetary union occurred on 1 July 1990, and full German unification was completed on 3 October 1990, shortly before the start of the intergovernmental conference. At this point, the German government could have abandoned the negotiations for European monetary union. Instead, the government and Bundesbank chose this point to continue the negotiations while making new demands. The Bundesbank published its opinion on monetary union, insisting on strict and quantitative convergence criteria that would apply to the second and third stages and central bank independence, and the government chose to add another issue to the negotiating table by pressing the other member states to open a parallel intergovernmental conference on political union.

Notes

1. Paul De Grauwe, "The Political Economy of Monetary Union in Europe," *The World Economy* 16, no. 6 (November 1993), 653–661; Geoffrey Garrett, "The Politics of Maastricht," *Economics and Politics* 5, no.2 (July 1993): 113; Joseph M. Grieco, "The Maastricht Treaty, Economic and Monetary Union, and the Neo-Realist Research Program," *Review of International Studies* 21 (1995): 21–40; Andrew Moravcsik, *The Choice for Europe: Social Purpose and State Power from*

Messina to Maastricht (Ithaca, NY: Cornell University Press, 1998); Thomas Oatley, *Monetary Politics: Exchange Rate Cooperation in the European Union* (Ann Arbor: University of Michigan Press, 1997); and Louis W. Pauly, "The Politics of European Monetary Union: National Strategies, International Implications," *International Journal* (Winter 1991–1992), 93–111.

2. David R. Cameron, "Transnational Relations and the Development of European Economic and Monetary Union," in *Bringing Transnational Relations Back In: Non-State Actors, Domestic Structures and International Institutions*, ed. Thomas Risse-Kappen (New York: Cambridge University Press, 1995); Kenneth Dyson, Kevin Featherstone, and George Michalopoulos, "Strapped to the Mast: EC Central Bankers Between Global Financial Markets and Regional Integration," *Journal of European Public Policy* 2, no. 3 (September 1995): 465–487; Kathleen R. McNamara, *The Currency of Ideas* (Ithaca, NY: Cornell University Press, 1998); and Wayne Sandholtz, "Choosing Union: Monetary Politics and Maastricht," *International Organization* 47, no.1 (Winter 1993): 1–39.

3. Loukas Tsoukalis, *The New European Economy: The Politics and Economics of Integration*, 2d ed. (Oxford: Oxford University Press, 1992), 193–205.

4. *Financial Times*, 15 March 1982, 16; and *Reuters North European Service*, 15 March 1982.

5. *Financial Times*, 13 March 1984, 1; see also Kenneth Dyson, *Elusive Union: The Process of Economic and Monetary Union in Europe* (London: Longman, 1994), 117; and *Financial Times*, 11 December 1984, 1.

6. *Financial Times*, 4 December 1985, 2.

7. *Economist*, 19 September 1987, 86; *Financial Times*, 14 September 1987, 1; and *Reuters*, 14 September 1987.

8. Dyson, *Elusive Union*, 123–125; and Karl Kaltenthaler, *Germany and the Politics of Europe's Money* (Durham, NC: Duke University Press, 1998), 56–68.

9. See, for example, Commission of the European Communities, "Annual Economic Report 1985–86," *European Economy* 26 (November 1985); and Jacques Drèze, *The Two–Handed Growth Strategy for Europe: Autonomy Through Flexible Cooperation*, Centre for European Policy Studies Working Paper No. 34 (Brussels: Centre for European Policy Studies, 1987).

10. Edouard Balladur, "Memorandum sur la Construction Monétaire Européenne," *Ecu Newsletter* 3 (March 1988).

11. *Financial Times*, 20 January 1988, 2; *Reuters*, 6 January 1988; and *Reuters*, 7 January 1988.

12. For the text of the treaty, see Commission and Council of the European Communities, *Treaty on European Union* (Luxembourg: Office of the Official Publications of the European Communities, 1992). Detailed overviews of the negotiations include Michael Baun, *An Imperfect Union* (Boulder, CO: Westview, 1996); Lorenzo Bini-Smaghi, Tommasso Padoa-Schioppa, and Francesco Papadia, *The Transition to EMU in the Maastricht Treaty,* Princeton Essays in International Finance (Princeton: Princeton University, 1994); Dyson, *Elusive Union;* Alexander Italianer, "Mastering Maastricht: EMU Issues and How They Were Settled," in *Economic and Monetary Union: Implications for National Policymakers*, ed. Klaus Gretschmann (Dordrecht: Martinus Nyjoff, 1993); Peter B. Kenen, *Economic and Monetary Union in Europe: Moving Beyond Maastricht* (New York: Cambridge University Press, 1995); Moravcsik, *The Choice for Europe;* and Horst Ungerer, *A Concise History of European Monetary Integration* (Westport: Quorum, 1997).

13. Interview with Banque de France official.

14. "Hanover European Council: Conclusions of the Presidency," in *Bulletin of the European Communities* (June 1988), 65–66. Genscher had proposed that the committee be made up solely of independent experts, but the Bundesbank and the British government rejected this idea, arguing that the central bank governors would produce a more "realistic" report. *Financial Times*, 27 February 1988, 2; and interview with a former Bank of England official.

15. Quotation from C. Randall Henning, *Currencies and Politics in the United States, Germany, and Japan* (Washington, DC: Institute for International Economics, 1994), 230; see also Kaltenthaler, *Germany and the Politics of Europe's Money;* David Marsh, *The Most Powerful Bank: Inside Germany's Bundesbank* (New York: Random House, 1992); Wilhelm Nölling, *Monetary Policy in Europe After Maastricht* (New York: St. Martin's Press, 1993); Oatley, *Monetary Politics;* Karl Otto Pöhl, "Statement on European Monetary Unification," (Frankfurt: Deutsche Bundesbank, 5 May 1988); and Heidemarie Sherman, *Central Banking in Germany and the Process of European Monetary Integration*, Tokyo Papers No. 3 (1990), 170–176.

16. Agence Europe, *Europe* 4730 (25 February 1988): 11.

17. Deutsche Bundesbank, *Report for the Year 1990* (Frankfurt: Deutsche Bundesbank, 1991), 10; and Dyson, *Elusive Union*, 130–132.

18. Interview with former Banque de France official.

19. *Financial Times*, 30 December 1988, 12; *Reuters*, 14 April 1989; and interview with former Banque de France official.

20. Amato's memorandum is reprinted in *Il Sole 24 Ore*, 25 February 1988, 1. See also Agence Europe, *Europe* 4731 (26 February 1988): 7; *Reuters*, 26 January 1988; and Guiliano Amato, *Due Anni al Tesoro* (Bologna: Il Mulino, 1990).

21. Quotation from Geoffrey Howe, *Conflict of Loyalty* (London: Macmillan, 1994), 533–534. During this period, Thatcher and Lawson both delivered major speeches criticizing the idea of EMU. See Dyson, *Elusive Union*, 134.

22. *Financial Times*, 27 June 1988, 1; and Margaret Thatcher, *The Downing Street Years* (New York: HarperCollins, 1993), 740.

23. Howe, *Conflict of Loyalty,* 576–577; Nigel Lawson, *The View from No. 11: Memoirs of a Tory Radical* (New York and London: Doubleday, 1993), 907–909; Robin Leigh-Pemberton, "The Future of Monetary Arrangements in Europe," Occasional Paper No. 82 (London: Institute of Economic Affairs, 1989); and Thatcher, *The Downing Street Years*, 708. The British seem not to have understood fully the conflict Pöhl faced between representing the Bundesbank's and the government's positions and blamed his willingness to agree to the Delors Report on "laziness." Interview with former Bank of England official.

24. Committee for the Study of Economic and Monetary Union, "Report on Economic and Monetary Union in the European Community," Brussels, 12 April 1989, paragraph 23. Hereafter cited as "Delors Report."

25. "Delors Report," paragraphs 51, 52, 57, 59, 60.

26. See also Moravcsik, *The Choice for Europe*.

27. Cameron, "Transnational Relations"; and Dyson, Featherstone, and Michalopoulos, "Strapped to the Mast."

28. Quotations from HM Treasury, *An Evolutionary Approach to Economic and Monetary Union* (London: HMSO, 1989); see also *Financial Times*, 12 September 1989, 8.

29. British Invisibles Export Council, *The Next Stage in an Evolutionary Approach to Economic and Monetary Union* (London: British Invisibles Export Council, 1990); HM Treasury, "EMU Beyond Stage I: The UK Approach," speech

by the chancellor to the German Industry Forum, London, 20 June 1990; HM Treasury, "Economic and Monetary Union Beyond Stage I: Possible Treaty Provisions and a Statute for a European Monetary Fund," London, January 1991; and interviews with officials of the European Commission and the Banque de France.

30. *Daily Telegraph*, 13 May 1991, 1; and Italianer, "Mastering Maastricht," 97.

31. *Financial Times*, 24 September 1991, 22; and interview with former Banque de France official.

32. Bini-Smaghi, Padoa-Schioppa, and Papadia, *The Transition to EMU in the Maastricht Treaty*, 17–20; *Financial Times*, 2 December 1991, 1; and Kenen, *Economic and Monetary Union in Europe*.

33. Éric Aeschimann, and Pascal Riché, *La guerre de sept ans: Histoire secrète du franc fort 1989–1996* (Paris: Calmann-Lèvy, 1996), 137, 158, 200; Dyson, Featherstone, and Micalopoulos, "Strapped to the Mast," 469; and interview with European Commission official.

34. Bini-Smaghi, Padoa-Schioppa, and Papadia, *The Transition to EMU in the Maastricht Treaty*, 23; *Reuters*, 18 September 1990; and interview with Banque de France official.

35. *Financial Times*, 6 December 1990, 2; Italianer, "Mastering Maastricht," 55; and interview with Banque de France official.

36. See C. Randall Henning, *Cooperating with Europe's Monetary Union*, Policy Analyses in International Economics No. 49 (Washington, DC: Institute for International Economics, 1997).

37. Bini-Smaghi, Padoa-Schioppa, and Papadia, *The Transition to EMU in the Maastricht Treaty*, 33; and Reimut Jochimsen, "Economic and Monetary Union: A German Central Banker's Perspective," in *Economic and Monetary Union: Implications for National Policy-Makers*, ed. Klaus Gretschmann (Dordrecht: Martinus Nyjoff, 1993), 198.

38. Bini-Smaghi, Padoa-Schioppa, and Papadia, *The Transition to EMU in the Maastricht Treaty*, 34.

39. Ibid., 36–37.

40. Ibid., 36–37; and Italianer, "Mastering Maastricht," 91.

41. Quotation from Bini-Smaghi, Padoa-Schioppa, and Papadia, *The Transition to EMU in the Maastricht Treaty*, 13–15; see also Aeschimann and Riché, *La guerre de sept ans*, 93; Guido Carli, *Cinquant'anni di Vita Italiana* (Bari: Laterza, 1993), 406–412; Italianer, "Mastering Maastricht," 63, 69–70; Jochimsen, "Economic and Monetary Union," 198–9; and interviews with former Banque de France official and European Commission official.

42. Bini-Smaghi, Padoa-Schioppa, and Papadia, *The Transition to EMU in the Maastricht Treaty*, 24–26; Italianer, "Mastering Maastricht," 99; and interview with European Commission official.

43. The selection of these reference values was somewhat arbitrary. The average debt-to-GDP ratio in the European Community was approximately 60 percent in 1990, whereas the deficit-to-GDP ratio was about 4 percent, and central bankers in particular wished to signal that this was unacceptably high (interview with European Commission official). Others hold that the French suggested that budget deficit criterion since this was the level Mitterrand pledged to achieve after the 1983 devaluation of the franc. See Aeschimann and Riché, *La guerre de sept ans*, 93.

44. Thatcher was under strong pressure from Chancellor Nigel Lawson to

bring sterling into the ERM. This debate between Thatcher and Lawson had been going on for some time, but Lawson's hand was strengthened prior to the Madrid summit by Foreign Secretary Geoffrey Howe. Howe favored a commitment to ERM membership for sterling as a demonstration of the British government's seriousness toward the EMU negotiations. He hoped that "an early UK move on ERM at Madrid . . . [would] prevent the Eleven convening an immediate Inter-Governmental Conference to draft EMU amendments to the Treaty" (Howe, *Conflict of Loyalty*, 557). Howe and Lawson threatened to resign unless Thatcher spelled out specific conditions under which the government would bring sterling into the ERM. For the principals' accounts, see Howe, *Conflict of Loyalty*, 576–580; Lawson, *The View from No. 11*, 926–936; and Thatcher, *The Downing Street Years*, 710–713, 750–752.

45. *Financial Times*, 29 June 1989, 2; and *Reuters*, 27 October 1989.

46. *Reuter Library Report*, 14 November 1989; and *Reuter Library Report*, 15 November 1989.

47. Deutsche Bundesbank, "Establishment of an Economic and Monetary Union in Europe," (Frankfurt: Deutsche Bundesbank, 19 September 1990).

48. Bini-Smaghi, Padoa-Schioppa, and Papadia, *The Transition to EMU in the Maastricht Treaty*, 21–22; and Italianer, "Mastering Maastricht," 63.

49. Bini-Smaghi, Padoa-Schioppa, and Papadia, *The Transition to EMU in the Maastricht Treaty*, 14, 22–23; and Italianer, "Mastering Maastricht," 71.

50. Quotations from Italianer, "Mastering Maastricht," 70; and Marsh, "The Most Powerful Bank," 206. See also Jochimsen, "Economic and Monetary Union," 196.

51. David M. Andrews, "The Global Origins of the Maastricht Treaty on EMU: Closing the Window of Opportunity," in *The State of the European Community,* vol. 2: *The Maastricht Debates and Beyond*, ed. Alan W. Cafruny and Glenda G. Rosenthal (Boulder, CO: Lynne Rienner, 1993), 107–123; Baun, *An Imperfect Union;* Garrett, "The Politics of Maastricht"; and Peter Loedel, *Deutsche Mark Politics: Germany in the International Monetary System* (Boulder: Lynne Rienner, 1999), 94, 145.

5

Exchange-Rate Politics, 1989–1999

Exchange-rate politics differed considerably in Britain, France, and Italy in the 1990s. The Thatcher government in Britain abandoned its focus on domestic monetary developments by joining the exchange-rate mechanism (ERM) of the European Monetary System (EMS) in 1990. But less than two years later, the government reverted to form by withdrawing from the ERM, allowing sterling to float, and focusing on keeping inflation low rather than on stabilizing the exchange rate. French governments gave greater attention to exchange-rate stability than to growth and competitiveness, reversing the priorities of the 1970s and 1980s. The French raised interest rates to defend the franc's ERM parity and cut the budget deficit during a period of slow economic growth, which provoked sharp domestic political conflict but did allow the country to meet the Maastricht Treaty's criteria for participation in monetary union in 1999. Italian governments also were committed to participating in the single currency but pursued a quite different set of economic policies to achieve this goal. They initially strengthened their commitment to European monetary institutions by refusing to devalue, eliminating capital controls, and narrowing the lira's fluctuation band in the early 1990s. But they withdrew the lira from the ERM in 1992 in the face of large-scale foreign exchange market speculation and allowed the currency to depreciate sharply until 1995. Thereafter, they rejoined the ERM and quickly reduced a very large budget deficit to join the single currency.

The evidence presented in this chapter supports the institutionalist explanation rather than the openness explanation for exchange-rate politics. Variation in bank-industry ties was associated with differences in groups' preferences and governments' policy choices, although in some cases the relationship was weaker in the 1990s than in earlier decades. Increased openness to trade and investment with Europe did not lead to changes in groups' preferences or government policy choices in Britain, although largely unchanged levels of openness accompanied a reversal of French policy priorities and overall continuity in Italian policy.

The next section of this chapter details the effects of exchange-rate changes, German unification, and the drive toward monetary union on exchange-rate policy coordination in Europe in the 1990s, focusing on the events surrounding the heavy speculation against ERM parities in 1992–1993. The following three sections describe exchange-rate politics and policy choices in each country, paying particular attention to the reactions of bankers, industrialists, and officials to exchange-rate instability and real appreciation. The concluding section compares the experiences of the three countries to the expectations of the openness and institutionalist explanations.

The Evolution of European Monetary Cooperation, 1989–1999

The ERM seemed to play an important role in promoting economic convergence and stable exchange rates in the late 1980s and early 1990s. The franc, lira, and pound sterling were much more stable against the mark than they had been during the 1970s and 1980s (see Figure 5.1) The only realignment that occurred in this period, the devaluation of the lira by 3.7 percent, was a technical adjustment of the currency's central parity more consistent with the narrow ERM fluctuation band that Italian authorities adopted in 1990. Participation in the ERM was associated with lower inflation rates in France, Italy, and other countries (see Table 5.1), and many observers saw pegging currencies to the mark as an effective way to prevent governments from implementing overly expansionary monetary policies.[1] This success in lowering inflation was one reason that Spain, Portugal, and Britain all joined the ERM with wide fluctuation bands and that Sweden and Finland informally pegged their currencies to the European currency unit (ECU). Many officials and international investors saw the well-functioning ERM as a sort of trial run for full monetary union and expected governments to privilege maintaining a stable exchange rate over other goals.

These successes masked underlying problems that emerged in a series of exchange-rate crises from 1992 to 1995. The most important underlying problem was the economic consequences produced by German unification. Unification led to increased private and public spending in Germany that was not fully offset by tax increases, and by 1993 the German public-sector borrowing requirement exceeded 7 percent of gross domestic product (GDP).[2] Stable exchange rates in Europe and higher demand and budget

Figure 5.1 Index of Monthly Mark Exchange Rates, 1988–1998 (January 1988 = 100)

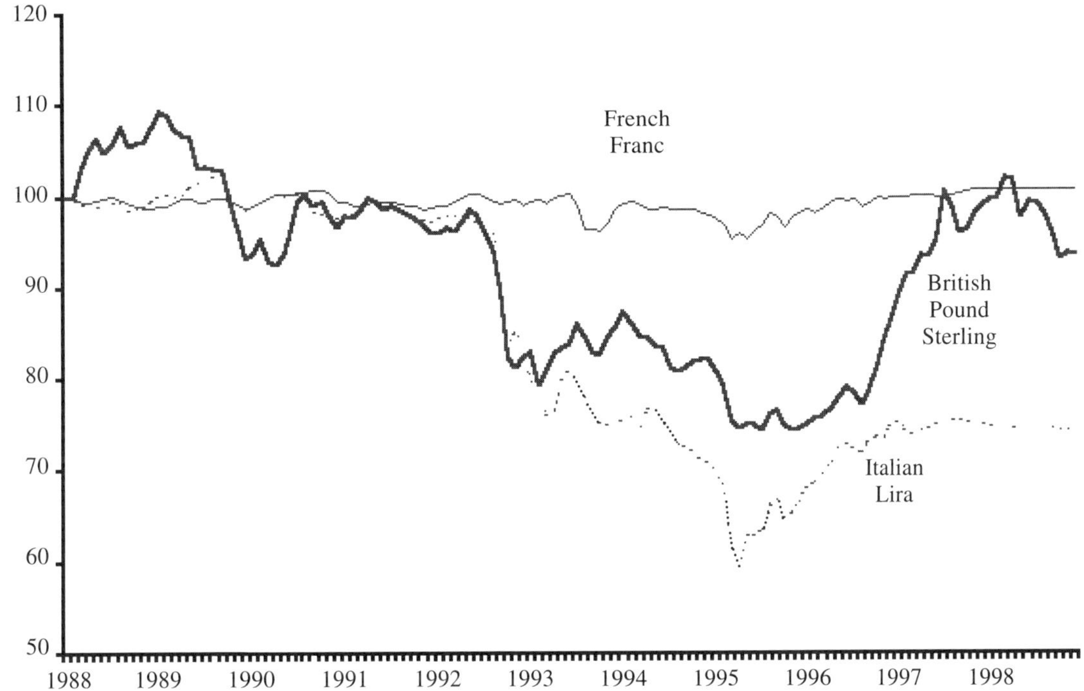

Source: Calculated from *Federal Reserve Economic Database.*

Table 5.1 Annual Percentage Changes in Consumer Prices, 1988–1997

	Britain	France	Italy	Germany
1988	4.9	2.7	5.0	1.3
1989	7.8	3.6	6.6	2.8
1990	9.5	3.4	6.1	2.7
1991	5.9	3.2	6.5	3.6
1992	3.7	2.4	5.3	5.1
1993	1.6	2.1	4.2	4.5
1994	2.5	1.7	3.9	2.7
1995	3.4	1.7	5.4	1.8
1996	2.4	2.0	3.8	1.5
1997	3.1	1.2	1.8	1.8

Source: Organization for Economic Cooperation and Development, *OECD Economic Outlook* 64 (December 1998): 206.

deficits in Germany could have been accommodated in one of three ways: increased inflation in Germany, nominal and real appreciation of the mark, or lower inflation in the rest of Europe. Political conflicts made it impossible for governments to agree on any of these solutions. The Bundesbank ruled out the first by countering inflationary pressures with increased interest rates. By the summer of 1992, the German Lombard rate was at the historically high level of 8.75 percent.

Other governments and central banks were unwilling to address the economic consequences of unification with exchange-rate changes. For reasons explored at length below, British, French, and Italian officials vetoed realignments that would devalue their currencies against the mark. Since Britain and Italy had higher inflation rates than did Germany, this nominal exchange-rate stability produced substantial real currency appreciation of sterling and the lira (see Figure 5.2). These were among the first currencies subject to speculation when investors questioned governments' commitment to stable exchange rates in mid-1992. Officials in the German government and the Bundesbank feared that this real appreciation would lead to speculation and require them to engage in potentially inflationary interven-

Figure 5.2 Annual Percentage Change in Real Effective Exchange Rates, 1988–1997 (based on relative normalized unit labor costs)

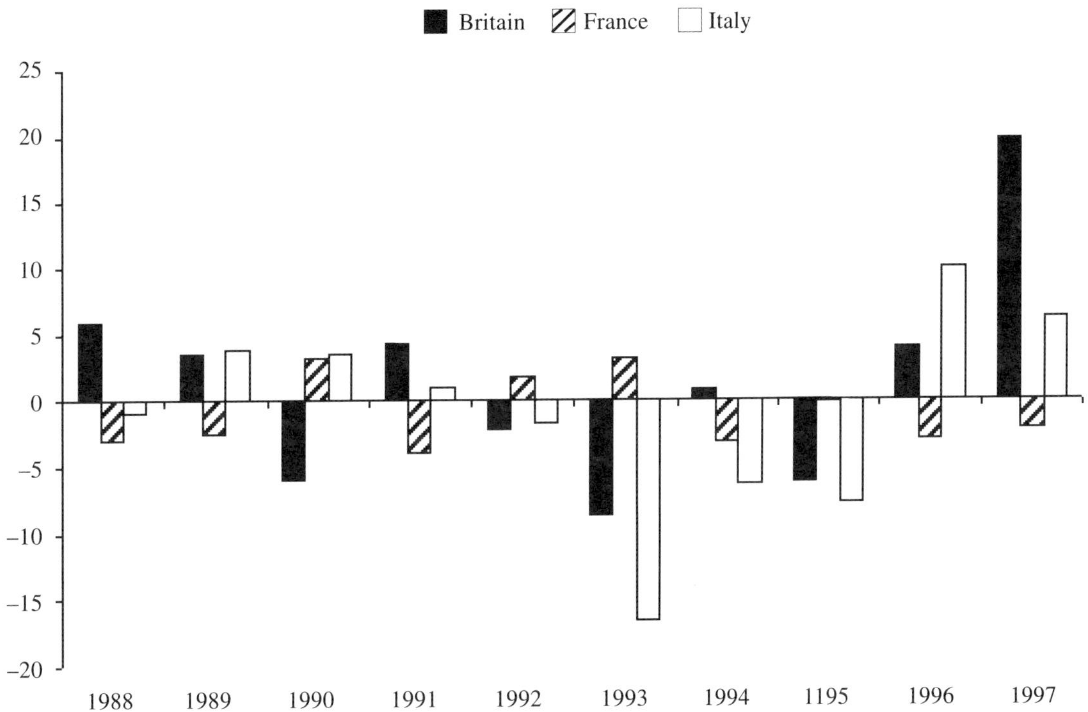

Source: Calculated from International Monetary Fund, *International Financial Statistics,* various years.

tion under the rules of the EMS. As early as mid-1989, German policymakers began advocating in private an effective revaluation of the mark against some ERM currencies, but this was blocked by the French, German, and other governments.[3] Rejecting exchange-rate changes meant that the economic shock of German unification would have to be accommodated with lower inflation and tighter monetary policies in other countries. But this disinflation came at the worst possible time, when the European economy was entering a very deep recession and governments preferred lower, not higher, interest rates.

The removal of capital controls in most countries by 1990 aggravated the tensions created by different national economic circumstances and political priorities. Capital controls had allowed weak currency countries such as France and Italy some leeway to hold domestic interest rates below offshore rates in the 1980s. Their removal made it easier for investors to speculate against ERM parities and more important for governments to coordinate their interest-rate policies. Since German interest rates effectively set a floor for rates throughout the ERM, this meant that other central banks had to follow the Bundesbank in tightening monetary policy beginning in 1989.

The contradiction between slower growth and higher interest rates did not create market tensions within the ERM until 1992, since "the knowledge that countries wished to qualify for monetary union convinced the markets of governments' commitment to policies consistent with the maintenance of fixed rates."[4] But on 2 June 1992, Danish voters failed to ratify the Maastricht Treaty in a referendum, increasing investors' doubts about the likelihood of a successful transition to full monetary union and the sustainability of overvalued currencies' parities. For the next year these doubts led to almost continuous speculation against ERM parities. Shortly after the Danish referendum, sterling and the lira depreciated toward the bottom of their fluctuation bands. Dollar depreciation in the spring and summer of 1992, driven by historically low U.S. short-term interest rates and high German interest rates, only aggravated these tensions (see Figure 5.3).

The British government, which held the European Community's rotating presidency, called a meeting of the Economics and Finance Council (Ecofin) in late August to discuss these developments. Ecofin ministers reaffirmed their opposition to parity changes, stating that "a change in the present structure of central rates would not be the appropriate response to the current tensions in the EMS."[5] Both British and Italian officials refused to consider devaluing unilaterally, although they might have accepted a "broad" devaluation of many currencies against the mark. French officials opposed any realignment prior to the national referendum on the Maastricht Treaty in September, fearing that it would reduce French voters' support for the treaty.

Figure 5.3 Index of Monthly Dollar Exchange Rates, 1988–1998 (January 1988 = 100)

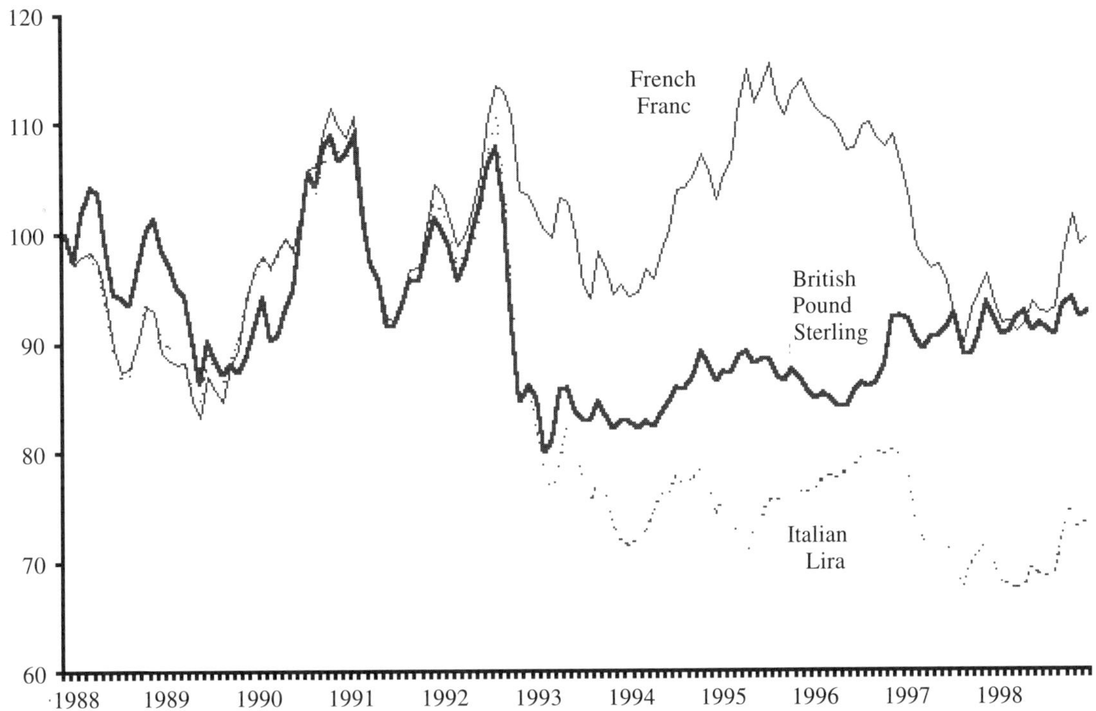

Source: Calculated from *Federal Reserve Economic Database.*

The Ecofin statement did not stop the heavy speculation against the lira and sterling, and a previously scheduled Ecofin meeting in early September in Bath allowed ministers to discuss the issue again. At that point, the Italians probably would have devalued if accompanied by other countries.[6] The French opposed a devaluation of the franc but did not rule out devaluations of other currencies. The British opposed devaluation that did not include the franc on the grounds that a unilateral devaluation of sterling, or one linked only with other "weak" currencies, would destroy the government's credibility. As chair of the meeting, British chancellor Norman Lamont was able to prevent any formal discussion of parity changes. Instead, he pressed the German representatives to lower interest rates, but the latter refused to do so, preferring some sort of change in ERM parities that would reduce their intervention obligations.[7] Given these different positions, the meeting resolved only to confirm the statement of a week earlier ruling out a realignment. Lamont and others interpreted the communiqué issued after the meeting as implying that the Germans might trade lower interest rates for a realignment, but Bundesbank president Helmut Schlesinger denied this.[8]

The failures to agree on a new course of action at Bath fueled speculation against sterling and the lira, and on 11 September 1992, the lira depreciated below its fluctuation band despite heavy intervention by the Bundesbank and the Banca d'Italia. Over the weekend, Bundesbank officials emphasized to senior German politicians the inflationary consequences of such large-scale intervention, and the latter authorized realignment discussions. Officials from the Italian and German central banks and finance ministries negotiated an effective 7 percent devaluation of the lira against other ERM currencies during the weekend of 12–13 September in exchange for a cut in German interest rates (when informed of the realignment discussions, the British refused to join by devaluing sterling). They hoped in vain that a modest reduction in the Lombard rate by 0.25 percent and in the discount rate by 0.5 percent would reduce pressures within the ERM. Speculation against ERM parities intensified, and sterling and the lira depreciated to the floors of their ERM fluctuation bands on 15 September. After briefly raising interest rates and intervening heavily on the foreign exchange markets, the British withdrew from the ERM on 16 September and allowed sterling to float. The next morning Italian authorities decided to follow suit and to suspend the lira's ERM membership as well.[9]

Speculation spread to the franc despite ratification of the Maastricht Treaty by a narrow majority in the French referendum on 20 September. The Banque de France raised interest rates and coordinated foreign exchange market intervention with the Bundesbank in a successful defense of the franc's parity. The currency was subject to further speculative attacks in late 1992 and early 1993, but these were rebuffed by coordinated action and increases in French interest rates, and confidence in the franc increased sufficiently by mid-1993 for the Banque de France to push French interest rates below German rates. This confidence vanished in July 1993, as increasing unemployment led many to believe that French political leaders—including Prime Minister Edouard Balladur, already effectively campaigning for the 1995 presidential election—might abandon the ERM in order to push interest rates lower still. By late July, the Bundesbank was unwilling to intervene further in support of the franc, and governments discussed the possibility of suspending the ERM, a withdrawal of Germany from the mechanism, and the widening of fluctuation bands. They chose the last option, widening the bands from ±2.25 percent to ±15 percent.

Europe did not see much monetary stability for the next two years. The pound sterling and lira both depreciated by about 20 percent shortly after withdrawal from the ERM. Sterling continued to depreciate through 1994 and in early 1996 reversed course and appreciated by almost 20 percent. Political uncertainty in Italy encouraged further speculation against the lira, which depreciated through mid-1995. A certain degree of political stability, combined with low inflation and strong export performance, stabilized the lira beginning in early 1995 and allowed the government to rejoin the ERM in late 1996. The franc remained stable within the new fluctuation bands of the ERM but required frequent central bank intervention and increases in French interest rates to ward off further speculative attacks.

An important motivation for French and Italian governments' desire to stabilize their currencies was to prepare the way for monetary union. The Maastricht Treaty held that only member states that had participated in the ERM for two years could adopt the single currency, and governments in both countries were successful in preventing speculation against their ERM parities in 1997 and 1998. Exchange-rate stability within Europe was combined with a welcome depreciation of ERM currencies against the dollar (see Figure 5.3). This increased the competitiveness of exports and helped promote economic growth during a period of sluggish domestic demand. French and Italian governments also weathered domestic political protests by launching crash programs to reduce their budget deficits below the Maastricht target of 3 percent of GDP by 1998.

Britain: In and Out of the Exchange-Rate Mechanism

British decisionmakers gave higher priority to reducing inflation than to stabilizing the currency at a competitive level in the 1990s. Reversing her earlier position, Prime Minister Margaret Thatcher brought sterling into the ERM in 1990. She took this step not out of a newfound interest in exchange-rate stability and industrial competitiveness but because of domestic political developments. ERM entry stabilized sterling's nominal exchange rate that, with inflation at 10 percent, led the currency to appreciate in real terms. This reduced import prices and placed downward pressure on the high inflation rate. The ERM also provided a more credible framework for monetary policy in the eyes of international investors. Currency appreciation and greater credibility allowed Thatcher and her Conservative successor, John Major, to reduce interest rates before the May 1992 general election. By mid-1992 inflation subsided and the economy entered a deep recession, but the government could not reduce interest rates further without threatening sterling's position in the ERM. Officials first pressed the Bundesbank to reduce interest rates. When it became clear in September 1992 that this would not succeed and speculation against sterling increased, they withdrew from the ERM and cut interest rates unilaterally. Policy choices outside the ERM explicitly focused on internal rather than external goals. The government announced a target rate for inflation and granted the Bank of England some influence over monetary policy but showed little interest in exchange-rate developments.

The Thatcher and Major governments made these choices despite pressures from British industrialists to stabilize sterling at a competitive level. The Confederation of British Industry (CBI) preferred that the government continue to "shadow" the mark in the late 1980s or at least intervene to prevent sterling from appreciating too rapidly. Industrialists supported ERM entry in 1990, but at a lower parity than the one chosen by the government. They also hoped that the authorities would use fully sterling's wide fluctuation band to prevent subsequent real appreciation of the currency. Neither of the two senior cabinet members supporting ERM entry—Nigel Lawson and Geoffrey Howe—devoted much attention to the possible effects on British industry. Lawson continued to emphasize that ERM entry would boost the credibility of monetary policy, and Howe hoped that ERM entry could increase Britain's influence in the monetary union negotiations.

Sterling Enters the Exchange-Rate Mechanism

In early 1988, the British government stopped shadowing the mark and raised interest rates on evidence that inflation was increasing rapidly. The subsequent appreciation of sterling caused dismay among industrialists. The CBI favored continuing to stabilize sterling against the mark, which had been "a major factor in helping businesses to expand their market share" in Europe. By May 1988, when it appeared that the appreciation of sterling might not be temporary, the CBI, the Institute of Directors, and some Conservative members of Parliament called on the government to intervene on the foreign exchange markets to stabilize the currency.[10] In contrast, many bankers and analysts in the City agreed with the government's decision to counter inflationary pressure with sterling appreciation and higher interest rates. The attitude of Kit McMahon, chairman of Midland Bank, was typical: although in principle ERM membership would provide a useful framework for monetary policy, in the present circumstances the priority had to be reducing inflation quickly.[11]

The decision to stop shadowing the mark also renewed the debate within the government over ERM membership. Both Foreign Secretary Geoffrey Howe and Bank of England governor Robin Leigh-Pemberton praised the lower inflation and exchange-rate stability achieved by members of the ERM, and Chancellor Nigel Lawson remained a strong proponent of ERM membership.[12] During the spring of 1989, Lawson and Howe hoped to persuade Thatcher to bring sterling into the ERM but knew that their usual arguments would not suffice, so they linked the issue to Britain's position regarding monetary union.[13] They argued to Thatcher that ERM membership would persuade other member states of Britain's seriousness about the monetary union negotiations and held that a commitment to enter the mechanism before the June 1989 summit of the European Council in Madrid could "prevent the Eleven [other member states] convening an immediate Inter-Governmental Conference to draft EMU [Economic and Monetary Union] amendments to the Treaty." Howe and Lawson threatened to resign when Thatcher initially refused to set a date for ERM entry. The prime minister acquiesced and at the Madrid summit committed to enter the mechanism when five conditions were met: inflation had gone down, all capital controls in the European Community had been removed, member states had made undefined "progress" toward completing the internal market, competition had been introduced in financial services, and European competition policy had been strengthened.[14]

Conflicts over the "Madrid conditions" created bitterness and suspicion among Thatcher, Howe, and Lawson; all would resign within little more than a year. In October 1989, the *Financial Times* published an excerpt from an article by Thatcher's economic policy adviser and Lawson nemesis, Alan Walters, in which he described the ERM as "half-baked." Lawson decided that either he or Walters had to leave the government; when Thatcher refused to dismiss Walters, Lawson resigned, and John Major replaced him as chancellor. Earlier the same year, Thatcher offered Howe a new position as either home secretary or leader of the House of Commons in order to reduce his influence over foreign policy; Howe reluctantly accepted the latter position. He resigned over Thatcher's intransigence during the monetary union negotiations at the Rome summit in October 1990. Howe's resignation prompted Michael Heseltine to mount a contest for the leadership of the Conservative Party against Thatcher. Thatcher won a majority of Conservative parliamentarians' votes but not enough for an outright victory under the leadership election rules. She resigned shortly thereafter, when it became clear to many Conservative members of Parliament that her handling of European issues, as well as the unpopular implementation of the poll tax in England, made her an electoral liability for the party. They chose Major as the new prime minister, and Norman Lamont replaced Major as chancellor.[15]

When Major took office as chancellor in late 1989, he faced a combination of high inflation, the beginning of what would become a deep recession, and a general election within the next two years. He quickly concluded that ERM entry was the best solution to all of these problems since it would reduce inflation by producing real appreciation, increase the government's credibility in financial markets, and therefore allow reductions in interest rates.[16] This logic, combined with the political pressures to join the ERM in order to buttress Britain's position in the monetary union negotiations, led Thatcher and Major to deemphasize the Madrid conditions for ERM entry.[17] By mid-June 1990, they had agreed to bring sterling into the ERM in the autumn, by which time sterling's effective exchange rate had appreciated by 8 percent. On 5 October, Major announced that sterling would enter the ERM with a wide fluctuation band and a parity of 2.95 marks. At the same time, he cut interest rates by a percentage point to 14 percent.[18]

Sterling Exits the Exchange-Rate Mechanism

Stabilizing sterling in the ERM was bound to lead to further real appreciation because of Britain's high inflation rate. Ministers and officials denied that sterling entered at an appreciated level; Major stated that the ERM parity was "a rate at which industry can compete" if it controlled its costs and argued that ERM membership would lead to "discipline" and lower inflation. But senior officials later admitted privately that they chose to enter when the market rate had appreciated in order to bear down on inflation. Most academic analysts also concluded that Britain entered the ERM at an overvalued parity.[19]

During the late 1980s, CBI officials had supported ERM entry to stabilize sterling and were disappointed when Thatcher and Lawson stopped shadowing the mark. CBI surveys in the spring of 1990 showed that a majority of firms favored entry at a lower parity of about 2.80 marks. Industrial firms did not immediately complain about the level of sterling's ERM parity; as Christopher Johnson observed, "the advocates of entry in both the government and the CBI were so relieved that Thatcher had dropped her opposition that they did not look the gift horse in the mouth, in case it was no longer on offer the following week." But disquiet with the level of sterling grew over the next few months; by early 1991, industrialists and some economists stated that although they supported ERM membership, the British recession required lower interest rates and, implicitly, currency depreciation.[20]

The government's strategy was to use the ERM to reduce inflation and create space for lower interest rates to offset a deep recession. Between joining the ERM in October 1990 and the Conservative Party's narrow victory in the general election of May 1992, the government was able to cut interest rates nine times, from 15 percent to 10 percent, while inflation fell from 10 percent to 4 percent. But by mid-1992, the recession had not ended, creating political pressure for interest rates to go even lower. Such a move was inconsistent with maintaining sterling's ERM parity, especially after the Bundesbank raised interest rates in mid-July and sterling began to depreciate.

The government's first responses were to intervene on the foreign exchange market and to reaffirm its commitment to the ERM. Lamont made a widely publicized speech in early July rejecting devaluation or withdrawal from the ERM on the grounds that either move would require higher interest rates; Major also reiterated the government's commitment to its ERM parity. When this did not end speculation against sterling, in early September the Treasury arranged a 10-billion ECU loan from international banks to augment the Bank of England's reserves and to demonstrate Britain's commitment to sterling's current exchange rate.[21]

Speculation against sterling continued, and Lamont tried unsuccessfully to persuade the Germans to reduce interest rates and refused to allow formal discussions of realignments at the Ecofin meeting in Bath in early September 1992. Although Treasury officials would later claim in interviews that they might have accepted a devaluation of sterling against the mark earlier in the summer if accompanied by many other ERM currencies, by the time market pressure became intense in early September, they did not want to be "forced" by speculation to devalue along with other weak currencies.[22] Over the weekend of 12–13 September, German officials contacted some of their European counterparts about a general realignment of ERM parities in exchange for a reduction in German interest rates. The British refused to participate in a general realignment that did not include the French franc, and in the end only the Italian lira was devalued, effective on 14 September. Most investors thought the small interest-rate reductions of the Bundesbank accompanying the devaluation would not allow the Bank of England to make large enough cuts in its own interest rates to stimulate the British economy while maintaining sterling in the ERM. On Tuesday, 15 September, sterling closed just above its lower ERM fluctuation band. That evening a wire service reported an interview given to the German newspaper *Handelsblatt* in which Bundesbank president Schlesinger seemed to imply that sterling and other currencies should devalue. When the foreign exchange markets in Europe opened the next day, the Bank of England had to intervene on the foreign exchange markets with about 15 billion pounds, or roughly half its reserves (in accordance with the rules of the ERM the Banque de France and Bundesbank also intervened heavily by buying sterling). The bank raised interest rates to 12 percent at 11 A.M. with little effect; a further increase to 15 percent that afternoon also failed to stop sales of sterling. Unwilling to raise interest rates further or to devalue, the British government indefinitely "suspended" sterling's participation in the ERM and allowed the currency to float. At an emergency meeting of the European Community's Monetary Committee that evening, the British tried to persuade other governments to suspend the entire ERM until after the French referendum the following Sunday, but the latter refused and in the communiqué simply "took note" of the British decision.[23]

Sterling Floats

Sterling depreciated rapidly after withdrawal from the ERM and by early 1993 had fallen about 20 percent below its former parity. Major and Lamont decided that the best way to proceed outside the ERM was to reduce interest rates aggressively to promote economic growth and the government's popularity. The interest rate increases of 16 September were reversed the next day, and by January 1993 interest rates had been cut from 10 percent to 6 percent. Despite comments from Major that there were "fault lines" in the ERM that needed to be corrected, at the next meeting of the Monetary Committee on 28 September, the British did not present any detailed plans to reform the mechanism and evinced little enthusiasm for rejoining.[24]

While other European countries tried to maintain their commitment to monetary union by reducing fiscal deficits and establishing the predecessor to the European Central Bank during the mid-1990s, the Major government developed a new monetary model that gave little direct attention to the exchange rate. The government announced that it would target the inflation rate with the intention of keeping the rate of increases in consumer prices (excluding mortgage interest rates) between 1 and 4 percent and below 2.5 percent by the end of the sitting Parliament in 1997. The government also announced "monitoring ranges" for the monetary aggregates M0 and M4 and stated that decisionmakers would take the exchange rate into account when implementing policy.

But announcing an inflation target was not enough; the government had to make its target credible to the financial markets after it had changed course and withdrawn from the ERM. Major chose to address this problem through institutional changes that gave the Bank of England some independence from the government. This was intended to convince investors that the Treasury would not wait until strong inflationary pressures developed before increasing interest rates. Beginning in 1993, the central bank produced and published its own forecast of the inflation rate. Although the chancellor remained responsible for ordering changes in interest rates, the Treasury institutionalized the monthly meetings between the chancellor and governor in which such changes were discussed. In April 1994, the government began releasing the minutes of these meetings with a six-week lag. The minutes summarized recent economic and financial developments, the views of the governor and chancellor, and the chancellor's decision regarding the level of interest rates.

Chancellor Kenneth Clarke and Bank Governor Eddie George often held different views about interest rates and the influence of the exchange rate on monetary policy. In April 1995, George argued that the condition of the domestic economy did not call for a change in interest rates, but he also felt that policy might have to be tightened if the recent depreciation of sterling to record lows against the mark was not reversed. Clarke disagreed and ruled out an immediate interest-rate increase. During the next three meetings, George held to his position, arguing that sterling's deprecation called for an increase in interest rates to maintain credibility and to keep inflation within the bottom half of the target range by 1997, but was again overruled by Clarke. The government and central bank resolved this conflict by allowing sterling's nominal effective exchange rate to appreciate by almost 17 percent between August 1996 and March 1997, despite complaints from industry that appreciation damaged its international competitiveness. Appreciation served the interests of the Bank of England by reducing import prices and inflationary pressures and allowed the government to delay increasing interest rates until after the 1997 general election.[25]

The Labour government elected in 1997 recognized that the partial autonomy granted to the Bank of England by its predecessor had serious political drawbacks. The government remained responsible for, and would be blamed for, unpopular monetary policy decisions. The potential for government interference also reduced the ability of the central bank to use its reputation as an independent guardian against inflation to keep interest rates lower than they otherwise would be. One of the first actions of Prime Minister Tony Blair and Chancellor Gordon Brown was to grant full independence to the Bank of England. On May 6, Brown announced the creation of a Monetary Policy Committee made up of Bank of England officials and outside experts that would have authority to control interest-rate policy in order to achieve the government's target inflation rate of 2.5 percent. This new policy did not mark a fundamental shift in the priority that both Conservative and Labour governments attached to domestic rather than external stability. It occurred less than a year before most other member states agreed to create an independent but supranational European Central Bank to manage the single currency. Although the Labour government was now convinced of the merits of central bank independence, it was unwilling to achieve this goal through international cooperation. Instead, ministers preferred to give up control over interest-rate policy to the domestic central bank that would be responsible for meeting a domestic inflation target rather than for ensuring exchange-rate stability. And Labour continued the Major government's policy of acquiesing to sterling appreciation, which produced strong complaints from industry and trade unions but had the advantages of keeping inflation and interest rates low.[26]

France: The Politics of Competitive Disinflation

Until 1993 the franc did not experience significant real appreciation because of France's low inflation rate. Decisionmakers used heavy foreign exchange market intervention coordinated with Germany and increases in interest rates to defend the currency from speculation in 1992. They felt that devaluation would have weakened their political and market credibility but would not have increased competitiveness significantly. But by the summer of 1993 the economy had entered a deep recession, and a new French government was less willing to continue raising interest rates to maintain the franc's ERM parity. The French agreed to widen the ERM fluctuation bands when the Bundesbank refused to lower its interest rates in August 1993 but did not take advantage of the wider bands to reduce interest rates or to depreciate the franc, despite the fact that the currency had now appreciated in real terms. During the mid-1990s, governments fought against opponents on both the left and the right in order to reduce the budget deficit below the Maastricht Treaty criterion of 3 percent of GDP.

French exchange-rate politics and policies in the 1990s differed from those of earlier periods in important ways. Governments placed priority on keeping the exchange rate stable and inflation low rather than on promoting growth and competitiveness through occasional devaluation. French industry continued to favor lower interest rates and currency depreciation, but banks and other financial firms had weaker ties to industry and preferred that the government concentrate on monetary and fiscal policies that would promote economic stability. This divergence of preferences reduced the political power of industry and created space for governments to concentrate on stabilizing the nominal exchange rate and reducing the budget deficit in preparation for participation in monetary union.

Competitive Disinflation

A major preoccupation of French governments in the late 1980s and 1990s was the ability of the Bundesbank to set a floor for interest rates in the

ERM, and they initiated monetary union negotiations to address this asymmetry. In late 1991, French officials also began complaining about the effects of German fiscal policy on the ERM, noting that large German budget deficits after unification led the Bundesbank to raise interest rates in Germany and thus in other states in the ERM. But with the French economy growing and inflation very low (by June 1991, French inflation was lower than German inflation for the first time in eighteen years), there was little political pressure for a devaluation to improve competitiveness or to allow a reduction in French interest rates.[27]

This benign environment facilitated implementation of a new monetary strategy called "competitive disinflation." In the early and mid-1980s, governments had devalued periodically to offset the loss of competitiveness brought about by real appreciation of the franc. By the end of the decade the franc was at a competitive level and the inflation rate had fallen to low levels. Competitive disinflation held that in these circumstances, the authorities should induce a real depreciation of the franc by pushing the French inflation rate below that of its major competitors while stabilizing the nominal exchange rate in the ERM. Governments resisted both market pressures and quiet suggestions from Bundesbank officials for devaluation of the franc or revaluation of the mark on several occasions between 1989 and 1992. Their justification was that devaluation would do little to improve the competitiveness of French industry during a period of rapid export growth and low inflation but would undermine any credibility with financial markets that the authorities had accumulated over the past few years.[28]

Competitive disinflation is often depicted as an abandonment of earlier priorities on growth and competitiveness in favor of achieving low inflation at any cost.[29] But competitive disinflation shared important similarities with earlier French policies. The long-term goal remained increasing the competitiveness of the French economy. As the following sections make clear, French governments remained far from indifferent to the level of the exchange rate and interest rates. They discouraged speculation when the exchange rate was at a competitive level from 1988 to 1992 but thereafter encouraged franc depreciation against the dollar and complained about the depreciation of other ERM currencies. Competitive disinflation also supported French governments' position in the monetary union negotiations. Their advocacy of low inflation and exchange-rate stability helped convince German negotiators to agree to share power over monetary policy.

Defending the Franc, 1992

The day after Danish voters rejected the Maastricht Treaty in a referendum in June 1992, Mitterrand declared that France would hold a referendum on the treaty on Sunday, 20 September. He hoped that a successful referendum would reinforce political support for monetary union throughout Europe and divide the right-wing opposition parties in France.[30] During the summer, most of the Union pour la Démocratie Française (UDF), as well as most senior bankers and the peak-level business association, the Patronat, came out in support of the Treaty, but elements of the Rassemblement pour la République (RPR) opposed it.[31] The Socialist government, supported by the UDF and parts of the RPR, mounted a forceful campaign in favor of approval (including opposing a realignment of the franc in early September), and on 20 September French voters narrowly approved the Treaty.

The franc became the next target of speculative attack after the suspension of sterling and the lira from the ERM on Wednesday, 16 September. When the positive results of the referendum failed to lift the franc from just above its floor in the ERM on Monday, 21 September, French and German officials implemented a joint defense of the currency that they had discussed the previous weekend. The Banque de France and Bundesbank undertook coordinated intervention in the foreign exchange markets, with the German central bank openly intervening "intramarginally" to support the franc. Early Wednesday morning, the Banque de France raised the 5-to-10 day repurchase rate from 10.5 percent to 13 percent and issued a joint statement of the French and German finance ministries and central banks, drafted over the weekend, which argued that the franc's ERM parity was justified by economic fundamentals and ruled out a devaluation. By the end of the week, the franc had appreciated to well above its floor against the mark, and the Banque de France was able to reduce its interest rates. Coordinated intervention, public statements, and increased French interest rates stopped speculation against the franc in November after the collapse of the Swedish krone's peg to the ECU and devaluations of the Spanish peseta and Portuguese escudo. Pressure on the franc declined in late January 1993 because of lower German interest rates and the fact that most weak currencies had either devalued within, or suspended their membership in, the ERM.[32]

The successful defense of the franc's parity was a remarkable event in the history of the EMS for a number of reasons. First, the Bundesbank intervened intramarginally to support the franc, one of the few times it had done so. Second, it announced its intervention; public statements from the Bundesbank, closely coordinated with French officials, helped convince investors that the franc's parity would be defended aggressively.[33] Third, the scale of intervention by the German and French central banks was enormous, exceeding the intervention European central banks undertook before the lira and sterling withdrew from the ERM. In the week after 16 September, the Banque de France spent the equivalent of 80 billion francs—about 80 percent of its foreign exchange reserves—and drew on credits of equal size from the Bundesbank. The Bundesbank, in turn, spent somewhere between 10 and 30 billion marks purchasing francs that week and more than 80 billion marks in September intervening on the foreign exchange markets.[34] Fourth, despite the significant liberalization of French financial markets in the late 1980s, officials successfully persuaded commercial banks to keep their three-month lending rates below the official short-term interest rates that the Banque de France raised to defend the currency.[35]

Defending the Franc, 1993

After the March 1993 parliamentary election delivered a victory to the right-wing UDF-RPR coalition, Edouard Balladur became prime minister, and Edmond Alphandéry took the post of finance minister. Like Major in Britain, Balladur was intent on lowering interest rates as it became clear that France was experiencing a serious recession. Lower interest rates also might placate the increasingly vocal complaints of French industrialists that the franc was overvalued against the many currencies that had devalued or withdrawn from the ERM. In a Louis Harris poll of 402 business leaders conducted in late 1992, 71 percent favored lower interest rates to promote growth rather than continuing with the policy of competitive disinflation. Major firms in the insurance, food processing, transportation, and other industries complained about France's high interest rates publicly and to Industry Minister Alain Madelin.[36] But the Bundesbank was reluctant to reduce interest rates quickly since German inflation still stood at 4 percent. By mid-June, the French had cut short-term interest rates to 7.25 percent, the same level as the Bundesbank's discount rate. The next week, after the Bundesbank decided not to reduce interest rates, the Banque de France reduced its intervention rate to 7 percent, just below the German discount rate, and the franc actually appreciated against the mark. French officials saw this as evidence of the credibility they had earned through competitive disinflation and openly called for the franc to share the mark's role as the anchor of the ERM or for the rapid development of some sort of monetary union among a small group of member states. German officials expressed hostility to both of these ideas.[37]

In early July 1993, Alphandéry gave an interview in which he suggested that the next Franco-German Economic and Finance Council meeting feature discussions about coordinated reductions in French and German interest rates. Interpreting Alphandéry's comments as an attempt to apply political pressure on the Bundesbank, German finance minister Theo Waigel canceled the meeting.[38] The next week, the Bundesbank did reduce interest rates, and the Banque de France followed this move. Nonetheless, the hint of open conflict between French and German governments led investors to begin selling large quantities of francs. On Monday, 12 July, the Bundesbank intervened intramarginally by buying francs, and Waigel issued a statement supporting the franc's ERM parity. The release of figures on 21 July showing that the German money supply was growing more quickly than the Bundesbank's target further increased pressure on the franc as it became less likely that the German central bank would reduce interest rates in the near future. The next day, both the Banque de France and the Bundesbank intervened, the German and French finance ministries and central banks issued another statement supporting the bilateral parity, and the Banque de France raised its overnight lending rate from 7.75 percent to 10 percent.[39]

These actions stabilized the franc until the next Thursday, when the Bundesbank Council lowered its Lombard rate from 8.25 percent to 7.75 percent but did not change its discount rate. Reading this as unwillingness to change domestic interest rates very much on the basis of exchange-rate considerations, investors began selling francs despite heavy intervention by European central banks.[40] By Friday the Banque de France had almost exhausted its reserves and stopped intervening when the franc reached the bottom margin of its ERM fluctuation band. The rules of the EMS required that the Bundesbank intervene marginally in unlimited quantities to support the franc, and French officials hoped that the Bundesbank would reduce interest rates again rather than intervene on a massive scale and swell the German money supply.[41]

Disturbed by the amount of Bundesbank intervention, German officials requested a meeting of the Monetary Committee for the next day, Saturday, 31 July, and Waigel called a meeting of Ecofin for Sunday. During the Monetary Committee meeting, the French refused to devalue or to raise interest rates and called on Germany to reduce its interest rates. German government and Bundesbank officials rejected the idea of changing interest rates for exchange-rate reasons and insisted that they could not intervene indefinitely to support the franc.[42] Having failed to reach agreement, the Monetary Committee left the problem to the Ecofin ministers. Balladur and Alphandéry proposed that Germany temporarily suspend its membership in the ERM, on the grounds that the inflation and high interest rates produced by German unification were the real cause of the speculation against the franc's ERM parity. The Dutch and Belgians scuttled this solution by threatening to follow Germany out of the mechanism. German negotiators countered with the idea of widening the ERM fluctuation bands, and the ministers eventually agreed to widen them to ±15 percent. This allowed the French to deny that they had devalued the franc while reducing both speculation against the currency and the Bundesbank's need to intervene to support it.[43]

Economic Austerity and the Drive Toward Monetary Union

The government did not take advantage of the new ERM fluctuation bands to quickly reduce interest rates and allow the franc to depreciate significantly against the mark for three reasons. First, the intervention in late July 1993 had depleted the Banque de France's foreign currency reserves. In early August, the central bank had a deficit in its foreign exchange holdings of 180 billion francs, and higher interest rates would allow it to replenish its holdings of foreign currency. Second, Balladur had good political reasons to stress his European credentials and support for monetary integration. He hoped to run for president in 1995, and although his government was a coalition of the RPR and the UDF, he had little support from the Gaullists. There was a near insurrection against the policy of competitive disinflation from both senior and rank-and-file RPR members, and the leader of the party and potential rival for the presidential nomination, Jacques Chirac, withheld support for the government during the monetary crises of 1993 until late July. This meant that Balladur would need the support of the pro-European UDF to have a chance of winning the presidency.[44]

Third, the government argued that on balance depreciation would harm the French economy. Leaders held that the franc was not greatly overvalued and that French firms should be able to compete in international markets at the prevailing exchange rate. Depreciation would erase in one stroke all the credibility that the government had earned since implementing the policy of competitive disinflation, and this credibility allowed the Banque de France to keep interest rates lower than they would be otherwise. They stressed that the widening of the ERM bands was a temporary response to market pressures that they hoped to undo in the near future.[45] In early 1994, the government granted independence to the Banque de France in accordance with the Maastricht Treaty. Central bank officials made it clear through their subsequent policy announcements and willingness to raise interest rates when the franc depreciated that their primary goal was to continue to stabilize the franc against the mark.[46]

Unlike in the 1970s and early 1980s, when economic downturns were met with exchange-rate depreciation, the Balladur government chose not to respond to the recession and high unemployment of the early 1990s with currency changes. This decision left it with fiscal policy as its only macroeconomic tool, and the government allowed the budget deficit to increase to nearly 6 percent of GDP in 1993. To begin meeting the Maastricht Treaty's fiscal convergence criteria, in September 1994 the government introduced a budget package that cut spending in 1995 by 25 billion francs. These efforts were undertaken despite the fact that unemployment stood at over 12 percent and showed few signs of falling.

Efforts to meet the Maastricht criteria soon became embroiled in the presidential election campaign of 1995. The two candidates of the center-right, Balladur and Chirac, both emphasized that unemployment was the biggest challenge facing France. Chirac, who won the election, was particularly ambiguous about the tensions between achieving the Maastricht Treaty's convergence criteria and reducing unemployment. But once Chirac won the election, his government under Prime Minister Alain Juppé was quick to emphasize monetary stability and fiscal consolidation over growth and employment.[47] Two factors seem to have been behind Chirac's newfound commitment to economic austerity and meeting the Maastricht criteria. First, he apparently believed that the short-run economic sacrifices necessary to join monetary union were in the long-run interests of both the country and his political career. Second, Chirac concluded that, with monetary policy now no longer under political control, the best way to boost domestic demand was with a tighter fiscal policy that would reduce inflationary pressures and allow the Banque de France to cut interest rates. The government's budget, introduced in September 1995, aimed to meet the Maastricht Treaty budget criteria by cutting the budget deficit to 3.5 percent of GDP in 1996 and under 3 percent of GDP in 1997. Particularly controversial was Juppé's plan to eliminate the social security system's deficit by 1997 by rejecting Chirac's campaign pledge of tax cuts, freezing civil service pay and limiting the growth of military spending, and effectively reducing pension benefits. In a widely publicized television interview Chirac backed this program by declaring that his priority was to reduce the budget deficit. Labor unions mobilized large-scale strike actions in November and December and shut down most of France's public transport and utilities, and on 7 December 1995, more than 1 million people took part in demonstrations throughout the country. Chirac again publicly backed the Juppé plan, although the government did agree to consult the unions and make modest changes to its budgetary program.[48] The Socialist-Communist government elected under the leadership of Lionel Jospin in 1997 made a similar choice. Jospin's campaign promised to tackle the problems of unemployment and slow growth more aggressively. But upon taking office, the government was faced with a choice between further fiscal consolidation to meet the Juppé government's target of a budget deficit of 3 percent of GDP in 1997 or abandoning this target and perhaps derailing monetary union. Jospin chose the former course, raising corporate and personal taxes and social security charges.[49]

Italy: Monetary Expansion and Fiscal Contraction

As discussed in Chapter 3, Italian governments offset real appreciation of the lira with devaluations to maintain competitiveness during the 1970s and

1980s. This policy stance changed to one of opposing devaluation and of accepting real appreciation in 1989–1992 for three reasons. First, large capital inflows kept the lira near the top of its ERM fluctuation band until mid-1992, making it difficult to arrange a devaluation even if one had been desired. Second, the central bank had to maintain high interest rates to finance the large government budget deficit. Cutting interest rates, which would have reduced capital inflows and weakened the lira, could have made it difficult or impossible to attract investment into government bonds.[50] Third, the Amato government that took office in mid-1992 was committed to reducing the budget deficit and to negotiating a new industrial relations and wage accord. Government and central bank officials felt that a devaluation would have made it much more difficult to "hold the line" during these negotiations, and they were willing to "live dangerously" by trying to maintain the exchange rate until the negotiations were completed.[51]

Industry initially was willing to put off a change in the lira's parity until after these goals had been achieved. But firms began agitating for a devaluation during 1992, and after the lira's withdrawal from the ERM, they encouraged governments to allow the currency to depreciate and to concentrate on reducing the budget deficit in order to lower interest rates and secure Italian participation in the single currency. Banks and financial firms either supported these goals or did not lobby the government to tighten monetary conditions.

Capital Inflows and Lira Appreciation

Italian monetary and fiscal policies moved in contradictory directions until 1992. Governments strengthened their commitment to the ERM by devaluing only once between 1987 and early September 1992, narrowing the lira's fluctuation band from ±6 percent to ±2.25 percent in 1990, and abolishing remaining capital controls. Given the fact that Italian inflation remained higher than German inflation (see Table 5.1), stabilization of the lira in the ERM meant that the currency appreciated in real terms. Fiscal policy aggravated this loss of competitiveness. Until the summer of 1992, governments failed to reduce large annual budget deficits. The Banca d'Italia had to keep short-term interest rates high to finance the budget deficit, and this attracted capital inflows and appreciated the lira toward the top of its ERM fluctuation band for much of 1990 and 1991.

By late 1989, high domestic interest rates made the lira one of the strongest currencies in the ERM, and some industrialists, including the vice president of Confindustria, Innocenzo Cipolletta, advocated devaluation to restore competitiveness. But officials responded by strengthening their exchange-rate commitment by narrowing the lira's fluctuation band in the ERM to ±2.25 percent. The governor of the Banca d'Italia, Carlo Azeglio

Ciampi, supported this as a way to increase the credibility of monetary policy and reduce interest rates. An implicit reason for central bank support was that a tighter external constraint on monetary policy, combined with real appreciation of the lira, would increase political pressure for a reduction of the fiscal deficit.[52]

The government and central bank carefully organized progress toward the narrow band and capital account liberalization in order to control further appreciation of the lira. By July 1989 capital inflows led the lira to surpass its theoretical narrow ERM upper band despite the fact that the Banca d'Italia had been trying to "practice" keeping the currency in a narrow band. The Banca d'Italia intervened on the foreign exchange markets to depreciate the currency and decided not to match interest-rate increases in other ERM countries in early October. As a consequence, the lira depreciated to 1.5 percent above its central parity by September and to 3 percent below its parity by December. In early January 1990 the authorities announced the move to the narrow band. This involved a "technical" devaluation of the lira's central parity of 3.7 percent, in which the new lower limit under the narrow band was the same as the old lower limit under the wider band. In late April, officials lifted the few remaining capital controls, a move that was timed to encourage foreign investment by Italian residents and to offset foreign exchange inflows and pressure for lira appreciation.[53]

These actions represented an important change in the conduct of monetary and exchange-rate policies. During the 1980s, Italian governments devalued periodically to compensate for much of the loss of competitiveness brought about by real appreciation of the lira. After 1990, the strategy of the Banca d'Italia, supported by Finance Minister Guido Carli, was to use exchange-rate and interest-rate policies to press for a more sustainable fiscal policy.[54] The political logic was that drawing attention to how the large deficit led to higher interest rates and lira appreciation could increase support for significant changes in fiscal policy. The economic logic held that a credible commitment to the ERM and the possibility that Italy might enter monetary union sometime in the 1990s reduced the risk premium attached to the lira and reassured foreign and domestic investors that the government would not resort to inflationary monetary policies to finance the deficit.

The real appreciation of the lira produced by this policy mix dismayed industrial firms and the peak employers' confederation, Confindustria. But instead of directly advocating a devaluation as it had in the past, Confindustria supported the central bank and drew attention to how the policy mix of tight monetary policy, loose fiscal policy, and real appreciation undermined competitiveness. Rapid growth and a lenient international environment (including strong export demand from Germany after unification) had prevented serious problems between 1988 and 1991, but Confindustria did not see this situation as sustainable for very long.[55] This shift in emphasis on the part of the central bank and employers was not very successful in the short term. A political crisis in the spring of 1991 led the government to abandon plans for a corrective minibudget. Instead, the legislature approved new spending without describing how to finance it, and the final budget exceeded the deficit target by 6 percent. The 1992 budget, approved in late 1991, omitted provisions for large-scale privatization meant to reduce the deficit because of a lack of political support within the governing majority for dramatic policy changes before new parliamentary elections in April.[56]

The Lira Exits the Exchange-Rate Mechanism

The Italian economy was in a dangerous position when the Danish referendum of June 1992 on the Maastricht Treaty prompted investors to reevaluate the sustainability of ERM parities and Italy's policy mix. The political situation did not help. By mid-1992, exporters were complaining about the overvaluation of the lira and advocating devaluation in private meetings with the government.[57] The general election of April 1992 saw Democrazia Christiana (DC) and the Socialists lose votes but did not produce a clear alternative coalition. Giuliano Amato, a Socialist untainted by the ongoing corruption scandals engulfing the major parties, emerged as prime minister in late June with the support of the DC, the Socialists, and small centrist parties. Amato's priorities included making significant cuts in current government spending, reforming wage agreements between unions and employers, and keeping the lira stable. But there were serious doubts in Italy and abroad that he would have enough political support to translate this program into legislation.[58]

Speculation against the lira occurred from June until September. The Banca d'Italia responded by raising the discount rate from 12 percent to 13.75 percent in July and by intervening intramarginally. Finance Minister Piero Barucci argued for a devaluation of about 10 percent on the grounds that the lira was overvalued and that devaluation would boost competitiveness and economic growth. Ciampi and others in the Banca d'Italia opposed a unilateral devaluation, arguing that it would ruin the central bank's credibility and reduce pressure for significant budget and wage reforms (although Ciampi also complained that German interest rates were "excessively high"). They preferred that Germany revalue the mark or that any devaluation of the lira be accompanied by realignments of most other currencies. Amato decided he could not risk devaluation during the wage and budget negotiations that began shortly after he took office.[59] But dollar depreciation pushed the lira to the bottom of its fluctuation band in the ERM by early September, despite agreement between the union confederations and Confindustria to abolish the wage indexation system and the passage of an emergency budget package by the legislature. The central bank raised the discount rate to 15 percent, the highest level since 1985, and with the Bundesbank intervened heavily.[60] When these measures failed to lift the lira, Barucci and Confindustria director-general Innocenzo Cipolletta convinced the government that a devaluation was necessary.[61] Over the weekend of 12–13 September 1992, Italian and German negotiators agreed on a lira devaluation of 7 percent against other ERM currencies and a reduction in German interest rates. The Italian negotiators apparently preferred a much larger devaluation on the order of 10–15 percent, but Ciampi emphasized that a change of this magnitude would attract French opposition and threaten to unravel the wage agreement of the previous month. Foreign exchange traders quickly took the view that this devaluation was too small to restore stability to the ERM. By Wednesday, the lira was below its floor against the mark, and the next day the government withdrew the lira from the ERM; the currency soon depreciated about 15 percent against the mark.[62]

Currency Depreciation and the Transition to Monetary Union

The Amato government initially hoped to return the lira to the ERM within a matter of days or weeks and did not support British criticisms of the rules of the EMS, but the lira did not reenter the ERM until late 1996 because of domestic political changes that altered governments' economic policy priorities. Beginning with Amato, Italian governments in the 1990s changed the policy mix of their predecessors by pursing fiscal contraction and allowing the exchange rate to depreciate. One reason for this policy change was that most of these governments lacked a strong base in parliament or a long mandate in office, which made it more difficult to convince investors to hold lira.[63]

A more important reason for this policy shift was a change in the social bases of the governing majority. The governments led by DC and the Partito Socialista Italiano (PSI) in the 1980s and early 1990s used their control over state spending to develop extensive patronage networks. The members of these patronage networks were concentrated in the nontradable sector of the economy, such as the civil service, farming, retail, and construction, all of which benefited from a lax fiscal policy.[64] During the early 1990s, Italy experienced a number of fundamental political changes—the moderation of the former Communist Party; the development of the Lega Nord, a regional political movement opposed to the status quo; and the revelation of systematic government corruption—that undermined the legitimacy of the DC and PSI and led to their sudden collapse by 1993.[65] The Amato government's initial tightening of fiscal policy was sustained by a new governing majority with a quite different base of societal support and policy preferences that favored a competitive exchange rate and smaller budget deficits. As discussed above, much of Italian industry felt that a tightening of fiscal policy combined with depreciation would improve their competitiveness, and they supported the emphasis of governments led by former Banca d'Italia officials Ciampi and Lamberto Dini on fiscal consolidation and their willingness to countenance currency depreciation and to delay reentering the ERM until late 1996. With the exception of the short-lived Berlusconi government, the Ciampi, Dini, and Prodi governments of the 1990s relied on the reformed Communist Party, the Partito Democratico della Sinistra (PDS), for support in parliament (see Table 5.2). These governments also secured the political backing of the three major labor confederations for their economic policies. The largest labor confederation and the one with the closest ties to the PDS—the Confederazione Generale Italiana del Lavoro—was more heavily concentrated in sectors exposed to international competition than the traditional ally of the DC (the Confederazione Italiana Sindacati Lavoratori) or that of the PSI (the Unione Italiana del Lavoro). The confederations negotiated changes to wage-bargaining institutions and pension spending with the Amato, Ciampi, and Dini governments and played a supportive role in formulating the governments' crash programs of fiscal adjustment.[66]

Beginning with the Amato administration, governments concentrated most of their political capital on fiscal policy. Coalition governments supported by the PDS managed to reduce the budget deficit from nearly 10 percent of GDP in 1993 to under 3 percent of GDP in 1997, during a period of slow economic growth and high unemployment. Most of labor and man-

Table 5.2 Composition of Italian Governments, 1989–1998

Government	Parties in Government	Period in Office
Andreotti VI	DC-PSI-PSDI-PRI-PLI	August 1989–April 1991
Andreotti VII	DC-PSI-PSDI-PLI	April 1991–June 1992
Amato	DC-PSI-PSDI-PLI	June 1992–April 1993
Ciampi	DC-PLI-PSDI-PSI-PDS[a]	April 1993–May 1994
Berlusconi	FI-AN-Lega Nord	May 1994–January 1995
Dini	PDS-PPI-Lega Nord[a]	January 1995–June 1996
Prodi	PDS-PPI-Dini-Verdi	June 1996–October 1998

Source: James I. Walsh, "Political Bases of Macroeconomic Adjustment: Evidence from the Italian Experience," *Journal of European Public Policy* 6, no. 1 (March 1999): 70.

a. Nonpolitical government; parties indicated in table supported government in confidence votes.

Abbreviations: AN (Alleanza Nazionale), DC (Democrazia Christiana), Dini (Lista Dini), FI (Forza Italia), PDS (Partito Democratico della Sinistra), PLI (Partito Liberale Italiano), PPI (Partito Popolaro Italiano), PRI (Partito Repubblicano Italiano), PSDI (Partito Socialista Democratico Italiano), PSI (Partito Socialista Italiano), and Verdi (Greens).

ufacturing industry supported this drastic retrenchment in order to improve competitiveness and to ensure Italian participation in monetary union. Yet these governments remained vulnerable to criticisms and defections from coalition partners. The nonpolitical governments under Prime Ministers Ciampi and Dini had to avoid contentious spending cuts in pensions, social security, and health care that some coalition members and public sector unions opposed. Even the government led by Prime Minister Romano Prodi had to move carefully after winning the 1996 legislative elections because of support it received in the legislature from the Rifondazione Comunista party.

Upon taking office, the government forecast a deficit of 4.5 percent of GDP in 1997, or 1.5 percent above the criterion for participation in monetary union. Initially, the government planned to reduce the deficit to 3 percent of GDP only in 1998 in order to avoid conflict with the RC and because it calculated that other member states would allow Italy into the first wave of monetary union if it came reasonably close to meeting the deficit criterion.[67] But in September 1996, the government reversed course and decided on a crash program to reduce the deficit below 3 percent of GDP in 1997 rather than in 1998, having been convinced that failure to do so would exclude Italy from initial participation in monetary union. Spanish prime minister Jose Maria Aznar made it clear that his government was determined to meet the convergence criteria in 1997 and was not interested in joining Italy in persuading the other member states to adopt a flexible interpretation of the deficit criterion. Prodi and Ciampi also received indications from European Commissioner Mario Monti and European finance ministers that France and Germany were unlikely to approve such a flexible interpretation. Prodi's shift in emphasis was backed by the PDS, and Prodi assured the RC and the union confederations that the issue of pension reform would not be discussed until 1998. The government's new budget, which the RC eventually supported, cut spending in other areas and raised taxes, including the introduction of a one-time "euro" tax that would be credited to taxpayers after Italy entered monetary union.[68]

In accordance with the Maastricht Treaty, the legislature granted the Banca d'Italia statutory independence from the government when implementing monetary policy in 1994. The central bank used its newfound independence to press for two goals. First, Governor Antonio Fazio encouraged governments to tighten fiscal policy and noted that smaller budget deficits would reduce inflationary pressures and create space for lower interest rates.[69] Second, the central bank focused on keeping inflation low by refusing to cut interest rates quickly or in large increments. It reduced rates only when inflation was falling, economic growth was slowing, and the government was cutting the budget deficit. This behavior led to complaints from the government, industry, and the union confederations, all of whom favored larger and more rapid reductions in borrowing costs.[70]

Although the government could no longer influence interest rates directly, it could and did delay reentry into the ERM. One of the criteria for joining monetary union was that each member state participate in the ERM for two years "without severe tensions" and without devaluing "on its own initiative." Italy had to rejoin the ERM sometime in 1996 if it wished to participate in the single currency. Reentry was one of the top priorities of the Prodi government elected in June 1996, but it delayed action until November as it tried to balance two competing interests regarding the lira's new central parity. Confindustria and prominent industrialists and bankers such as Cesare Romiti of FIAT and Mario Sarcinelli of the Banca Nazionale del Lavoro warned against entering at an uncompetitive rate. Conversely, the French, who had complained vociferously about the depreciation of the lira after 1992 and in 1995, warned against a "hasty" reentry at an overly competitive parity. After a weekend of hard bargaining in Brussels, the lira reentered the ERM on 25 November. The Italian delegation, led by Budget and Finance Minister Ciampi, requested a parity against the mark near the prevailing market rate between 1,000 and 1,010 lire; most other member states preferred a more appreciated rate between 950 and 960 lire. They eventually settled on a parity of 990 lire after a "masterful performance" by Ciampi in persuading his colleagues that this parity was sustainable and not too competitive.[71]

Comparisons and Conclusions

A modest preponderance of the evidence in this chapter supports the institutional explanation for group preferences and government policy choices. British financial and industrial firms continued to hold different policy preferences, and governments consistently chose to ignore industry's demands. This occurred despite the fact that the British economy was quite open to trade and investment with Europe in the 1990s. The preferences of French finance and industry began to diverge in the 1990s as their ties weakened, and decisionmakers gave less priority to keeping the franc at a competitive level than they had in the 1970s and 1980s. This shift in preferences and policies was not associated with significant changes in the openness of the French economy. Exceptional circumstances led finance and industry in Italy to support currency appreciation in the early 1990s, but thereafter their preferences and governments' exchange-rate policies shifted back to keeping the lira at a competitive level.

With the exception of Italy in 1990 and 1991, industry in all three countries opposed policy measures that produced real currency appreciation. British industry supported ERM entry for sterling in the late 1980s but opposed the government's efforts to encourage appreciation before entry in 1990. The CBI preferred a lower parity than the one chosen and then hoped that sterling's wide fluctuation band could be used to offset further real appreciation. In contrast, some representatives of the City supported "uncapping" sterling's informal mark parity in 1988 to reduce domestic inflation (see Chapter 3) and felt that sterling's real appreciation before and after joining the ERM also would help reduce inflation.

French industry was not very politically active on exchange-rate policy because the franc was stable and did not appreciate significantly in real terms until late 1992. French industrialists began advocating depreciation and lower interest rates when the franc appreciated following the suspension of sterling and the lira from the ERM, the devaluation of other European currencies, and the continued depreciation of the dollar. But in contrast to earlier periods, French banks supported efforts to maintain the franc's ERM parity even when the currency experienced real appreciation. Government and central bank officials persuaded French commercial banks not to raise their lending rates when the Banque de France increased its short-term interest rates in the early 1990s, thus easing the impact on domestic borrowers, including industry, of stabilizing the currency. But these steps also meant that banks sided with the government's priorities rather than those of industry. By 1996 both finance and industry were reasonably satisfied with the combination of low inflation, stable exchange rates in Europe, and appreciation of the dollar.

For most of the 1990s, Italian industry opposed real currency appreciation. Confindustria advocated devaluation to restore competitiveness in 1992, supported the government's decisions to delay rejoining the ERM, and lobbied hard to ensure that the lira reentered the mechanism at a competitive rate in 1996. Italian financial firms either supported or did not oppose industry's demands. The exception was the period 1989–1992, when Confindustria abandoned the goal of an immediate improvement in competitiveness through devaluation and supported the Amato government's efforts to secure significant changes to fiscal policy and industrial relations.

On balance, these preferences accord more closely with the expectations of the institutionalist explanation. Weak ties between finance and industry continued to be associated with different exchange-rate policy preferences. Although French industry continued to prioritize stabilizing the franc at a competitive level, the preferences of banks and financial firms changed in important ways. French finance supported occasional devaluations to restore competitiveness during the 1980s, but not during the 1990s. Banks began to endorse the strategy of competitive disinflation not long after the deregulation and capital market liberalization that weakened ties between finance and industry in the late 1980s. Italy, in contrast, experienced little structural change to its financial system, so it is not surprising that for most of the 1990s banks and industry continued to favor policies such as devaluation that kept the lira at a competitive level. The exception to this generalization was the period from 1989 to early 1992, when Confindustria felt that the real appreciation induced by stabilizing the lira in the ERM would pressure the government to reduce the budget deficit and the labor unions to reform the wage indexation system. This shift in industry's preferences proved to be only temporary for two reasons. First, real exchange-rate appreciation initially was not very costly because of strong domestic and export demand. Industry shifted back to its traditional position of backing a devaluation once the Italian and European economies entered recession in 1992. Second, Confindustria hoped that commitment to the ERM and the goal of monetary union would allow the Banca d'Italia to reduce industry's borrowing costs. Heavy speculation in the summer of 1992 undermined this tactic by forcing the central bank to raise interest rates to defend the lira's ERM parity.

Table 5.3 summarizes governments' responses to changes in the level and stability of exchange rates in the 1990s. The Thatcher, Major, and early Blair governments preferred to place the burden of adjustment on industry by countering inflationary pressures in 1989–1992 and 1997–1998 with real currency appreciation rather than with higher interest rates. Although British industry favored ERM entry in the late 1980s to stabilize sterling, senior Conservative party politicians were divided on the issue. Thatcher and Major agreed to join the ERM at an appreciated parity only when they concluded that this was a viable way to increase the government's credibility and to reduce both inflation and interest rates before the next election. Thus they dropped most of the "Madrid conditions" for entry, encouraged sterling appreciation in the summer of 1990, and decided to enter the ERM when the predicted path of inflation turned down, rather than waiting for actual inflation to fall. These actions ensured that sterling subsequently appreciated in real terms and allowed the Bank of England to reduce interest rates from 15 percent in October 1990 to 10 percent by September 1992. When the Conservative Party was reelected in April 1992, the political logic of this strategy was finished. The Major government therefore had little reason to counter speculation against ERM parities in the summer of 1992 as forcefully as the French and Italians. British officials first pressed the Germans to reduce interest rates rapidly and significantly but refused to raise British interest rates to stabilize sterling in the ERM. Until almost literally the last hour, the government countered speculation against sterling solely with foreign exchange market intervention rather than interest-rate increases. When it became clear that substantial increases in interest rates

Table 5.3 Changes in Exchange Rates and Policy Choices, 1988–1999

Britain		France		Italy	
Changes in Exchange Rate	Policy Choices	Changes in Exchange Rate	Policy Choices	Changes in Exchange Rate	Policy Choices
Real appreciation, 1988–1990	Encouraged appreciation and brought sterling into ERM to reduce inflation	No real appreciation, 1988–1992	"Competitive disinflation," refused to devalue	Real and nominal appreciation, 1988–1990	Narrowed fluctuation band; encouraged outward investment
Real appreciation, 1990–1992	Reduced interest rates as sterling appreciated	Speculation against ERM parity, 1992	Defended parity with intervention and interest rate increases	Real appreciation, 1990–1992	Accepted appreciation to encourage fiscal and labor market reforms
Speculation against ERM parity, 1992	Defended parity with intervention only; withdrew from ERM	Real appreciation and speculation against ERM parity, 1993	Defended parity, then widened fluctuation bands; subsequently opposed depreciation	Speculation against ERM parity, 1992	Defended parity with interest rate increases and intervention; devalued and withdrew from ERM
Nominal and real depreciation, 1993–1995	Acquiesced to depreciation and cut interest rates during period of low inflation	Speculation against ERM parity and slow economic growth, 1995	Defended parity with intervention and interest rate increases; also began reducing budget deficit to qualify for monetary union	Nominal and real depreciation, 1993–1995	Accepted depreciation and focused on reducing budget deficit
Nominal and real appreciation, 1997–1998	Encouraged appreciation to counter inflationary pressures			Nominal stabilization and real appreciation	Rejoined ERM and continued to reduce budget deficit in order to qualify for monetary union

might be the only way to maintain sterling in the ERM, the British floated the currency and rapidly reduced interest rates. Thereafter they instituted new monetary policy arrangements—inflation targeting and central bank independence—that gave priority to keeping inflation low rather than to stabilizing the exchange rate. British exchange-rate policy choices in the 1990s were quite similar to those of the earlier decades analyzed in Chapter 3.

In contrast, French governments in 1993–1995 and Italian governments in 1989–1992 broke with earlier choices by acquiescing to real currency appreciation. But the Italian and possibly the French episodes involved exceptional circumstances rather than fundamental alterations of governments' policy priorities. French officials made two arguments against devaluation. First, they pointed out that devaluation would contribute little to industry's competitiveness because of the very low inflation rate, but that it would lead to higher rather than lower interest rates as investors lost confidence in the government's commitment to price stability. Second, they held that devaluation might provide some short-term relief to French industry but would undermine the long-term project of monetary union in the late 1990s. French officials were determined to keep the franc's exchange rate stable in the ERM with huge levels of foreign exchange market intervention and higher interest rates during a period of sluggish economic growth. Although it is difficult to draw definitive conclusions from a single episode, it is possible that the weakening of ties among banks, industry, and government officials in the late 1980s and early 1990s led financial firms to attach greater importance to low inflation and less importance to a competitive value for the franc, breaking their earlier pattern of allying with industry on exchange-rate issues. This, in turn, would have reduced pressures on policymakers to maintain the franc at a competitive level and allowed them to turn their attention to increasing their credibility in financial markets by meeting the conditions for monetary union laid out in the Maastricht Treaty: low inflation, small budget deficits, and a stable exchange rate.

Further support for this contention comes from comparing the French and Italian experiences. During the recession of 1992–1995 the French stuck to the franc's ERM parity by keeping interest rates high. After 1993 they began reducing the budget deficit, producing a quite restrictive and anti-inflationary policy mix. Italian governments, in contrast, chose to offset a tighter fiscal policy with currency depreciation that boosted industry's competitiveness. Although governments in both countries wanted to tighten fiscal policy in order to qualify for participation in monetary union, the fact that bank-industry ties and the political importance of competitiveness remained strong may have been one reason that Italian officials were unwilling to tighten monetary policy as well.

To a much greater extent than in earlier periods, officials, especially in the Banca d'Italia, used the exchange rate both to enhance their credibility and to press for labor market and fiscal policy reforms from 1989 to 1992. What explains this shift in emphasis? An accurate description of Italian economic policy during this period must look to political immobility and crisis. The Italian political system, characterized by weak coalition governments with short time horizons, made political leaders unwilling and unable to confront the structural problems of the Italian economy. Repeated failure to control government spending was the best example of this trend. Although deficit spending during the late 1970s and early 1980s was a possibly appropriate response to recession, large deficits after the mid-1980s threatened the central bank's ability to vary monetary policy over the business cycle. Industry's position shifted from advocating devaluation to accepting appreciation of the lira in the early 1990s to secure changes in other areas of economic policy. Industrialists and senior central bank officials hoped that a stronger commitment to the ERM would force politicians to implement changes in fiscal and labor market policies that would improve long-term competitiveness. In some ways, this attitude mirrors the British experience of using real exchange-rate appreciation in the early 1980s to force industrial firms to restructure and to reduce their costs. But it took long-term political crisis to prompt this pattern of Italian policy, whereas the British pattern had been consistent since the 1970s. Thus, while both British and Italian governments maintained overvalued currencies in the early 1990s and both suspended membership in the ERM after heavy speculation in September 1992, the Italian experience was an exception to earlier patterns of political mobilization and policy choice, but the British experience was not.

Notes

1. See, for example, Francesco Giavazzi and Marco Pagano, "The Advantage of Tying One's Hands: EMS Discipline and Central Bank Credibility," *European Economic Review* 32 (1988): 1055–1082; Jilleen R. Westbrook, *The Effects of Exchange Rate Pegging on the Credibility of Stabilization Programs: An Empirical Investigation of the European Monetary System* (Ph.D. diss., Claremont Graduate School, May 1993).
2. *Economist*, 3 July 1993, 45.
3. *Reuters*, 17 July 1989; *Financial Times*, 7 October 1989, 28; *Reuters*, 4 February 1991; and interviews with officials of European central banks.
4. Barry Eichengreen and Charles Wyplosz, "How to Save the EMS," in *The Monetary Economics of Europe: Causes of the ERM Crisis*, ed. Christopher Johnson and Stefan Collignon (Rutherford: Fairleigh Dickinson University Press, 1994), 168.
5. The full statement is reprinted in *Financial Times*, 29 August 1992, 2.

5. Piero Barucci, *L'Isola Italiana del Tesoro: Ricordi di un Naufragio Evitato 1992–1994* (Milan: Rizzoli, 1995), 51.

7. *Financial Times*, 11 December 1992, 2; and *Guardian*, 2 December 1992, 1.

8. *Financial Times*, 7 September 1992, 1; and *Financial Times*, 15 September 1992, 2.

9. *Financial Times*, 11 December 1992, 2; and interviews with Treasury officials.

10. See the comments of David Nickson, the chairman of the CBI, reported in *Financial Times*, 11 March 1988, 1; see also *Financial Times*, 16 May 1988, 1; and CBI press releases dated 16 March and 10 October 1988.

11. *Reuters*, 26 October 1988; and interviews with official of the British Bankers' Association and a senior banker.

12. *Financial Times*, 25 March 1988, 11; *Reuters*, 28 March 1988; *Reuters*, 13 May 1988; and Nigel Lawson, *The View from No. 11: Memoirs of a Tory Radical* (New York: Doubleday, 1993), 835–845.

13. See, for example, Thatcher's comments about discussions on this issue with Lawson in early May in Margaret Thatcher, *The Downing Street Years* (New York: HarperCollins, 1993), 709, and on announcing the Conservative Party's manifesto for elections to the European Parliament on June 15, reported in *Financial Times*, 23 May 1989, 24.

14. Geoffrey Howe, *Conflict of Loyalty* (London: Macmillan, 1994), 577, 580, 582; Lawson, *The View from No. 11*, 932–934; and Thatcher, *The Downing Street Years*, 712.

15. *Reuters*, 28 October 1989; *Reuters*, 29 October 1989; and *Financial Times*, 31 October 1989, 13; a good review of these developments is Philip Norton, "The Conservative Party from Thatcher to Major," in *Britain at the Polls, 1992*, ed. Anthony King (Chatham, NJ: Chatham House Publishers, 1993).

16. *Financial Times*, 24 February 1990; and *Independent*, 12 March 1990, 22.

17. *Daily Telegraph*, 31 March 1990, 1; Thatcher, *The Downing Street Years*, 719–720; and *Sunday Times*, 20 May 1990, 1.

18. *Financial Times*, 6 October 1990, 1; *Independent*, 17 June 1990, 9; and Thatcher, *The Downing Street Years*, 722–723.

19. Major's comments are reported in *Financial Times*, 12 October 1990, 8; and *Financial Times*, 16 October 190, 13. Senior treasury officials told me in confidential interviews that the desire to reduce inflation drove the timing and rate of sterling's ERM membership. A good independent analysis that comes to the same conclusion is Ray Barrell, Andrew Britton, and Nigel Pain, "When the Time Was Right? The UK Experience of the ERM," in *European Monetary Upheavals*, ed. David Cobham (Manchester: Manchester University Press, 1994).

20. Quotation from Christopher Johnson, "The UK and the Exchange Rate Mechanism," in *The Monetary Economics of Europe: Causes of the EMS Crisis*, ed. Christopher Johnson and Stefan Collignon (Rutherford: Fairleigh Dickinson University Press, 1994), 89. On the evolution of industry's views, see CBI press release dated 16 May 1989; *Financial Times*, 11 October 1989, 1; Confederation of British Industry, "Exchange Rate Mechanism and UK Manufacturing Exports" (London: Confederation of British Industry, March 1990); *Financial Times*, 6 April 1990, 12; *Financial Times*, 31 January 1991, 9; *Financial Times*, 20 February 1991, 12; and *Financial Times*, 24 December 1991, 6.

21. *Financial Times*, 11 July 1992; *Financial Times*, 13 July 1992, 1; and *Financial Times*, 4 September 1992, 1.

22. Interviews with Treasury officials.

23. *Financial Times*, 18 September 1992, 1.

24. Secretariat General, Conseil des Communautés Européennes, "1604ème session du Conseil Economie/Finances," 8854/92, Brussels, 28 September 1992.

25. David Cobham, "The UK's Search for a Monetary Policy: In and Out of the ERM," manuscript, University of St. Andrews, November 1995, 17–19, 26–27; and Philip Stephens, *Politics and the Pound: The Conservatives' Struggle with Sterling* (London: Macmillan, 1996), 294–295.

26. *The Times*, 11 July 1997; and *The Times*, 28 July 1997.

27. See the speech of Banque de France governor Jacques de Larosière reported in *Reuters*, 17 September 1991; see also *Financial Times*, 8 February 1991, 3; and *Reuters*, 26 September 1988.

28. Jean-Claude Trichet, "Dix Ans de Désinflation Compétitive en France," *Les Notes Bleues de Bercy*, 16–31 October 1992, 1–12; and interviews with former Banque de France and European Commission officials; see also Bérégovoy's comments reported in *Reuters*, 6 November 1989.

29. Jean-Paul Fitoussi, *Le Débat Interdit: Monnaie, Europe, Pauvreté* (Paris: Arléa, 1995).

30. *L'Année Politique, Économique et Sociale 1992* (Paris: Éditions du Grand Siècle, 1993), 215; and *Financial Times*, 4 June 1992, 4.

31. *L'Année Politique, Économique et Sociale 1992*, 552–553; *Financial Times*, 11 June 1992, 2; *Financial Times*, 16 September 1992, 2; and interview with senior banker. A minority of firms in the Patronat opposed the treaty, and the organization did not take an official position on the referendum. However, the president of the Patronat made a widely publicized appeal to French voters to approve the treaty.

32. *Financial Times*, 20 November 1992, 2; *Financial Times*, 3 December 1992, 1; *Le Monde*, 4 December 1992, 3; *Le Monde*, 5 January 1993, 14; *Le Monde*, 6 January 1993, 1; *Financial Times*, 6 January 1993, 1; *Financial Times*, 5 February 1993, 2; and *Le Monde*, 6 February 1993, 1.

33. Pierre Jacquet, "La Désunion Monétaire Européenne," *Politique Étrangère* 58, no. 1 (1993): 443–453.

34. *Le Monde,* 24 September 1992, 1; *Financial Times*, 2 October 1992, 1; and *Monthly Report of the Bundesbank* 44, no. 11 (November 1992): 14.

35. *Financial Times*, 3 October 1992, 2; and interview with senior French banker.

36. Éric Aeschimann and Pascal Riché, *La guerre de sept ans: Histoire secrète du franc fort 1989–1996* (Paris: Calmann–Lèvy, 1996), 160, 178–180; and Philippe Bauchard, *Deux Ministres Trop Tranquilles* (Paris: Belfond, 1994), 152, 163.

37. See, for example, the comments of André Icard of the Banque de France, reported in *Financial Times*, 23 June 1993, 16; see also *Le Monde*, 10 February 1993, 24; and *Financial Times*, 30 June 1993, 2.

38. *Financial Times*, 25 June 1993, 1.

39. *Financial Times*, 10 July 1993, 1; *Le Monde*, 14 July 1993, 1; *Le Monde*, 19 July 1993, 20; *Financial Times*, 23 July 1993, 1; *Le Monde*, 24 July 1993, 1.

40. *Financial Times*, 30 July 1993, 2.

41. Aeschimann and Riché, *La guerre de sept ans*, 222–226; *Le Monde*, 2 August 1993, 1; *Financial Times*, 31 July 1993, 1; and *Financial Times*, 3 August 1993, 1.

42. *Financial Times*, 2 August 1993, 1, 4; and Bauchard, *Deux Ministres Trop Tranquilles*, 164–165.

43. Bauchard, *Deux Ministres Trop Tranquilles*, 165; David R. Cameron, "British Exit, German Voice, and French Loyalty: Defection, Domination, and Cooperation in the 1992–93 ERM Crisis," paper prepared for the Annual Meeting of the American Political Science Association, Washington, DC, September 1993, 46–48; *Financial Times*, 2 August 1993, 1; and *Financial Times*, 3 August 1993, 3; and *The Times*, 12 August 1993, 1. The Dutch and German central banks separately agreed to keep their bilateral exchange rates within the old band of ±2.25 percent.

44. Aeschimann and Riché, *La guerre de sept ans*, 242.

45. *Financial Times*, 3 August 1993, 3; *Le Monde*, 3 August 1993, 13; *Financial Times*, 13 August 1993, 2; and *L'Année Politique, Économique et Sociale 1993* (Paris: Éditions du Grand Siècle, 1994), 469–470.

46. *Financial Times*, 28 January 1994, 2; and *Financial Times*, 22 April 1994, 2.

47. *Le Monde*, 23 June 1995, 1.

48. Aeschimann and Riché, *La guerre de sept ans*, 301–317; *Financial Times*, 21 September 1995, 2; *Financial Times*, 14 December 1995, 1; and *Le Monde*, 27 October 1995, 1.

49. *Financial Times*, 21 July 1997; and *La Tribune*, 24 September 1997.

50. Barucci, *L'Isola Italiana del Tesoro*, emphasizes this.

51. Quotations from interview with senior Banca d'Italia official.

52. Istituto Affari Internazionali, *L'Italia Nella Politica Internazionale: Anno Diciottesimo 1989–1990* (Rome: Franco Angeli, 1991), 195–202; and *La Repubblica*, 12 December 1989, 1.

53. "Accostamento al 1 Luglio," *Bancaria* (December 1989): 21; Istituto Affari Internazionali, *L'Italia Nella Politica Internazionale: Anno Diciottesimo 1989–1990*, 208–212; and Angelo De Mattia, "La Lira Stretta," *Politica ed Economia* 21, nos. 1–2 (January–February 1990): 50–51.

54. Guido Carli, *Cinquant'anni de Vita Italiana* (Bari: Laterza, 1993), 395–396; and "La Tenuta del Cambio," *Bancaria* (November 1990): 23.

55. "I Piccoli Passi della Liberalizzazione Valutaria," *Bancaria* (February 1990), 50–51; *Reuters*, 24 May 1990; *Il Mondo Economico*, 7 July 1990, 24–27; and interview with Banca d'Italia official.

56. *Financial Times*, 30 December 1991, 2; *Il Mondo Economico*, 29 April 1991, 20–21; and *Il Mondo Economico*, 15 June 1991, 20–21.

57. *Il Mondo Economico*, 6 July 1991, 22–23; *Il Mondo Economico*, 21 September 1991, 24–25; and *Il Mondo Economico*, 22 February 1992, 26–27; *Il Mondo Economico*, 2 May 1992, 40–42; and interview with Banca d'Italia official.

58. *Il Mondo Economico*, 13 July 1992, 30–33; and interview with former Banca d'Italia official.

59. Barucci, *L'Isola Italiana del Tesoro*, 38; *Financial Times*, 11 September 1992, 1; *Il Mondo Economico*, 1 August 1992, 31–33; *Il Mondo Economico*, 22 August 1992, 6; Carlo Santini, "An Italian Perspective," in *The European Currency Crisis*, ed. Paul Temperton (Cambridge: Probus, 1993), 238, 240; and interview with former Banca d'Italia official.

60. *Il Mondo Economico*, 19 September 1992, 8; and Santini, "An Italian Perspective," 242.

61. Barucci, *L'Isola Italiana del Tesoro*, 53.

62. *Financial Times*, 11 December 1992, 2; and Barucci, *L'Isola Italiana del Tesoro*, 53, 351.

63. This section draws on James I. Walsh, "L'incerto cammino verso l'Unione monetaria," *in Politica in Italia*, ed. Luciano Bardi and Martin Rhodes (Bologna: Il

Mulino, 1998), 109–130; and James I. Walsh, "Political Bases of Macroeconomic Adjustment: Evidence from the Italian Experience," *Journal of European Public Policy* 6, no. 1 (March 1999), 66–84.

64. Luigi Graziano, *Clientelismo e sistema politico: Il caso dell'Italia* (Milan: Franco Angeli, 1980); and Gianfranco Pasquino, "Rappresentanza degli interessi, attività di lobby e processi decisionali: Il caso italiano di istituzioni permeabili," *Stato e Mercato* 21 (1987): 403–429.

65. A good overview is Mark Gilbert, *The Italian Revolution: The End of Politics Italian Style?* (Boulder, CO: Westview, 1995).

66. Michael Braun, "The Confederated Trade Unions and the Dini Government: 'The Grand Return to Neo-Corporatism?'" in *Italian Politics: The Stalled Transition*, ed. Mario Caciagli and David I. Kertzer (Boulder, CO: Westview, 1996), 205–221; Carlo Chimenti, *Il Governo dei professori* (Florence: Passigli Editori, 1994); and Jeffry Frieden, "Making Commitments: France and Italy in the European Monetary System, 1979–1985," in *The Political Economy of European Monetary Integration*, ed. Barry Eichengreen and Jeffry Frieden (Boulder, CO: Westview, 1994), 25–46.

67. *Financial Times*, 17 July 1996.

68. *Financial Times*, 27 September 1996; *La Stampa*, 22 September 1996; and *La Stampa*, 1 October 1996.

69. For example, see the overview of Governor Antonio Fazio's attitudes toward fiscal policy in *Financial Times*, 14 February 1996.

70. Walsh, "L'incerto cammino verso l'Unione monetaria."

71. *Financial Times*, 26 November 1996; see also *La Stampa*, 22 May 1996; *La Stampa*, 28 September 1996; *Financial Times*, 15 October 1996; and *La Stampa*, 24 November 1996.

6

Conclusions and Prospects

The successful implementation of monetary union in 1999 is one of the most important instances of international cooperation since World War II. My purpose in this book has been to explain the political processes that contributed to this dramatic development. To do so, I gathered and analyzed evidence to test theories of exchange-rate politics and the creation of international institutions. The primary contribution of this book, then, is empirical; rather than seeking to develop new theories, I use evidence to compare and test the explanatory power of existing ones.

This concluding chapter serves three purposes. I first pull together the evidence from the preceding four chapters to summarize the findings regarding political sources of exchange-rate policy and international institutions. I also discuss the findings' implications for theoretical work on the role of institutions in structuring actors' preferences and in promoting learning and the development of shared beliefs. The second section analyzes European monetary institutions negotiated in the 1990s, such as the Stability and Growth Pact that governs national fiscal policies, to see if these more recent developments accord with the finding that distributional bargaining rather than learning drives agreement on specific institutional rules. The concluding section explores the findings' implications for future societal exchange-rate policy preferences, the operation of the European Central Bank, and the development of new European institutions to underpin the single currency.

The Findings: Exchange-Rate Politics

Chapters 3 and 5 evaluate the ability of the openness and institutional approaches to explain variations in groups' preferences and exchange-rate policy from the 1970s through the 1990s. The key difference between these approaches is how they explain the origins of groups' preferences. The openness approach holds that the principal cleavage is between producers in the tradable goods sector, who are exposed to overseas competition, and those in the nontradable goods sector, who are limited to the domestic market. Tradable goods producers, such as manufacturing industry, prefer policies that keep their goods competitive on world markets by preventing real appreciation of the exchange rate; nontradable goods producers prefer the opposite set of policies to reduce the prices of imports. The political power of each group depends in large measure on their economic importance; the influence of tradable goods producers over the government's exchange rate policy increases as the economy becomes more open to international trade and investment.

The institutional explanation agrees that industry has a strong and indisputable preference for policies that prevent real currency appreciation. But the exchange-rate preferences of banks and financial firms in the nontradable goods sector vary with their ties to industry. In countries where banks have strong ties to industry, such as France and Italy, the policy preferences of banks and industry become interdependent: industry relies on banks for most of its outside finance, and banks must ensure that their industrial clients remain profitable and can repay their loans. Having only weak exchange-rate preferences of their own, banks come to share industry's preferences for stable and competitive exchange rates. Where banks do not have close ties to industry, as in Britain, their principal preference is for economic policies that keep inflation low. Close bank-industry ties have two political effects. First, they enlarge the coalition favoring fixed and competitive exchange rates. Second, a small number of banks aggregate the preferences of a large and heterogeneous industrial sector and effectively transmit these preferences to monetary authorities. Weak ties between banks and industry lead each group to favor the preferences outlined by the openness approach. In such a situation, the authorities face a divided set of preferences and are more likely to subordinate exchange-rate policy to other goals, such as reducing inflation or unemployment.

The evidence in Chapters 3 and 5 supports the contention of both approaches that industry opposed real currency appreciation and instability and also supports the hypothesis that institutionalized ties to industry structure the preferences of banks. Consider the response of industry to episodes of real currency appreciation in each country. Sterling experienced significant real appreciation in the early 1980s, early 1990s, and late 1990s. On each occasion, representatives of British industry lobbied the government to take actions to reverse appreciation. Representatives of the peak business organization, the Confederation of British Industry (CBI), as well as individual industrialists close to government ministers, actively pushed in the early 1980s for a looser monetary policy and exchange-rate depreciation. Sterling appreciation after 1988 also attracted the opposition of the British manufacturing sector. The CBI supported bringing sterling into the exchange-rate mechanism (ERM) in 1990 to reduce currency instability but objected to the way this policy was implemented. The Thatcher and Major governments used ERM entry to appreciate sterling and reduce inflation quickly, not to bring about currency stability. Once Britain was a member of the ERM, industrialists called on the government to reduce interest rates more quickly and to utilize sterling's wide fluctuation band to allow the currency to depreciate. Industry also demanded lower interest rates and depreciation when sterling appreciated sharply outside of the ERM in 1997–1998.

The French franc appreciated in real terms until 1987, and French industry advocated devaluations within the ERM to maintain competitiveness. This lobbying activity was particularly forceful in the early 1980s, when the relatively high French inflation rate, combined with stable nominal exchange rates between devaluations, led to rapid real appreciation. During this period, representatives of French industry and finance split between those favoring devaluation of the currency within the ERM and those who advocated withdrawal from the ERM. The former group eventually won out in this struggle, but what is notable is that neither faction questioned the need for devaluation to restore competitiveness. Representatives of French industry did not lobby very actively on exchange-rate questions from 1988 until the currency experienced further real appreciation in 1993, when they pushed for lower interest rates even if this threatened the franc's position in the ERM.

The real exchange rate of the Italian lira faced constant pressure for appreciation from the late 1970s to the early 1990s because Italian inflation was consistently higher than inflation rates in the rest of Europe. This pressure was particularly severe in the early 1980s and early 1990s. During the early 1980s Italian industry successfully advocated devaluation as the best way to maintain its competitiveness. The peak business association, Confindustria, directed attention to the real appreciation of the currency in its publications and meetings with political leaders. The heads of both private and state-owned firms advocated devaluation privately and in public. Although industrialists also supported policies to reduce inflation and increase the Italian economy's long-term competitiveness, especially through cutting budget deficits and reforming wage-bargaining institutions, they did not do so at the expense of advocating short-term improvements in competitiveness through devaluation. This position changed somewhat in the early 1990s, when industry briefly attached more importance to structural changes in fiscal and wage policies and downplayed the importance of devaluation in order to achieve these changes.

Although industry shared common preferences across the three countries, banks and financial firms did not. The primary preference of British finance was to reduce inflation quickly. During the early 1980s, economists and bankers in the City supported the Conservative government's attempts to target the money supply, increase interest rates, and encourage sterling appreciation. Few called for Britain to join the ERM during this period, although this attitude changed somewhat after sterling began a long period of depreciation in late 1981. Representatives from the financial sector (as well as the Treasury and Bank of England) then began to view ERM membership as a useful way to limit sharp depreciation of the currency. An additional but related reason for growing support for ERM membership after 1984 was the government's failure to meet its money supply targets; ERM entry could provide a new nominal anchor for monetary policy. Thus financial firms gradually began to support ERM entry, but this support had little to do with concerns about the competitiveness of British industry. Rather, ERM membership was interpreted as a way to hold the government accountable by providing a clear nominal anchor for policy choice. Indeed, some representatives of the City opposed ERM membership in 1988 on the grounds that entry would lead the government to loosen, not tighten, monetary policy when inflation seemed to be increasing.

In contrast, banks in France and Italy usually allied with industry on exchange-rate policy questions. The preferences of French banks, industrial firms, and economic policy officials were quite similar until the early 1990s. During the early 1980s, two of the most prominent representatives of those calling for withdrawal from the ERM or a steep devaluation were leading members of the French financial community—Georges Plescoff of Suez and Jean Deflassieux of Crédit Lyonnais. Also during this period, no one in the government or the financial sector advocated the British approach of deliberate currency appreciation to reduce domestic inflation. The institutions of French finance experienced significant changes in the second half of the 1980s, including the weakening of the ties between banks and industry. When the franc appreciated in real terms in 1993, French bankers did not advocate devaluation but kept domestic interest rates low to support the government's policy of remaining in the ERM.

Italian finance also supported the preferences of industry. Some bankers and officials in the early 1980s did feel that real appreciation was an appropriate way to force Italian industry to reduce its costs, challenge the unions, and become more competitive. But these individuals were exceptional; most did not complain when the authorities decided to seek devaluations. The exception to this pattern was the early 1990s, when the private sector acquiesced to real appreciation of the lira in the hope that this would help achieve the goals of reducing the budget deficit and labor costs.

These variations in the preferences of banks and financial firms were associated with different exchange-rate policy choices. British governments exhibited the least interest in stabilizing the exchange rate at a competitive level, preferring instead to focus on reducing inflation. The Conservative Thatcher government that took office shortly after the negotiation of the EMS in 1979 made reducing the high inflation rate its primary goal, with a domestic strategy of raising interest rates, targeting the money supply, and abolishing capital controls. This led to sharp real and nominal appreciation of sterling, which ministers publicly encouraged in order to reduce import prices and to place additional downward pressure on inflation. Beginning in late 1981, sterling started to depreciate and continued to do so until late 1986. The government accepted the fact that the currency could not remain at the high levels reached at the beginning of the decade but did not encourage quick depreciation toward more a more realistic exchange rate. Instead, it engaged in foreign exchange market intervention and increased interest rates when depreciation threatened to accelerate and feed back into domestic inflation.

By 1982 technical problems with the relationships among interest rates, inflation, and the rate of growth of the money supply led the Thatcher government to begin searching for a more reliable nominal anchor for monetary policy. Many ministers, officials, and financial analysts now backed membership in the ERM as a secure and easily understood anchor for policy and the expectations of financial markets. They also felt that ERM membership would provide assistance from European central banks during periods of sharp exchange-rate depreciation. British industry also favored ERM entry but for different reasons, namely to stabilize sterling against European currencies after it had depreciated to a competitive level. Despite strong support for ERM entry among some senior cabinet members, some financial firms, and the CBI, Margaret Thatcher refused to bring sterling into the mechanism until 1990. She gave many reasons for opposing entry, including an ideological position favoring market determination of exchange rates, the asymmetry of the ERM, and an unwillingness to give up control over interest-rate policy for political reasons. With the exception of the CBI, even proponents of ERM membership did not interpret it in terms of its impact on domestic industry. The most forceful advocate of entry, Nigel Lawson of the Treasury, saw the ERM as an external constraint on monetary policy that, like targeting the money supply, would provide a clear signal of the government's intentions and willingness to maintain a restrictive monetary policy and to keep inflation low.

Sterling's entry into the ERM in 1990 bears out this point. Only after intense and direct pressure from some of her most senior advisers, as well as from industry, did Thatcher agree in principle to entry in 1989. The conditions and timing of entry were carefully calculated to support the Conservative Party's electoral goals. By mid-1990 Chancellor John Major was able to convince Thatcher that joining the ERM would allow reductions in interest rates to offset slowing economic growth and rising inflation. The government encouraged sterling to appreciate over the summer of 1990 to further reduce inflation—the exact timing of entry seems to have been chosen to distract attention from the Labour Party's annual conference. The Thatcher and Major governments cut interest rates five times between October 1990 and the summer of 1992. Major wished to continue reducing interest rates in 1992 below levels prevailing in Germany but now was prevented from doing so by the need to stabilize sterling against other ERM currencies. This explains why the government waited until the last possible moment to raise interest rates in an unsuccessful attempt to end speculation against sterling's ERM parity in September 1992. The subsequent choices of the Major and Blair governments to target the domestic inflation rate and to grant independence to the Bank of England, even when sterling appreciated at the end of the 1990s, continued this pattern of giving priority to internal rather than external stabilization.

French and Italian governments attached greater weight to exchange-rate stability at competitive levels even when this conflicted with reducing the inflation rate. The French devalued frequently—once every year from 1981 to 1987, with the exceptions of 1984 and 1985—to compensate for the loss of competitiveness implied by the relatively high inflation rate. Italian governments secured even more and larger devaluations of the lira. They also allowed the currency to fluctuate within larger bands than the other ERM currencies, which permitted gradual depreciation before a devaluation.

At first sight, the clear cross-national differences in exchange-rate policies during the 1980s seem to break down in the 1990s as governments in France and Italy allowed their currencies to appreciate in real terms in the ERM. Closer analysis demonstrates that unusual circumstances led to this shift in policy, which was sustained only in France.

French governments began attaching more importance to reducing inflation and maintaining their credibility in financial markets with the March 1983 decision to devalue but to remain in the ERM. By the end of the decade, stabilizing the franc became the centerpiece of monetary policy, and the emphasis shifted to the long-term process of improving competitiveness by achieving low inflation rather than by devaluing. The adoption of this "competitive disinflation" strategy coincided with reforms to French financial institutions that increased the transparency and liquidity of capital markets and that removed government incentives for banks to lend to industry. These reforms weakened French finance's dependence on lending to industry and led it to articulate preferences for maintaining the government's anti-inflation credibility by pegging the franc in the ERM. The latent conflict between the preferences of industrial and financial firms surfaced in late 1992, when the economy entered recession and the franc appreciated in real terms due to sharp depreciation of the dollar and many European currencies. A substantial majority of French industrial (but not financial) firms advocated lower interest rates and, implicitly, a devaluation of the franc. For the first time the French government refused these requests, and when necessary raised interest rates to high levels to ward off speculation against the franc's ERM parity before agreeing to widen the regime's fluctuation bands. The Balladur and Juppé governments continued to resist depreciation until 1996, when some relief was provided by the appreciation of the dollar. This changing pattern of exchange-rate politics resulted in part from the weakening of strong ties and shared preferences among bankers, industrialists, and state officials. But it would be an exaggeration to claim that exchange-rate politics in France came to mirror those of Britain. Recall from Chapter 1 that although French capital markets increased in importance and bank lending decreased in importance in the late 1980s, the size, liquidity, and importance of French capital markets do not come close to matching those of Britain, and that some banks and financial firms retained ties to industrial firms through networks of shareholdings.

Italian monetary and exchange-rate policies underwent a gradual shift during the mid-1980s. The primary goal during the 1970s and early 1980s was to accommodate economic shocks and maintain the growth of output. Later in the decade, the Italian authorities placed more emphasis on reducing the still-high inflation rate and stopped devaluing in the ERM, which led to a gradual but noticeable real appreciation of the lira by the early 1990s. Industry temporarily stopped complaining about this real appreciation and joined the central bank in pressing the government to devote political resources to reducing the large budget deficit and tax burden and to reforming wage-bargaining institutions. Industry reverted to its earlier preferences for currency depreciation once the Amato government had begun to reduce the deficit and had brokered an initial agreement between the union confederations and the employers' association. After the devaluation and withdrawal of the lira from the ERM in September 1992, subsequent Italian governments acquiesced to continual depreciation, which promoted industrial profitability and exports.

The simple conclusion that "institutions matter" for politics and policy is trivial alone; a great deal of work by political scientists and economists has demonstrated that institutions such as property rights, executive-legislative relations, politically autonomous regulatory agencies, and so on have an important influence on public policy. But most such work, particularly in the rational choice tradition, starts with assumptions about actors' preference orderings and then demonstrates that institutional arrangements influence how successful these actors are in realizing their preferences. In other words, most institutional analysis focuses on the implications of institutions for actors' strategies of achieving a given goal. In the context of this study, for example, banks that have institutionalized ties with industry can mobilize a large number of firms and transmit their preferences to monetary authorities, which makes industry lobbying more effective. But in addition to shaping actors' strategies, institutions also influence their preference orderings. Thus strong and institutionalized ties with industry lead banks' preferences to shift from keeping inflation low to stabilizing the exchange rate at a competitive level. Relatively little work acknowledges that the institutional environment can shape actors' preference orderings in this way.[1] Thorough analysis must pay attention to both types of institutional effects. Analyzing only institutions' strategic effects might lead one to misspecify actors' preference orderings, whereas focusing solely on the effects of institutions on preferences ignores how actors try to translate their desires into public policy.

The Findings: International Institutions

Chapters 2 and 4 investigate the benefits of creating and strengthening international monetary institutions and the reasons member states agree on particular rules for these institutions. In particular, I investigated why the snake, EMS, and full monetary union closely reflect German preferences for rules that would keep inflation low. I find little support for the contention that policy failure in Britain, France, and Italy led authorities to learn the advantages of the German model for monetary policy or to change their preference orderings regarding institutional rules. Instead, the pattern of outcomes is consistent with the propositions of the distributional bargaining approach, which predicts that national preferences are stable and that outcomes most closely reflect the preferences of the state least interested in reaching agreement.

The negotiations surrounding the creation of the EMS in the 1970s illustrate this conclusion well. Member states' institutional preferences reflected a desire to minimize the cost of adjustment to fixed exchange rates. Germany's low inflation and politically powerful central bank made negotiators unwilling to agree to rules that might require an unwanted relaxation in monetary policy or foreign exchange market intervention. France, Italy, and initially Britain favored rules that would stabilize exchange rates by providing generous credit lines to finance intervention and by having both low and high inflation countries adjust monetary policy. German preferences were met in the final agreement to create the EMS.

The EMS is a difficult test against which to measure the explanatory power of the learning approach, since it was negotiated only a few years after European countries began to experience serious economic difficulty. We are more likely to see the effects of learning in the negotiations in the 1980s over changing the rules of the EMS and creating a full monetary union since these occurred after it became clear that German institutions and practices produced superior economic outcomes in terms of inflation, unemployment, and trade performance. Yet this was not the case; British, French, and Italian negotiators retained the institutional preferences they held in the 1970s. British governments showed no interest in participating in, much less strengthening, the ERM. Thatcher and most of her colleagues opposed the idea of monetary union and reluctantly approved the mandate of the Delors Committee in 1988 to study its implementation. Displeased with the support the committee's report received from other member states, British negotiators tried to delay adoption of its conclusions at the Madrid and Rome summits in 1989 and 1990 and proposed alternatives such as competing currencies and the hard ECU in order to delay moves to monetary union. When presented with the obvious desire of other states to sign a treaty, the British negotiated a clause allowing it to choose to opt out of the most important parts.

French governments pushed to change the rules of European monetary institutions from the 1970s to the 1990s. They preferred rules that would have distributed the burden of policy adjustment more equally and favored using monetary policy to promote economic growth. French negotiators understood that Germany would not agree to rules that threatened higher inflation and eventually accepted all of Germany's major demands regarding the EMS. In the early 1990s, they proved willing to accept a Maastricht Treaty with a very independent European Central Bank, a long delay before the start of full monetary union, and multilateral restrictions on fiscal policies. Like the French, Italian negotiators advocated rules that would distribute the burden of adjustment more symmetrically among countries with different rates of inflation and economic growth. Italian authorities played active and constructive roles during the negotiation of the Maastricht Treaty. Along with the French, they supported a rapid move to full monetary union, rather than the long transition process included in the treaty, and opposed convergence criteria that would stand in the way of Italian participation.

In sum, governments' preferences regarding the rules of European monetary institutions continued to be shaped more by the importance they attached to stabilizing the exchange rate than by the lessons they learned from policy failures and interaction with German officials. With the exception of ERM entry in 1990–1992, British governments had little interest in stabilizing sterling in the context of a formal institution and therefore had no interest in setting international rules for the conduct of macroeconomic policy. French and Italian governments considered it more important to keep their exchange rates stable in the context of European monetary institutions. They were consistent but largely unsuccessful in pressing for changes to the rules of such institutions that would redistribute the burden of policy adjustment onto Germany.

We are left, then, with two seemingly contradictory empirical findings. On the one hand, institutionalized interaction and learning had little effect on states' preferences regarding the design of European monetary institutions. But on the other hand, the institution of close bank-industry ties did influence groups' exchange-rate policy preferences. How, then, are we to explain the fact that institutions influenced preferences at the domestic but not the international level? The reason may have to do with the different ways that international and domestic institutions acquire legitimacy. National patterns of economic and security policy often remain consistent because they are based on long-standing and politically legitimate institutions such as democratic elections, particular forms of state and social organization, and national memories and ideologies that promote shared beliefs and learning about political practices and policy priorities.[2] Few international institutions, including the EMS, possess such powerful sources of legitimacy. Instead, states and other actors evaluate and legitimate international institutions based on their ability to solve specific functional problems, such as encouraging exchange-rate policy cooperation. Even international institutions that do a good job of solving such problems may have difficulty acquiring enough deep-rooted legitimacy to promote learning since decisionmakers from different states may continue to hold different, domestically rooted beliefs about the proper policy tools and goals.[3]

The Transition to Monetary Union

Although Chapters 2 and 4 demonstrated that little learning about rules for European monetary institutions occurred in the 1970s and 1980s, it is possible that more recent institutional developments might show stronger evidence of learning. To address this issue, I consider the fates of three major proposals in the 1990s for institutional innovations to be implemented with the move to full monetary union: the creation of a Stability and Growth Pact to limit national fiscal policies, negotiations over a Euro Council to manage the external monetary policy of the single currency and to further strengthen mechanisms for economic policy coordination, and the creation of a new ERM. I also analyze the decisions taken in 1997 and 1998 as to which member states would participate in monetary union and the composition of the leadership of the European Central Bank. With the exception of the negotiation of the new ERM, each of these episodes support the contention that power-based bargaining, rather than learning, continued to drive agreement on institutional rules.

The Stability and Growth Pact and the Euro Council

In late 1995 the German government, backed by the Bundesbank, proposed negotiation of a Stability Pact that would place permanent constraints on national fiscal policies after the move to full monetary union in 1999. Two concerns motivated this proposal. First, the Germans feared that some member states might continue to have difficulty keeping their budget deficits within acceptable limits after they adopted the single currency, the euro. Second, both the government and the Bundesbank thought that although the Maastricht Treaty laid out straightforward fiscal policy guidelines that would apply *before* the transition to full monetary union, it was unclear what would happen after the introduction of the single currency. In particular, German negotiators felt that the Maastricht Treaty did not make it clear that the 3 percent of gross domestic product (GDP) ceiling for budget deficits would apply after 1999 and that its provisions for sanctions against member states determined to have excessive deficits were too complicated and subject to political judgment. Finance minister Theo Waigel proposed three core elements to the Stability Pact: (1) that the rate of growth of public spending should be held below the rate of GDP growth over the medium term, (2) that member states continue to respect the 3 percent budget deficit ceiling even during economic recessions (with exceptions approved by Ecofin) and pledge to keep deficits to 1 percent of GDP over the business cycle, and (3) that member states violating these prescriptions be required to make a non-interest-bearing deposit that would be converted into a fine if the deficit was not reduced.[4]

All member states except France and the Netherlands came out against the idea of a Stability Pact, and even these two countries had serious reservations about the severity and automatic imposition of sanctions implied by Waigel's proposal. There was general agreement that member states should have a limited amount of time to correct an excessive deficit, but most governments opposed the idea that monitoring begin as soon as such a deficit was detected, preferring to take action only after a deficit had existed for a period of time. Germany compromised on this point in September 1996, agreeing to give member states up to a year to correct an excessive deficit before the imposition of sanctions. Key differences remained, however, over how Ecofin would decide that an excessive deficit in violation of the pact existed, and this issue was not resolved until the European Council summit meeting in Dublin in December 1996. German negotiators preferred that the pact enumerate quantitative criteria that member states would have to meet or face automatic penalties. The French, joined by most other member states, opposed the idea of automatic decisions according to quantitative criteria and preferred that Ecofin have some leeway to make political judgments about "exceptional circumstances" that impinged on fiscal policy before declaring that an excessive deficit existed or imposing sanctions. The Germans made a modest concession on this issue, but the remainder of the pact addressed Germany's major concerns. The political agreement reached in Dublin required member states to keep the budgets close to balance over the medium term and to submit annual "stability programs" to Ecofin. On the question of defining and sanctioning an excessive deficit, the Stability Pact held that a decrease in the rate of growth of 2 percent or more would qualify as exceptional circumstances, and Ecofin would vote by qualified majority on whether exceptional circumstances existed when the decline in economic growth fell between 2 percent and 0.75 percent. Member states with output declines of less than 0.75 percent could not claim exceptional circumstances. Ecofin could impose sanctions in the form of a non-interest-bearing deposit on member states that had not corrected an excessive deficit within a year and convert this deposit to a fine after two years. At French insistence, the Germans also agreed to soften the tone of the agreement by renaming it the Stability and Growth Pact.[5]

The Juppé government in France was ambivalent about the proposed Stability Pact, fearing that it could limit member states' ability to deal with unemployment and slow growth, and acquiesced only after winning some flexibility in Dublin. The Jospin government that took office in spring 1997, shortly before the European Council in Amsterdam that would formally approve the pact, forcefully reiterated these concerns and argued that the agreement needed to be renegotiated. Italian officials initially supported Jospin's plea that the pact place more emphasis on growth and employment and create a political counterpart to the European Central Bank.[6] Faced with a potential breakdown in the agreement reached in Dublin, the European Commission and member states started working on a compromise.[7] Commission president Jacques Santer, in discussions with the French, argued that the Stability Pact could not be renegotiated but did propose a supplemental declaration on employment based on articles 102a and 103 of the Maastricht Treaty, which the French and German governments found attractive.[8] The agreement at Amsterdam included the creation of an employment committee that could recommend steps to reduce unemployment as part of the process of surveillance of member states' economic policies, and encouraged the European Investment Bank to open a new lending facility for small and medium-sized firms and for European-wide infrastructure projects, but at the insistence of Germany did not include significant spending on employment and did not alter other parts of the pact.[9]

The French counterpoint to the Stability Pact was a call for the creation of a Euro Council consisting of finance ministers only from member states adopting the single currency. The Euro Council would oversee implementation of the Stability and Growth Pact and be responsible for formulating external exchange-rate policy, coordinating fiscal policy, and serving as a political counterweight to the European Central Bank by advising it on monetary policy. To the Germans this looked like a revival of French demands during the negotiation of the Maastricht Treaty for an "economic government" that might threaten price stability and central bank independence. Bundesbank and German government officials refused to endorse the French ideas until March 1997, when they won a series of important concessions, including that the Euro Council would be an informal, consultative body not subject to the European Union's regular decisionmaking procedures, that it would not discuss monetary policy or impinge on the independence of the European Central Bank, and that political responsibility for exchange-rate policy would remain with the full Ecofin Council.[10] But after reaching agreement among themselves, the French and Germans had difficulty securing formal Ecofin approval for the informal Euro Council. The four member states unlikely to participate in full monetary union from the beginning—Britain, Denmark, Greece, and Sweden—opposed creating a Euro Council limited only to countries adopting the single currency, fearing that it might in effect take over from the full Ecofin group. The compromise reached at the Luxembourg summit in late 1997 held that Ecofin would remain the sole decisionmaking body but that the Euro Council could invite other member states to its discussions that concerned "matters of common interest."[11]

The rules of the Stability and Growth Pact and Euro Council reflected German preferences and power. German negotiators succeeded in pushing through the Stability and Growth Pact's new requirements for the management of the single currency over the opposition of most other member states, although they did concede that member states could temporarily run excessive deficits under restricted circumstances and that Ecofin have some political leeway in interpreting national fiscal policies.[12] The German government also succeeded in whittling down the long-standing French desire for a political counterweight to the European Central Bank by insisting that the Euro Council remain an informal consultative body that would not question the European Central Bank's power to make monetary policy decisions.

The New Exchange-Rate Mechanism

There was little question in the mid-1990s that Britain and Denmark would choose not to participate in the single currency or that economic difficulties in other member states, such as Italy, might prevent them from doing so.

The new exchange-rate mechanism negotiated in 1996–1997 was intended to govern monetary and exchange-rate policy coordination between the euro and such member states. Two questions dominated the negotiations: First, how should the new ERM distribute the burden of adjustment? And second, should participation in the new institution be a requirement for member states that wished to join the single currency after 1999?

The French and German governments hoped that a new ERM would ensure that member states outside monetary union avoided policies that produced large depreciation or heavy speculation against the euro. Upset by the competitive effects of British and Italian withdrawal from the ERM in 1992, the French called for something approaching compulsory participation in the new ERM.[13] German officials' priority was that the major responsibility for exchange-rate stabilization be placed on the countries outside the eurozone to ensure that the European Central Bank's intervention obligations would be limited. In contrast, the Italians, Spanish, and Portuguese, who had devalued in the recent past and feared exclusion from monetary union, favored greater reliance on European Central Bank intervention to support currencies participating in the new ERM.[14] Both groups of countries quickly agreed on the desirability of wide fluctuation bands to make it difficult for speculators to target currencies for devaluation, but they continued to disagree on the distribution of obligations for policy changes and foreign exchange market intervention.[15]

Ecofin reached preliminary agreement on this issue in April 1996, although details were not completed until the Amsterdam summit of the European Council in 1997. The general aim of the new ERM was to stabilize exchange rates while not compromising the European Central Bank's primary mandate of internal price stability. A second aim was to "foster convergence" of member states outside the eurozone by providing them with "a reference for their conduct of sound economic policies." The new ERM is based on bilateral exchange rates against the euro. Currencies may fluctuate within wide bands of 15 percent, although the European Central Bank and individual member states might negotiate tighter bands based on the degree of economic convergence. The member states outside the eurozone, rather than the European Central Bank, bear the principal responsibility to undertake policy adjustments to keep exchange rates stable. When a currency reaches the margin of its fluctuation band, intervention is automatic and unlimited "in principle," but the European Central Bank could stop its intervention "if this were to conflict with their primary objective" of low inflation.[16] The agreement also makes it clear that a major purpose of the new ERM is to promote the convergence of economic policy toward that of the European Central Bank with the aim of facilitating adoption of the single currency.

The British objected to this presumption that the monetary union "outs" would be expected to synchronize their economic policies with those countries in the eurozone. They also feared that the creation of a new ERM would require them to abide by the Maastricht Treaty's convergence criterion that member states participate in the ERM for two years before adopting the single currency. The first concern was met when the other member states agreed that participation in the new ERM would be voluntary, but the second remains unresolved. The British argued that widening the ERM fluctuation bands in August 1993 from 2.25 to 15 percent essentially did away with the ERM and that the criterion therefore would not apply, should Britain apply to join monetary union. Most other member states, as well as the European Commission, hold that the treaty provision applies to the new ERM, therefore requiring British participation for two years before joining monetary union.

There is evidence that learning facilitated agreement on the rules of the new ERM. The member states were quick to agree on the desirability of wide fluctuation bands, having learned in the early 1990s that narrow bands could create inviting targets for speculation against exchange-rate parities. Member states with the best chances of participating in monetary union, including France and Germany, also realized that the size of the eurozone economy and the independence of the European Central Bank would give them a great deal of power to resist pressures to adjust economic policy to balance-of-payments problems. Therefore, they demanded that the burden of adjustment fall on member states not adopting the single currency. Clearly, they had learned from the German experience with the ERM in the 1980s and 1990s the advantages of having a dominant currency and the rules that would facilitate the implementation of an autonomous monetary policy.

The Endgame: Moving to Monetary Union and Creating the European Central Bank

The heads of state and government planned to decide which member states met the Maastricht Treaty's convergence criteria at a meeting of the European Council in early 1998. In 1995 governments agreed that the difficulty of meeting the convergence criteria would make it impossible to move to monetary union in 1997, the first possible date set in the Maastricht Treaty. As late as mid-1997, there were serious doubts that Italy, and perhaps France and Germany, would meet the deficit and debt criteria because their budget deficits exceeded 3 percent of GDP in 1996.[17] France and Germany were likely to allow some leeway interpreting this criterion for each other, since a monetary union without them would make little political or economic sense. But strong opposition within Germany to monetary union with fiscally profligate member states made the participation of

Italy and other Mediterranean states less certain. Many politicians, Bundesbank officials, and a substantial part of the German public feared that a monetary union including Italy would produce a weak euro.[18] Chancellor Helmut Kohl and Finance Minister Theo Waigel responded by reassuring these constituencies that they would interpret the Maastricht criteria rigorously. This was one reason that the government of Romano Prodi launched a crash program of fiscal consolidation not long after taking office (see Chapter 5).

The possibility of excluding Italy from monetary union was rumored frequently in 1997. In early February, the *Financial Times* reported that "senior European Union central bankers and monetary officials" had been discussing a deal that would assuage German concerns by delaying Italy's adoption of the euro for twelve to eighteen months. In the interim, the European Central Bank would allow Italy to narrow its fluctuation band in the new ERM and might reserve one or two positions on its executive board for Italy and other countries that joined later. Prodi rejected this idea and reiterated his government's commitment to participating in monetary union from the beginning; French and German officials also denied that such a deal was in the works, and in early April Kohl and Jacques Chirac again denied rumors of a secret agreement to exclude Italy.[19]

Italian participation seemed more certain by the summer of 1997 because of the reduction in the deficit and the strong support of the recently elected Jospin government in France. But in July, European Commissioner Mario Monti warned that the French and Germans might interpret the debt criterion rigorously to maintain monetary stability and German public support. Although the debt-to-GDP ratio was over 120 percent in both Belgium and Italy, this was less of a problem for Belgium because of the government's success in introducing structural reforms to spending.[20] Reports circulated that at the July Ecofin meeting, the French and German finance ministers had discussed this issue off the record. Italian finance minister Carlo Azeglio Ciampi replied that his government agreed that further structural reforms of pension and social security spending were necessary in order to make Italy's fiscal position more sustainable.[21] Prodi and others also made (not very credible) threats that, if excluded from the first wave of monetary union, Italy might seek to block the admission of other member states or scuttle agreement on issues such as the eastward enlargement of the European Union.[22]

In the end, in May 1998 the Council followed the recommendations of the Commission and the European Monetary Institute and decided that eleven countries desiring to participate in monetary union, including France, Germany, and Italy, met the convergence criteria.[23] All eleven easily met the criteria for long-term interest rates and inflation. Faster economic growth also allowed them to meet the deficit criterion, with Italy managing to reduce its budget deficit to 2.8 percent of GDP in 1997. A flexible interpretation of the ERM participation requirement allowed Italy to pass this test, since more than two years would pass between when the lira rejoined the mechanism in late 1996 and the introduction of the euro in January 1999. Italy (and Belgium) clearly did not meet the debt criterion, but the Council recognized the progress that both had made in reducing debt in the 1990s and cautioned that further progress would be necessary in the future.

British politicians made it clear quite early that they would exercise the opt-out clause in the Maastricht Treaty that allowed them not to participate in monetary union even if Britain met the convergence criteria. Strong opposition to the single currency within the Conservative Party and the cabinet led the Major government to promise a referendum on the issue before joining and to declare repeatedly that in any case it was "highly unlikely" that the euro would be introduced on schedule in 1999.[24] The Labour government elected in May 1997 portrayed itself as more pragmatic on the issue, holding that it would base a decision on a "hard-headed assessment of Britain's economic interests" rather than ideological opposition to further European integration. But even before the election, Labour proved unwilling to abandon sterling in the immediate future and pledged that it would move to monetary union only after the decision had cleared challenging economic and political hurdles. Monetary union would have to pass five economic tests before Britain joined, including a synchronization of economic cycles in Britain and Europe, a positive influence on employment, international investment, and British financial firms, and there would have to exist sufficient labor market flexibility to respond to unforeseen economic shocks. In addition to these economic tests, a decision to move to monetary union would have to receive political approval at three levels: the cabinet, Parliament, and the electorate in a referendum. After taking office, the Blair government stated that it favored joining the single currency "in principle" but would not do so until after the next general election in 2002.[25]

By late 1997, it was clear to most observers that the necessary degree of political commitment and economic convergence had been achieved for some, and perhaps a majority, of member states to move to full monetary union in 1999. Member states and European institutions began finalizing technical preparations for irrevocably fixing exchange rates. Most of these preparations proceeded smoothly, with the exception of the naming of the president of the European Central Bank. Dutch central banker Wim Duisenberg had accepted the presidency of the European Monetary Institute with the understanding that governments in 1998 would name him to the eight-year term as head of the more powerful European Central Bank. Although the French (and Italian) governments did not object to this agreement, in 1997 French president Jacques Chirac put forward Banque de France governor Jean-Claude Trichet as a candidate for the job.

All the other member states came out in support of Duisenberg, and many thought that the French intended to acquiesce to his nomination in exchange for Italian admission to monetary union or a stronger Euro Council. Various parties floated solutions such as nominating a third, compromise candidate or having Duisenberg retire after a few years to be replaced by Trichet.[26] But the German and Dutch governments were committed to securing the job for Duisenberg and feared that a compromise would weaken the political independence and legitimacy of the new central bank before it even began operations.

Governments did not settle the issue until the last possible moment at the meeting of the European Council in Brussels in early May 1998. With British prime minister Tony Blair serving as mediator, the French, Germans, and Dutch agreed that Duisenberg would "voluntarily" promise to take early retirement sometime after the introduction of euro notes and coins in 2002, made a political commitment that Trichet would succeed Duisenberg, and nominated French finance ministry official Christian Noyer as the European Central Bank's vice president.[27]

Implications

The successful transition to monetary union raises a host of questions about the future, including the political legitimacy of the European Central Bank, the difficulty of coordinating fiscal policies according to the terms of the Stability and Growth Pact, external monetary policy, and the implications of different national wage-bargaining institutions for a single European monetary policy.[28] In conclusion, I want to focus on three issues for which this book has direct implications: the development of a single European capital market, relationships between the member states and the European Central Bank, and the evolution of European institutions.

First, it is widely held that the euro will facilitate the development of a single market for capital by eliminating the risk of exchange-rate changes.[29] This might weaken the traditionally strong ties between banks and industry in continental Europe if large, creditworthy firms replace some of their bank borrowing with issues of euro-denominated shares and bonds and come to rely on financial firms principally for advice and short-term fund management. Such a change in the structure of European finance could undermine the close connections between banks and industry that give firms a strong voice in the making of exchange-rate policy and shift the preferences of banks toward low inflation and euro appreciation. Along with its political independence and mandate for internal price stability, the

European Central Bank would gain more political space to avoid formal international monetary policy cooperation and to treat the exchange rate as the residual of internal monetary policy.

Second, the small degree of learning about the desirable rules for institutions underpinning monetary union may pose difficulties for the European Central Bank. Monetary union may not be managed by like-minded authorities working out technically superior policies within a commonly accepted intellectual and institutional framework. Instead, it is possible to imagine that a serious economic shock could accentuate member states' differences regarding economic priorities and management. Some may continue to lean toward a pro-growth stance and urge the European Central Bank to relax monetary policy, whereas others will want the central bank to give priority to low inflation. Conflicts such as this would pose an important challenge for the European Central Bank's ability to preserve its political independence and to garner legitimacy with governments, interest groups, and citizens.

Finally, the successful transition to monetary union will create pressures for further institution building at the European level. The current design for monetary union, with a single currency, an independent central bank, and the Stability and Growth Pact's controls over fiscal policy, makes it difficult for member states to adjust to unforeseen economic shocks through budgetary or exchange-rate changes. Henceforth, adjustment will have to occur in other ways, such as through the labor market or changes to national patterns of taxation, expenditure, and social provision. This is one reason that many people support measures to increase the flexibility of labor markets or to create corporatist bargaining arrangements between management and labor at the European level. Yet previous attempts at institution building have been driven by power-based bargaining, with each member state seeking rules that impose the fewest costs on it. This may make it difficult for the member states to agree on politically sensitive changes to their welfare states, which are grounded in long-standing domestic institutions and practices.

Notes

1. Exceptions include Matthew Evangelista, "Stalin's Revenge: Institutional Barriers to Internationalization in the Soviet Union," in *Internationalization and Domestic Politics,* ed. Helen Milner and Robert Keohane (New York: Cambridge University Press, 1996); Peter Hall, *Governing the Economy* (New York: Oxford University Press, 1986); C. Randall Henning, *Currencies and Politics in the United States, Germany, and Japan* (Washington, DC: Institute for International Economics, 1994); Ellen M. Immergut, "The Theoretical Core of the New Institutionalism," *Politics and Society* 26, no. 1 (March 1998): 5–34; James G.

March and Johan P. Olsen, "The New Institutionalism: Organizational Factors in Political Life," *American Political Science Review* 78, no. 3 (September 1984): 734–749; Kathleen Thelen and Sven Steinmo, "Historical Institutionalism in Comparative Politics," in *Structuring Politics: Historical Institutionalism in Comparative Perspective*, ed. Sven Steinmo, Kathleen Thelen, and Frank Longstreth (New York: Cambridge University Press, 1992), 1–32; and John Zysman, *Governments, Markets, and Growth* (Ithaca, NY: Cornell University Press, 1983).

2. See, among many, Peter J. Katzenstein, ed., *Between Power and Plenty* (Madison: University of Wisconsin Press, 1978); Peter J. Katzenstein, ed., *The Culture of National Security* (New York: Columbia University Press, 1996); Peter J. Katzenstein and Noburo Okawara, "Japan's National Security: Structures, Norms, and Policies," *International Security* 17, no. 4 (1993): 84–118; Elizabeth Keir, *Imagining War: French Military Doctrine Between the Wars* (Princeton: Princeton University Press, 1997); Jeffrey W. Legro, "Culture and Preferences in the International Cooperation Two-Step," *American Political Science Review* 90, no. 1 (1996): 118–137; and Andrew Shonfield, *Modern Capitalism* (Oxford: Oxford University Press, 1965).

3. This notion of legitimacy and learning draws heavily on Mary Douglas, *How Institutions Think* (Syracuse: Syracuse University Press, 1986); and John Rawls, "Two Concepts of Rules," *Philosophical Review* 64 (1955): 3–32; see also Robert Keohane, "International Institutions: Two Approaches," *International Studies Quarterly* 32 (1988): 379–396; and Oran Young, "International Regimes: Toward a New Theory of Institutions," *World Politics* 39 (1986): 104–122.

4. Horst Ungerer, *A Concise History of European Monetary Integration* (Westport: Quorum, 1997), 279.

5. "Dublin European Council Presidency Conclusions: Annexes," 14 December 1996.

6. *La Repubblica*, 10 June 1997; and *Times*, 3 June 1997.

7. *Financial Times*, 11 June 1997.

8. *Financial Times*, 12 June 1997.

9. *La Repubblica*, 17 June 1997.

10. *Les Echos*, 13 March 1997, 6; and *La Tribune*, 16 October 1997, 1.

11. *La Tribune*, 18 November 1997, 1; *Financial Times*, 2 December 1997, 2; and *Financial Times*, 18 December 1997, 1.

12. Compare Barry Eichengreen and Charles Wyplosz, "The Stability Pact: More Than a Minor Nuisance?" *Economic Policy* (1998): 67–104; and Dorothee Heisenberg, *The Mark of the Bundesbank* (Boulder, CO: Lynne Rienner, 1999), 162.

13. *Financial Times*, 29 March 1996, 8.

14. *Financial Times*, 12 April 1996, 1.

15. *Financial Times*, 21 February 1996, 1.

16. Quotations from "Presidency Conclusions, Amsterdam European Council, Annex II: Resolution of the European Council on the Establishment of an Exchange-Rate Mechanism in the Third Stage of Economic and Monetary Union," June 1997.

17. European Monetary Institute, *Progress Towards Convergence 1996* (Frankfurt: European Monetary Institute, November 1996), iv.

18. Peter Henning Loedel, *Deutsche Mark Politics: Germany in the European Monetary System* (Boulder, CO: Lynne Rienner, 1999), 209–211.

19. *Financial Times*, 5 February 1997; *Financial Times*, 6 February 1997; *The Times*, 10 April 1997; and *Agence France Presse*, 17 April 1997.

20. *La Repubblica*, 14 July 1997.

21. For Ciampi's remarks, see *La Repubblica*, 20 July 1997; for speculation on using the debt to exclude Italy, see *Il Sole 24 Ore*, 19 July 1997.

22. James I. Walsh, "L'incerto cammino verso l'Unione monetaria," in *Politica in Italia*, ed. Martin Rhodes and Luciano Bardi (Bologna: Il Mulino, 1998), 109–130.

23. These member states were Belgium, Germany, Spain, France, Ireland, Italy, Luxembourg, the Netherlands, Austria, Portugal, and Finland. Britain and Denmark chose to exercise the provisions of the Maastricht Treaty allowing them to opt out of monetary union, whereas the Swedish government used a technicality to remain outside the euro. Greece did not meet the convergence criteria. See European Commission, "Commission Recommends 11 Member States for EMU" (IP/98/273, 25 March 1998); European Monetary Institute, *Convergence Report: Report Required by Article 109j of the Treaty Establishing the European Community* (Frankfurt: European Monetary Institute, March 1998).

24. *Financial Times*, 29 January 1999, 9.

25. Quotation from Labour Party election manifesto, 3 April 1997; see also *Financial Times*, 20 February 1997, 1; and *Financial Times*, 28 October 1997, 1.

26. See, for example, *La Tribune*, 30 January 1998.

27. *Financial Times*, 1 May 1998, 1; and *Financial Times*, 4 May 1998, 2.

28. General surveys include Christopher Allsopp and David Vines, "The Assessment: Macroeconomic Policy After EMU," *Oxford Review of Economic Policy* 14, no. 3 (1998): 1–23; David R. Cameron, "Economic and Monetary Union: Underlying Imperatives and Third-Stage Dilemmas," *Journal of European Public Policy* 4, no. 3 (September 1997): 455–485; Rudi Dornbusch, Carlo Favero, and Francesco Giavazzi, "Immediate Challenges for the European Central Bank," *European Economy* (April 1998): 17–52; Martin Feldstein, "The Political Economy of the European Economic and Monetary Union: Political Sources of an Economic Liability," *Journal of Economic Perspectives* 11, no. 4 (Fall 1997): 23–42; and Charles Wyplosz, "EMU: Why and How It Might Happen," *Journal of Economic Perspectives* 11, no. 4 (Fall 1997): 3–22. On the legitimacy of the European Central Bank, see Sheri Berman and Kathleen R. McNamara, "Bank on Democracy: Why Central Banks Need Public Oversight," *Foreign Affairs* (March–April 1999): 2–8; Randall D. Germain, "The European Central Bank and the Problem of Authority," paper prepared for the Annual Meeting of the American Political Science Association, Boston, 3–6 September 1998; and Amy Verdun, "The Institutional Design of EMU: A Democratic Deficit?" *Journal of Public Policy* 18, no. 2 (1999): 107–132. On wage bargaining institutions, see Peter A. Hall and Robert J. Franzese, "Mixed Signals: Central Bank Independence, Coordinated Wage Bargaining, and European Monetary Union," *International Organization* 52, no. 3 (Summer 1998): 505–535; and Erik Jones, "The Politics of Economic and Monetary Union: Playing with Money," in Andrew Moravcsik, ed., *Centralization or Fragmentation? Europe Facing the Challenges of Deepening, Diversity, and Democracy* (New York: Council on Foreign Relations Press, 1998), 59–93. On fiscal policy, see Antonio Fatas, "Does Europe Need a Fiscal Federation?" *European Economy* (April 1998): 165–192; and Eichengreen and Wyplosz, "The Stability Pact: More Than a Minor Nuisance." For external monetary policy, see C. Randall Henning, "Systemic Conflict and Regional Monetary Integration: The Case of Europe," *International Organization* 52, no. 3 (Summer 1998): 537–573; and C. Randall Henning, *Cooperating with Europe's Monetary Union,* Policy Analyses in International Economics No. 49 (Washington, DC: Institute for International Economics, 1997).

29. Alessandro, Pati, and Garry J. Schinasi, "European Monetary Union and International Capital Markets: Structural Implications and Risks," IMF Working Paper WP/97/62 (Washington, DC: Research Department, International Monetary Fund, May 1997); a more skeptical view is Adam Posen, "Why EMU Is Irrelevant for the German Economy," Institute for International Economics Working Paper 99-5, April 1999.

Selected Bibliography

Abdelal, Rawi. "The Politics of Monetary Leadership and Followership: Stability in the European Monetary System Since the Currency Crisis of 1992." *Political Studies* 46 (1998): 236–259.

Aeschimann, Éric, and Pascal Riché. *La guerre de sept ans: Histoire secrète du franc fort 1989–1996*. Paris: Calmann-Lèvy, 1996.

Allsopp, Christopher, and David Vines. "The Assessment: Macroeconomic Policy After EMU." *Oxford Review of Economic Policy* 14, no. 3 (1998): 1–23.

Alogoskoufis, George, Lucas Papademos, and Richard Portes. *External Constraints on Macroeconomic Policy: The European Experience*. New York: Cambridge University Press, 1991.

Andrews, David M. "European Monetary Diplomacy and the Rolling Crisis of 1992–1993." In *The State of the European Union,* vol. 3: *Building a European Polity?* ed. Carolyn Rhodes and Sonia Mazey, 159–176. Boulder, CO: Lynne Rienner, 1995.

———. "The Global Origins of the Maastricht Treaty on EMU: Closing the Window of Opportunity." In *The State of the European Community,* vol. 2: *The Maastricht Debates and Beyond,* ed. Alan W. Cafruny and Glenda G. Rosenthal, 107–123. Boulder, CO: Lynne Rienner, 1993.

Andrews, David M., and Thomas D. Willett. "Financial Interdependence and the State: International Monetary Relations at Century's End." *International Organization* 51, no. 3 (Summer 1997): 479–511.

Barkin, Samuel. "Hegemony Without Motivation: Domestic Policy Priorities and German Monetary Policy." *German Politics and Society* 14, no. 3 (Fall 1996): 54–72.

Barrell, Ray, Andrew Britton, and Nigel Pain. "When the Time Was Right? The UK Experience of the ERM." In *European Monetary Upheavals,* ed. David Cobham. Manchester: Manchester University Press, 1994.

Baun, Michael J. "The Maastricht Treaty as High Politics: Germany, France, and European Integration." *Political Science Quarterly* 110, no. 4 (1995–1996): 605–624.

Begg, David, and Charles Wyplosz. "The European Monetary System: Recent Intellectual History." In *The Monetary Future of Europe,* ed. Centre for Economic Policy Research. London: CEPR, 1993.

Berman, Sheri, and Kathleen R. McNamara. "Bank on Democracy: Why Central Banks Need Public Oversight." *Foreign Affairs* (March–April 1999): 2–8.

Bini-Smaghi, Lorenzo, Tommaso Padoa-Schioppa, and Francesco Papadia. *The Transition to EMU in the Maastricht Treaty.* Princeton Essays in International Finance No. 194. Princeton: International Finance Section, Department of Economics, Princeton University, November 1994.

Britton, Andrew, and David Mayes. *Achieving Monetary Union in Europe*. London: Sage, 1992.

Brown, Richard. "British Monetary Policy and European Monetary Integration." In *Monetary Implications of the 1992 Process,* ed. Heidemarie Sherman. New York: St. Martin's Press, 1990.

Burdekin, Richard C. K., Jilleen R. Westbrook, and Thomas D. Willett. "Exchange Rate Pegging as a Disinflation Strategy: Evidence from the European Monetary System." In *Varieties of Monetary Reform: Lessons and Experiences on the Road to Monetary Union,* ed. Pierre L. Siklos. Boston: Kluwer Academic Publishers, 1993.

Cameron, David R. "British Exit, German Voice, French Loyalty: Defection, Domination, and Cooperation in the 1992–93 ERM Crisis." Paper prepared for the annual meeting of the American Political Science Association, Washington, DC, September 1993.

———. "Economic and Monetary Union: Underlying Imperatives and Third-Stage Dilemmas." *Journal of European Public Policy* 4, no. 3 (September 1997): 455–485.

———. "Exchange Rate Politics in France, 1981–83: The Regime-Defining Choices of the Mitterrand Presidency." In *The Mitterrand Era: Policy Alternatives and Political Mobilization in France,* ed. Anthony Daley, 56–82. New York: New York University Press, 1996.

———. "From Barre to Balladur: Economic Policy in the Era of the EMS." In *Remaking the Hexagon: The New France in the New Europe,* ed. Gregory Flynn, 117–159. Boulder, CO: Westview, 1995.

———. "Transnational Relations and the Development of European Economic and Monetary Union." In *Bringing Transnational Relations Back In: Non-State Actors, Domestic Structures and International Institutions,* ed Thomas Risse-Kappen, 37–78. New York: Cambridge University Press, 1995.

Canzoneri, Matthew, Vittorio Grilli, and Paul Masson, eds. *Establishing a Central Bank for Europe*. New York: Cambridge University Press, 1992.

Cobham, David. "European Monetary Integration: A Survey of Recent Literature." *Journal of Common Market Studies* 29, no. 4 (June 1991).

Cohen, Benjamin J. "Beyond EMU: The Problem of Sustainability." *Economics and Politics* 5 (July 1993): 187–202.

———. "European Financial Integration and National Banking Interests." In *The Political Economy of European Integration: States, Markets and Institutions,* ed. Paolo Guerrieri and Pier Carlo Padoan. Savage, MD: Barnes and Noble Books, 1989.

———. "Europe's Money, America's Problem." *Foreign Policy* 35 (1979): 31–47.

Collignon, Stefan, ed. *European Monetary Policy*. London: Pinter, 1997.

Collignon, Stefan, et al. *Europe's Monetary Future*. Rutherford: Fairleigh Dickinson University Press, 1994.

Collins, Susan, and Francesco Giavazzi. "Attitudes Toward Inflation and the Viability of Fixed Exchange Rates: Evidence from the EMS." In *A*

Retrospective on the Bretton Woods System: Lessons for International Monetary Reform, ed. Michael D. Bordo and Barry Eichengreen. Chicago: University of Chicago Press, 1993.

Curzio, Alberto Quadrio. "Riflessioni sull'Unione Economica e Monetaria Europea." *Il Mulino* 333 (January–February 1991).

Danthine, Jean-Pierre, Paul De Grauwe, Louka Katseli, and Niels Thygesen. *North/South in the EMS: Convergence and Divergence in Inflation and Real Exchange Rates*. CEPS Paper No. 50. London: Brassey's, 1991.

Dastoli, Pier Virgilio. "The Stone Guest: Italy on the Threshold of European Monetary Union." In *Italian Politics: The Stalled Transition,* ed. Mario Caciagli and David I. Kertzer, 169–185. Boulder, CO: Westview, 1996.

De Boissieu, Christian. "The EMS Crisis and the French Franc." In *The Monetary Economics of Europe: Causes of the EMS Crisis,* ed. Christopher Johnson and Stefan Collignon. Rutherford: Fairleigh Dickinson University Press, 1994.

De Cecco, Marcello. "The European Monetary System and National Interests." In *The Political Economy of European Integration: States, Markets and Institutions,* ed. Paolo Guerrieri and Pier Carlo Padoan. Savage, MD: Barnes and Noble Books, 1989.

De Cecco, Marcello, and Alberto Giovannini, eds. *A European Central Bank? Perspectives on Monetary Unification After Ten Years of the EMS*. New York: Cambridge University Press, 1989.

De Grauwe, Paul. "The Economics of Convergence Towards Monetary Union in Europe." Centre for Economic Policy Research Discussion Paper No. 1213, July 1995.

———. "The Political Economy of Monetary Union in Europe." *The World Economy* 16, no. 6 (November 1993): 653–661.

Dell, Edmund. "Britain and the Origins of the European Monetary System." *Contemporary European History* 3, no. 1 (1994): 1–60.

Dennis, Geoffrey, and Joseph Nellis. "The EMS and UK Membership: Five Years On." *Lloyds Bank Review* (October 1984): 13–31.

Dornbusch, Rudi, Carlo Favero, and Francesco Giavazzi. "Immediate Challenges for the European Central Bank." *European Economy* (April 1998): 17–52.

Dowd, Kevin. "The Case Against a European Central Bank." *World Economy* 12, no. 3 (September 1989): 361–372.

Dyson, Kenneth. *Elusive Union: The Process of Economic and Monetary Union in Europe*. London: Longman, 1994.

Dyson, Kenneth, and Kevin Featherstone. "EMU and Economic Governance in Germany." *German Politics* 5, no. 3 (December 1996): 325–355.

———. "Italy and EMU as 'Vincolo Esterno': Empowering the Technocrats, Transforming the State." *South European Society and Politics* 1, no. 2 (Autumn 1996): 272–299.

Dyson, Kenneth, Kevin Featherstone, and George Michalopoulos. "Strapped to the Mast: EC Central Bankers Between Global Financial Markets and Regional Integration." *Journal of European Public Policy* 2, no. 3 (September 1995): 465–487.

Eichengreen, Barry. "European Monetary Integration." *Journal of Economic Literature* 31 (September 1993): 1321–1357.

———. *Should the Maastricht Treaty Be Saved?* Princeton Studies in International Finance No. 74. Princeton: International Finance Section, Department of Economics, Princeton University, 1992.

Eichengreen, Barry, and Jeffry Frieden. "The Political Economy of European

Monetary Unification: An Analytical Introduction." *Economics and Politics* 5 (July 1993): 85–104.
Eichengreen, Barry, and Charles Wyplosz. "The Stability Pact: More Than a Minor Nuisance?" *Economic Policy* 26 (1998): 67–113.
———. "The Unstable EMS." *Brookings Papers on Economic Activity* 1 (1993).
Emerson, Michael, ed. *One Market, One Money: An Evaluation of the Potential Benefits and Costs of Forming an Economic and Monetary Union.* Oxford: Oxford University Press, 1992.
Feldstein, Martin. "EMU and International Conflict." *Foreign Affairs* (November–December 1997): 60–72.
———. "The Political Economy of the European Economic and Monetary Union: Political Sources of an Economic Liability." *Journal of Economic Perspectives* 11, no. 4 (Fall 1997): 23–42.
Fitoussi, Jean-Paul. *Le Débat Interdit: Monnaie, Europe, Pauvreté.* Paris: Arléa, 1995.
Fratianni, Michele, and Jürgen von Hagen. *The European Monetary System and European Monetary Union.* Boulder, CO: Westview Press, 1992.
Fratianni, Michele, Jürgen von Hagen, and Christopher Waller. *The Maastricht Way to EMU.* Essays in International Finance No. 187. Princeton: International Finance Section, Department of Economics, Princeton University, June 1992.
Frieden, Jeffry. "The Euro: Who Wins? Who Loses?" *Foreign Policy* (Fall 1998): 25–40.
———. "The Impact of Goods and Capital Market Integration on European Monetary Politics." *Comparative Political Studies* 29, no. 2 (April 1996): 193–222.
———. "Making Commitments: France and Italy in the European Monetary System, 1979–1985." In *The Political Economy of European Monetary Integration,* ed. Barry Eichengreen and Jeffry Frieden, 25–46. Boulder, CO: Westview, 1994.
Frieden, Jeffry A., Daniel Gros, and Erik Jones, eds. *The New Political Economy of EMU.* Boulder, CO: Rowman & Littlefield, 1998.
Garrett, Geoffrey. "The Politics of Maastricht." *Economics and Politics* 5, no. 2 (July 1993): 105–123.
Giavazzi, Francesco, and Alberto Giovannini. *Limiting Exchange Rate Flexibility.* Cambridge, MA: MIT Press, 1989.
Giavazzi, Francesco, Stefano Micossi, and Marcus Miller, eds. *The European Monetary System.* New York: Cambridge University Press, 1988.
Giavazzi, Franceso, and Marco Pagano. "The Advantage of Tying One's Hands: EMS Discipline and Central Bank Credibility." *European Economic Review* 32 (1988): 1055–1082.
Giovannini, Alberto. "Economic and Monetary Union: What Happened? Exploring the Political Dimension of Optimum Currency Areas." In *The Monetary Future of Europe,* ed. Centre for Economic Policy Research London: CEPR, 1993.
———. "How Do Fixed-Exchange Rate Regimes Work? Evidence from the Gold Standard, Bretton Woods and the EMS." In *Blueprints for Exchange-Rate Management,* ed. Marcus Miller, Barry Eichengreen, and Richard Portes. New York: Academic Press, 1989.
———. *The Transition to European Monetary Union.* Essays in International Finance No. 178. Princeton: International Finance Section, Department of Economics, Princeton University, November 1990.
Goodhart, Charles. "Economists' Perspectives on the EMS: A Review Essay." *Journal of Monetary Economics* (December 1990).

Goodman, John B. *Monetary Sovereignty: The Politics of Central Banking in Western Europe*. Ithaca, NY: Cornell University Press, 1992.

Grieco, Joseph M. "The Maastricht Treaty, Economic and Monetary Union, and the Neo-Realist Research Programme." *Review of International Studies* 21 (1995): 21–40.

Gros, Daniel. "Paradigms for the Monetary Union of Europe." *Journal of Common Market Studies* 27, no. 3 (March 1989): 219–230.

Gros, Daniel, and Niels Thygesen. *European Monetary Integration*. New York: St. Martin's, 1992.

Hall, Peter A., and Robert J. Franzese, Jr. "Mixed Signals: Central Bank Independence, Coordinated Wage Bargaining, and European Monetary Union." *International Organization* 52, no. 3 (Summer 1998): 505–535.

Harasty, H., and J. Le Dem. "Les Consequences Macroeconomiques de la Reunification Allemande." *Economie Prospective Internationale* 43, no. 3 (1990).

Harmon, Mark D., and Dorothee Heisenberg. "Explaining the European Currency Crisis of September 1992." *German Politics and Society* 28 (Summer 1993).

Heisenberg, Dorothee. *The Mark of the Bundesbank*. Boulder, CO: Lynne Rienner, 1999.

Henning, C. Randall. *Cooperating with Europe's Monetary Union*. Policy Analyses in International Economics No. 49. Washington, DC: Institute for International Economics, 1997.

———. *Currencies and Politics in the United States, Germany, and Japan*. Washington, DC: Institute for International Economics, 1994.

———. "Europe's Monetary Union and the United States." *Foreign Policy* 102 (Spring 1996): 83–100.

———. "Systemic Conflict and Regional Monetary Integration: The Case of Europe." *International Organization* 52, no. 3 (Summer 1998): 537–573.

Italianer, Alexander. "Mastering Maastricht: EMU Issues and How They Were Settled." In *Economic and Monetary Union: Implications for National Policymakers,* ed. Klaus Gretschmann, 51–113. Dordrecht: Martinus Nyjoff, 1993.

Jacquet, Pierre. "La Disunion Monétaire Européenne." *Politique Etrangere* 58, no. 1 (1993): 443–453.

Johnson, Christopher. "The UK and the Exchange Rate Mechanism." In *The Monetary Economics of Europe: Causes of the EMS Crisis,* ed. Christopher Johnson and Stefan Collignon. Rutherford: Fairleigh Dickinson University Press, 1994.

Jones, Erik. "The Politics of Economic and Monetary Union: Playing with Money." In *Centralization or Fragmentation? Europe Facing the Challenges of Deepening, Diversity, and Democracy,* ed. Andrew Moravcsik, 59–93. New York: Council on Foreign Relations Press, 1998.

Kaelberer, Matthias. "Hegemony, Dominance or Leadership? Explaining Germany's Role in European Monetary Cooperation." *European Journal of International Relations* 3, no. 1 (1997): 35–60.

Kaltenthaler, Karl. *Germany and the Politics of Europe's Money*. Durham, NC: Duke University Press, 1998.

Kenen, Peter B. *Economic and Monetary Union in Europe: Moving Beyond Maastricht*. Princeton: Princeton University Press, 1995.

Loedel, Peter Henning. *Deutsche Mark Politics: Germany in the European Monetary System*. Boulder, CO: Lynne Rienner, 1999.

Lohmann, Susanne. "Federalism and Central Bank Independence: The Politics of

German Monetary Policy, 1957–92." *World Politics* 50, no. 3 (1998): 401–446.

Ludlow, Peter. *The Making of the European Monetary System: A Case Study of the Politics of the European Community*. Boston: Butterworth Scientific, 1982.

Martial, Enrico. "Un Dicembre a Maastricht: Il Nuovo Trattato dell'Unione." *Il Mulino* 338 (November–December 1991): 1001–1012.

Martin, Lisa. "International and Domestic Institutions in the EMU Process." *Economics and Politics* 5 (July 1993): 125–144.

Masera, Rainer S. "Single Market, Exchange Rates and Monetary Unification." *The World Economy* 17, no. 3 (May 1994): 249–279.

McNamara, Kathleen R. *The Currency of Ideas*. Ithaca, NY: Cornell University Press, 1998.

Mélitz, Jacques. "French Monetary Policy and Recent Speculative Attacks on the Franc." In *European Monetary Upheavals,* ed. David Cobham. Manchester: Manchester University Press, 1994.

———. "Monetary Discipline and Cooperation in the European Monetary System: A Synthesis." In *The European Monetary System,* ed. Francesco Giavazzi, Stefano Micossi, and Marcus Miller. New York: Cambridge University Press, 1988.

Moravcsik, Andrew. *The Choice for Europe: Social Purpose and State Power from Messina to Maastricht*. Ithaca, NY: Cornell University Press, 1998.

Nölling, Wilhelm. *Monetary Policy in Europe After Maastricht*. New York: St. Martin's Press, 1993.

Oatley, Thomas H. *Monetary Politics: Exchange Rate Cooperation in the European Union*. Ann Arbor: University of Michigan Press, 1997.

Padoa-Schioppa, Tommaso. "Dopo la tempesta di settembre: il futuro dell'unione monetaria." *Il Mulino* 345 (January–February 1993): 198–206.

———. "The European Monetary System: A Long-Term View." In *The European Monetary System,* ed. Francesco Giavazzi, Stefano Micossi, and Marcus Miller. New York: Cambridge University Press, 1988.

Pauly, Louis W. "The Politics of European Monetary Union: National Strategies, International Implications." *International Journal* (Winter 1991–1992): 93–111.

Portes, Richard. "EMS and EMU After the Fall." *The World Economy* 16, no. 1 (January 1993): 1–16.

Rotte, Ralph, and Klaus F. Zimmerman. "Fiscal Restraint and the Political Economy of EMU." *Public Choice* 94 (1998): 385–406.

Sandholtz, Wayne. "Choosing Union: Monetary Politics and Maastricht." *International Organization* 47, no. 1 (Winter 1993): 1–39.

———. "Monetary Bargains: The Treaty on EMU." In *The State of the European Community,* vol. 2: *The Maastricht Debates and Beyond,* ed. Alan W. Cafruny and Glenda G. Rosenthal, 125–142. Boulder, CO: Lynne Rienner, 1993.

———. "Money Troubles: Europe's Rough Road to Monetary Union." *Journal of European Public Policy* 3, no. 1 (March 1996): 84–101.

Smith, Michael E., and Wayne Sandholtz. "Institutions and Leadership: Germany, Maastricht, and the ERM Crisis." In *The State of the European Union,* vol. 3: *Building a European Polity?* ed. Carolyn Rhodes and Sonia Mazey, 245–265. Boulder, CO: Lynne Rienner, 1995.

Story, Jonathan. "The Launching of the EMS: An Analysis of Change in Foreign Economic Policy." *Political Studies* 36 (1988): 397–412.

Story, Jonathan, and Marcello De Cecco. "The Politics and Diplomacy of Monetary

Union, 1985–1991." In *The New Europe,* ed. Jonathan Story. Oxford: Basil Blackwell, 1993.

Tew, Brian. "Onwards to EMU." In *The Single European Market and Beyond: A Study of the Wider Implications of the Single European Act,* ed. Dennis Swann. New York: Routledge, 1992.

Thompson, Helen. *The British Conservative Government and the European Exchange Rate Mechanism, 1979–1994*. London: Pinter, 1996.

Tsoukalis, Loukas. *The Politics and Economics of European Monetary Integration.* London: Allen and Unwin, 1977.

Ungerer, Horst. *A Concise History of European Monetary Integration.* Westport: Quorum, 1997.

Verdun, Amy. "The Institutional Design of EMU: A Democratic Deficit?" *Journal of Public Policy* 18, no. 2 (1999): 107–132.

von Hagen, Jürgen. "Monetary Policy Coordination in the European Monetary System." In *Monetary Policy in Developed Economies,* ed. Michele U. Fratianni and Dominick Salvatore. Westport, CT: Greenwood Press, 1993.

Walsh, James I. "International Constraints and Domestic Choices: Economic Convergence and Exchange-Rate Policy in France and Italy." *Political Studies* 42, no. 2 (June 1994): 243–258.

Weber, Axel A. "Reputation and Creditability in the European Monetary System." *Economic Policy* 12 (April 1991): 58–102.

Welfens, Paul J. J., ed. *European Monetary Integration: From German Dominance to an EC Central Bank.* Heidelberg: Springer, 1991.

Woolley, John T. "Policy Credibility and European Monetary Institutions." In *Euro-Politics: Institutions and Policymaking in the New European Community,* ed. Alberta Sbragia. Washington, DC: Brookings Institution, 1992.

Wyplosz, Charles. "Asymmetry in the EMS: Intentional or Systemic?" *European Economic Review* 33 (1989): 310–320.

———. "EMU: Why and How It Might Happen." *Journal of Economic Perspectives* 11, no. 4 (Fall 1997): 3–22.

Ypersele, Jacques van, and Jean-Claude Koeune. *The European Monetary System: Origins, Operation and Outlook.* Luxembourg: Commission of the European Communities, 1985.

Zis, George. "The European Monetary System 1979–84: An Assessment." *Journal of Common Market Studies* 23, no. 1 (September 1984).

Index

About the Book

This book explains why three countries—Britain, France, and Italy—that faced similar problems of high inflation and currency depreciation since the 1970s pursued very different international monetary strategies.

Walsh argues that international monetary policies produce predictable sets of winners and losers, and that policy choice is a function of how industrial firms, banks, and labor unions organize and deploy their political resources. He draws on a wealth of primary data and interviews to reconstruct the domestic politics and international bargaining behind Europe's single currency.

James I. Walsh is assistant professor of political science at the University of North Carolina, Charlotte.

Donated by
Ian Thomson